EUROPE
ON THE
FIDDLE

EUROPE ON THE FIDDLE

The Common Market Scandal

NIGEL TUTT

CHRISTOPHER HELM
London

100781730

© 1989 Nigel Tutt
Christopher Helm (Publishers) Ltd, Imperial House,
21–25 North Street, Bromley, Kent BR1 1SD

ISBN 0–7470–3207–6

A CIP catalogue record for this book
is available from the British Library

Typeset by Opus, Oxford
Printed and bound in Great Britain by Billing and Sons Ltd, Worcester

CONTENTS

Section 3 – Pollution, the Third World, Mafia and the
1990s

Acknowledgements

I would like to thank Keith Elliott for his invaluable advice and editing of the text; Curtis Bollington for the diagrams; Nick Kochan for making the introduction to Richard Wigmore; Anselmo Guarraci MEP and Giovanni Angelo for their practical help; and all those across Europe who generously gave their time to be interviewed and provided information.

Figures

Tables

xi

INTRODUCTION

To many people the Common Market conjures up a shoddy agricultural policy, the tantalising economic dream of '1992' and Mrs Thatcher once again upsetting her European counterparts. The popular view also is of an overweening bureaucracy making up unnecessary rules for industry. Certainly there are elements of truth in them all, but investigations reveal a far more alarming picture. There is fraud, mismanagement and incompetent officials.

Taxpayers' money is being wasted in scandalous proportions. Those who look after the cash cannot be trusted and are not properly punished when uncovered. The filling of top civil service posts is often rigged, and merit is rarely the arbiter of promotion. National authorities cannot keep a grip on EC agricultural subsidies. And the EC's own financial watchdog is not up to the job. Laws, particularly controls on pollution and the environment, are a farce and there is little attempt to adhere to them. The overall picture uncovers a pressing need for a top-to-bottom overhaul of the Common Market – the European Community – and all its organisations.

This book is an antidote to the worthy words on European unity and co-operation. It's not that the sentiments aren't worthy, but in practice European co-operation has been badly mishandled. The internal workings and the way individual policies are put in place bodes ill for ambitious plans for closer economic working of the twelve countries by 1992. Many trade barriers will remain. Even the heavily targeted telecommunications sector is putting up new barriers as fast at it tears down the old ones.

The EC and its cumbersome organisation is widely misunderstood. Its largest institution is the European Commission, mainly based in Brussels. It is led by a team of Commissioners, usually politicians from each member country. They give the EC civil service some muscle and scope for executive action. The Commission alone can propose pan-European legislation, such as directives. Its directorates cover all policy areas, do the groundwork for these plans and police limited aspects of commercial policy.

Commission proposals have to get the agreement of the majority of the twelve governments which are members of the EC club before becoming law. In some cases, such as on tax policy, they have to be unanimous. With Spain and Portugal joining in January 1986, the EC's geographical coverage extends north as far as Denmark and south to Greece. The member governments have their own institution, called the Council of Ministers, to house working groups of officials and ministerial meetings.

The Council takes decisions and wields power. This is in marked contrast to the European Parliament, the third major arm of the EC. Since 1979 it is directly elected by the people of Europe, or at least by those who turn out to vote. In the UK's case this was 33 per cent in 1984, by far the lowest. The next was Ireland with 48 per cent. It gives 'opinions' on proposed legislation – which can be ignored by the Council. Its power lies in a veto over the EC's own £25 billion budget and the opportunity to sack the Commissioners (though only en masse).

EuroMPs can play a useful role in exposing the impact of EC policies in their areas and on their constituents. But too often their activities have been seen as junketing or in the arms of lobbyists.

The fourth institution is the Economic and Social Committee of industrialists, trade unionists and professionals appointed by governments. This too provides an opinion on legislative proposals but is regarded as duplicating the work of the Parliament, though its opinions are often better researched and more thoughtful.

The line of EC institutions is completed with the European Court of Justice, which arbitrates between Commission, governments and business, and the European Court of Auditors, which vets EC spending. Both of these are based in Luxembourg, 200 kilometres from Brussels, as are some Commission and Parliament officials.

This is the cumbersome framework which formulates and manages EC policy. Its influence comes in two forms: direct spending from its budget and setting Europe-wide legislation. The £25 billion EC budget is not large compared to national public spending, amounting to £78 per head. UK public spending is £140 billion, or £2,500 for each member of the UK population. And about 80 per cent of the EC cash goes straight back into government hands for dispensing as grants and subsidies.

Across industrial sectors, the influence of the EC varies. In agriculture, the influence is heavy. Two-thirds of the EC budget goes on subsidising farming. Prices and subsidies are set in Brussels. It has controlled iron and steel production through quotas and regulations on national subsidies. In private industry sectors, the impact has been less through controlling subsidy levels, more via the overall business environment. In the petrochemical and plastics industry, the Commission has fined price-fixing cartels.

Setting the business environment has meant laying down common rules for company accounts, value-added tax, social security, and sex discrimination. Protecting the environment from pollution and conserving nature has also imposed a burden on business. These directives require individual governments to put in their own national laws.

A few random examples suggested the EC machine is not running efficiently. There is no check that governments are paying their full subscriptions to the club. In December 1986 the EC's own financial watchdog said that only five governments, out of ten, had let it check their contributions. These are based on a share of the country's VAT receipts, but Italy and Luxembourg refused to supply tax statistics to the Court. Auditors have also been hampered in West Germany and France.

On the spending side, over-generous subsidies have produced food mountains and wine lakes. Apart from the poor forecasting and incorrect signals to the industry that led to the surpluses, there were many other doubts. The stockpiles resulted in huge sums in storage contracts and financing but they were declining in quality and value, eventually costing £2 billion. The Commission had not taken account of this possibility. At the same time the drip-drip of fraud turned into a deluge as officials argued over the scale of the problem.

Internal management of the institutions was also suspect. The putting out of contracts to tender to find the best and cheapest bidder has often provoked fixing claims. In other cases, sizeable contracts have been negotiated privately. One example involved a plan to hire a converted cross-channel ferry for a travelling trade fair to south-east Asia to win export sales. Commissioner from France, Claude Cheysson, vigorously backed the scheme despite opposition from national and Commission trade promotion experts.

The Netherlands Council for Trade Promotion was paid £350,000 to drum up support for this operation. Only a quarter of the space on the ship was sold and the project was scrapped in 1987. Exporters said the ship was not suitable for large-scale exhibits and did not give them enough time during the three-week timetable to follow up sales leads at the six ports. A three-day stop in Malaysia was criticised because it was twenty-eight miles outside Kuala Lumpur, the capital, and spanned a bank holiday and a prayer day.

The cancellation of the £7 million project did not deter officials. They looked for other ways to spend their trade promotion budget, specially re-jigged to cope with the ship. The ASEAN countries were building a trade surplus with the EC and efforts were neeeded rapidly.

And why is the Commission investing in so many sports, culture and television stations? Why did the Antwerp-based European Champions Championship tennis in 1985 become the European Community Championships in 1986, especially when the Belgian tax authorities mounted a tax investigation into the tennis championship soon after? There was £17,500 spent promoting media coverage. Another £10,000 went to help put an EC flag of yellow stars on a blue background on top of the K2 Himalayan mountain. A similar sum was spent on a North Pole expedition.

Looking beyond the limited financial regularity of transactions carried out by the EC's own financial watchdog has revealed some further failings. The Court of

Auditor's aim is to uncover corruption, waste and misman-agement, to draw conclusions and suggest some remedies. But it is guilty of many of the shortcomings it is supposed to be investigating.

EC policies for the Third World are run like the rest of the operation, perhaps even worse. Development projects go awry, food aid is delayed and arrives in a poor state. And those who run the policy are often treated like second-class employees while the senior men enjoy free first-class flights, top hotels and a champagne lifestyle.

This book investigates all these areas along with several other topics, such as Mafia involvement, and looks at the prospects for improvement, especially given the EC's plans for a single market in 1992.

Note: Finances originally stated in ecu have been consis-tently translated at 1 ecu = 70 pence.

Nigel Tutt, October 1988, Brussels and London.

Section 1
ORGANISATION

1 LOCATION
THE EC's SPREADING TENTACLES

Brussels' identification with the European Community is firmly placed in the public mind. It is where policy is discussed and decisions are taken. Yet in reality it is just one of three EC capital cities, part of an inefficient merry-go-round that no one can decide to jump off. It is the capital where the EC institutions have paid over the odds for rent and where developers have left a wretched record with local residents. If the EC was judged on performance in its hometown then it would score few points out of ten.

If the European Parliament decided not to decamp once a month to Strasbourg in France from its committee rooms in Brussels and moved the major part of its staff from Luxembourg, it could save up to £50 million a year. Each time it tries, there is diplomatic infighting and the whole issue is put aside. If EC institutions had taken the advice of auditors 10 years ago to buy their buildings, then they could have avoided paying exorbitant rents. The very presence of the EC in Brussels has led to property developers charging prices way over the odds, and buildings showing little or no architectural merit destroying the character of one of the city's oldest quarters.

The EC's forerunner, the European Coal and Steel Community, was built on the post-war ruins of continental Europe. Its aim was to put the making of iron and steel for armaments under common control and rebuild the post-war industry. The choice of locations for offices and meeting places was either historical or to help the smaller states. It 'provisionally' agreed to base the coal and steel offices and Court of Justice in Luxembourg in July 1952.

Its Assembly, later the Parliament, held its meetings in the Alsatian city of Strasbourg on the French side of the Rhine.

The full-blown European Economic Community was founded by the Treaty of Rome in 1957 by the six governments from France, West Germany, Italy, The Netherlands, Belgium and Luxembourg. They said they would choose a single location for EC organisations before 1 June 1958. Well, June 1958 came and went and thirty years later the issue is still undecided, although Brussels has become the largest EC centre by far. A decision in 1967 confirmed Luxembourg's right to host ministerial meetings in April, June and October – forcing hundreds of needless 200-kilometre trips by officials, interpreters and journalists from Brussels.

Only the European Parliament regularly used all three locations. Each month it holds committee meetings in Brussels, serviced by permanent officials from Luxembourg. For one week 518 EuroMPs, committee officials, political aides and many administrative officials travel to Strasbourg for the monthly plenary session. Many top European Commission and government officials are obliged to do the same. Each Friday before the session, or earlier in some cases, papers are stuffed into trunks and the Parliament's fleet of pantechnicons rumbles off.

The strict cost in lost time, expenses of this operation and the journeying can be measured, though no figure can quantify the inefficiency of the system and the sheer waste of time to those involved. Peter Price, Tory MEP for London South-east, has monitored the cost and reckons that a single centre would save a minimum of £20–25 million – about 10 per cent of Parliament's budget.

'The assumption for that figure is that the European Parliament becomes more efficient and does more work. The staff time previously wasted becomes effective. If MEPs do the same amount of work, then you get the staff down. You could then double the savings to £50 million with reduced staff numbers. It is more likely in practice that this place would hum more – what organisation sheds staff? Therefore I don't think the £50 million is realistic,' Price says.

He is critical of a 1983 study by Ernst & Whinney, the international accountants, which five years later is still seen

3

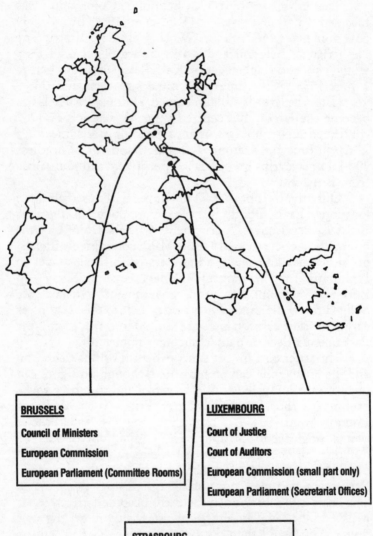

BRUSSELS

Council of Ministers

European Commission

European Parliament (Committee Rooms)

LUXEMBOURG

Court of Justice

Court of Auditors

European Commission (small part only)

European Parliament (Secretariat Offices)

STRASBOURG

European Parliament (Assembly Chambers)

as the main argument for preserving the status quo. He says that the Parliament's officials underestimated the cost of the time wasted packing up trunks on Friday every month for the session in Strasbourg, unpacking on the following Monday and then going through the same ritual at the end of the week. It is very disruptive. He suggests four whole days a month are spent in this process and believes the main boost from a single centre comes from efficiency in the way members and their offices work.

But cost is unlikely to settle the question where the Parliament is located or holds its plenary session. Even Price, a strict budget disciplinarian, says: 'The extra cost is not so huge to be a major argument for change. If it had been that big, the member states would have had to take action and they have not. You are talking about percentages of the Community budget. £25 million or £50 million is 0.1 or 0.2 per cent of the total EC budget. It is not that insignificant, but it is not a compelling figure.

'The real motivation for change is much more in the view taken of the European Parliament externally – the public being able to see a Parliament like Westminster. If people could see the Parliament in Brussels, they could envisage it better. Now they see it in Brussels, Luxembourg or Strasbourg. People think it is ridiculous because MEPs choose to have this itinerant life style. If member states can't agree, we have to take action unilaterally.'

Two moves will bring the issue to a head in the run-up to the June 1989 European Parliament elections. First, the practical effects of the Parliament's September 1988 legal victory on a Brussels base will be clearer. The French, who had no obvious supporters, had argued that only governments can decide where the Parliament sits. The Parliament won on its claim that a Brussels building will be used in an emergency and that using Strasbourg for sessions is not obligatory. The second move will be further pressure from UK Tories to centralise on Brussels.

In practice many of the political groups have moved their staff to Brussels, retaining only a skeleton service in Luxembourg. This itself has prompted court action by individual officials, based in Luxembourg and not keen to move. One possible option mooted has been a political trade-off involving the location of a new institution, the

European Trade Marks Office, which will shortly get underway. Under this plan Luxembourg would take on ETMO and give up the Parliament's secretariat, probably to Brussels.

Luxembourg diplomats query this option and stress the economic importance of EC institutions on their soil. Jean Dondelinger, Secretary General of the Foreign Ministry and tipped as a future European Commissioner, said: 'They are vitally important on political as well as economic grounds. There are 7,000 people who work for the EC, plus their families which makes one out of ten of the inhabitants.'

The Luxembourg ETMO move is unlikely, if only because it is an uneven trade-off. The Parliament's staff in Luxembourg comprise 2,600 and those from the ETMO may be as few as 200. There are other bidders to host the ETMO, which is the only major new institution planned. Ten countries put in bids (having an EC institution in your backyard is both lucrative and prestigious) and the European Commission produced a shortlist of four on grounds of suitable facilities and cost. The Hague is widely regarded as the best candidate. London, Munich and Madrid reached the final four.

Government officials have agonised over the site and decisions have been delayed. Luxembourg, threatening court action under its claim to site quasi-judicial institutions, believed it had many second choice votes, particularly from countries which were not pitching or were not in the last four. The British regard this as 'a bloody stupid idea. It should be done on first choices.' Many were prepared to call Luxembourg's bluff. As industry waited for its 'technical' decisions on the new trade mark regime, governments were haggling over the 'political' choice.

In mid-1988 two new sites put in their claims, to complicate (and delay) things further. France put up Strasbourg for the site of the ETMO. Spain said the south of Europe needed its share of EC institutions and pressed its case for Madrid. The Italians tried to put their flashy Venetian palazzi back on the agenda. London believed its leasehold building in St Katherine's dock site still stood a chance. The clear danger was that industry, for which the ETMO was designed, would get an inefficient service. (The political choice on languages in which the documents would be produced also had to be made. More than three would prevent it being self-financing. 'Over three, and the economics would go through the roof', said one official.)

Parliament's bid to find a single location was pressed hard by the Tories during 1988. Derek Prag, MEP for Hertfordshire, was piloting a report through the Parliament's political affairs committee calling for a single location. He believes Parliament's low standing in opinion surveys – fewer than half of Europe's citizens even know of its existence – could be improved. In the UK and The Netherlands, half had a 'generally unfavourable' view of the place, and only Italy and Portugal have a favourable opinion. In Brussels it could face off its rivals for power, the European Commission and the governments' Council of Ministers.

He complained of thirty-five years of delay by governments, marked by one attempt to resolve the issue in 1981 leading only to a statement confirming the status quo. Prag appealed to the Parliament's 'self-evident right' as a parliament elected by universal suffrage to decide on its main place of work. But he faces opposition from other MEPs, Luxembourg and French governments, and it would be astonishing if the Parliament decided anything positive, even in the next five years.

And polycentricity – having more than one centre – has its supporters. Pierre Pflimlin, French Christian Democrat MEP, former President of the Parliament and former Mayor of Strasbourg is one. He told a Brussels-based magazine in 1988: 'It is perfectly feasible and is a solution which has worked for many years. The inconveniences are greatly exaggerated'. He went on to explain how air flights between Brussels and Strasbourg took only 55 minutes and that MEPs always had to journey from their constituencies.

Pflimlin, not surprisingly, supports Strasbourg with pride. He knows that many enjoy their week there. It has an historic centre with good shops and restaurants. It is well-placed for visiting the German Black Forest across the Rhine. He says visitors are not fond of 'technocratic Europe symbolised by Brussels. They feel more at home in Strasbourg'. He says buildings are put up more quickly in

7

Strasbourg. Some take only eighteen months from scratch, whereas contracts Pflimlin signed two years before in Brussels had yet to begin.

'It just does not work in Brussels. Why not? Because Brussels is a city cut across by tension. It is always difficult to know who exactly to address yourself to; tensions between local, regional and national authorities are such that it is impossible to get anything done. I was responsible for security matters. It took me half a day to settle the problem with the French police and the Lower Rhine Prefect, compared with two years in Brussels.'

Brussels is the third Belgian region in this community of warring tribes of Flanders in the north and Wallonia in the south. For many, the excellent motorways provide a quick route around the city. Though it has an historical centre, those who stay in Brussels find it to be no architectural showpiece, with the EC presence having a significant influence on this. Its best boulevards have been turned into dual carriageways or car parks. The EC institutions have generated their own planning blight. Belgian speculators have let rip as the supra-national EC has remained diplomatically on the sidelines.

The EC institutions are on the eastern side of the city and only two or three kilometres from the centre of Brussels. Most of the expanding set of buildings lie between the Belgian ministries close to the centre and the Parc Cinquentenaire, two kilometres further east. Two five-lane tracks, Rue de la Loi and Rue Belliard, take traffic west and east respectively. They handle the commuter flows efficiently but are dark, dirty and with narrow pavements. They straddle the area between the European Commission's main building on Rue de la Loi and the Parliament's committee rooms on Rue Belliard.

In 1988 the last patches of grass and open space were being devoured for a massive new building for the governments' Council of Ministers secretariat, which currently has a less grandiose building across the street. The last gap along the Rue de la Loi five-lane highway was being blocked up. Temporary flyovers, road deviations and the infilling of a lake were all part of works expected to last for a number of years. One part of the development involved slicing vertically through a ten-storey office

8

block. Offices in one part remained occupied as a demolition gang removed the rest to make way for the controversial development.

Construction of the Council building has had a rocky history. A Belgian minister first gave the construction contract to a single firm without putting it out to tender to get the best bid on quality and price. This prompted complaints that an EC directive putting large works contracts out to competitive tendering had been breached. The much-abused 1971 EC directive was put in jeopardy at the very institution which has agreed to it – the Council of Ministers. The Belgian minister relented and groups of 'promoters-conceptualists-entrepreneurs' were asked to bid. It all sounded above board at last – but the dirty tricks department was still at work.

EC civil servants, their trade union and the Council's staff committee have monitored the building and the tendering of bids closely. According to one of the local unions: 'Fifteen projects will be put forward: but the improvisation is such that the wolves have entered the flock of sheep. It appears that one of the groups knew the programmes a month before the others, that the results of the competition were already known before the deliberations of a "jury" of which an important member – a European representative – was officially advised by a study group legally connected to one of the candidate groups.'

After the first round, the fifteen bids were whittled down to eleven and of these, ten replied to a request from the minister of public works to present one or more sets of plans for the Council building. Five consortia, including the UK's Costain Construction, were given the work in early 1980 to prepare detailed designs, architecture and to find financiers for the project. The work was divided between two groups from the five consortia, one to work on the buildings, the other on the infrastructure.

The contract tendering may still have breached the European directive – the invitation was not published in the EC's Official Journal as required. In exceptional cases, the regulation allows a contract to be negotiated. But all too often, the aim of the directive is breached in this way. The Commission's legal service intervened to see if the Belgians were breaking the rules, but the final resolution was a Belgian undertaking to publish future contracts for construction and services which will run up to FB9 billion (£150 million). It was all a big cover-up.

It's not just the fact that abuse of the rules had been taking place right under the EC's nose. The design of the building has angered Council staff too. (Sometimes these officials with a tough white-collar union appear fussy. They refused a move into the refurbished Residence Palace, a former apartment block opposite their present Charlemagne premises. While calling for the building to be preserved because of its elegant art deco interior, they refused to use it for offices. Instead, various Belgian government departments occupy the somewhat irregular shaped interior.)

Council staff agree with the aim to create a single site instead of their present four locations in Brussels. They urged designs and architecture 'in the best traditions of Europe' and avoiding 'monoliths'. A new development ought to 'present the structure of a small town' with corridors that are not 'tubelike' and of one dimension, but like streets with 'meeting places and some small areas allowing informal contact'. Working areas must be grouped to allow a view of outside life, they said. These fine ideas fell on deaf Belgian ears.

During 1984, Belgian royal decrees to allow the expropriation of property and land for the Council site prompted court retaliation by residents, Inter-Environment-Bruxelles and the civil servants' Union Syndicale. Their hearing before the Conseil d'Etat, the highest civil court in Belgium, was unsuccessful and their plea declared inadmissible. But the hearing allowed a further airing of the complaint over the contract tendering. Two of the five successful consortia (not Costain) had made proposals of only 'medium quality', the vetting by experts in 1979 had said.

But the design was still not decided despite the years of planning and legal delays, and the first sketches in early 1987 caused an outcry. They proposed a building outlined by three 40-metre high, seven-metre thick pillars and a 100-metre crosspiece which formed an 'E' on its side. It was the frontpiece to ten storeys of offices. As the Council staff quickly asked: ' "E" for Europe or "M" for monster?

It presents a massive construction out of all proportion, which is the expression of an authoritarian regime, totally contrary to the idea of a democratic Europe of citizens.'

The government authorities themselves asked for a re-think while the staff committee engaged their own architect to propose an alternative facade. Its proposal broke up the solid lines and removed the crossbar of the upturned 'E' and replaced it with five irregular spaced pillars and a more varied frontage. The finally-agreed design is for one of Brussels' largest developments comprising 214,000 square metres of meeting rooms, office space, and 2,000 parking places in a series of interlocking islands.

It is a complex building offering space for ministers, and, at times, heads of government, to meet. The meeting rooms must provide interpretation facilities. Fast transla-tion for documents must also be on hand. Security is a factor here. But it is also a place where 2,000 officials, secretaries and other staff will spend their working days all year round. Several hundred square metres have been set aside for a café, fitness and social centre, and chapel. The original hopes for a mini-town have disappeared. There is only one shop – for books, newspapers and cigarettes.

The battle against ugly and intrusive buildings is one taken up by residents as well as the officials who work for the EC institutions. The staff representatives have joined residents on the south edge of the quarter to campaign against a conference centre and office development. This is a private development but the centre, with its debating chamber, is being lined up for the European Parliament if it moves *en masse* to Brussels. It may be one of the last major developments in the area as the remaining land is fought over. The EC ghetto is nearly complete.

First firm plans in April 1987 cover a site not far behind the Parliament's committee rooms and would extend over an old defunct Stella Artois brewery and the adjacent Gare du Luxembourg railway station. The initial cost would be FB5 – 6 billion (£90 million) but rising to FB 20 billion as the development extended over the railway tracks up to the year 2000. Planning application for the congress centre arrived first. It was a building of ten storeys with a cupola roof and would later connect to the adjacent exhibition and office space.

The application said there would be shops, housing and offices to meet 'the wishes of the people of Brussels as much as of Europe. We want to avoid too large a contamination in the residential areas and to improve the use of public transport.' Public consultation brought a call for an impact assessment by Jean-Louis Thys, government minister for the Brussels region, on its technical and financial feasibility.

Residents were stunned by the April 1987 plans, not least because the announcement came halfway through completion of a study of the quarter by Thys. It raises a large question mark over Thys's objectivity. The Espace Bruxelles-Europe study had taken evidence since June 1986 from the local groups, the EC unions, government departments and a host of urban experts. It was not due to be published until November 1987 and its recommendations would have a major impact, subject only to adaptation by the three local councils (communes) and the central departments of public works and transport.

It was already clear that those preparing the study and those developing the International Congress Centre came from the same stable. The main authors of the EBE study were town planners Centre d'Etude et de Recherche d'Architecture et d'Urbanisme (CERAU), assisted by Bureau Vanden Bossche, a firm of architects. CERAU had also prepared the ICC planning application and Vanden Bossche were the architects. Thys had clearly not set up an independent study and was involved closely himself as a member of its technical committee.

Another group of activists, the Brussels Council for the Environment (BRAL), made a vitriolic intervention and pinpointed the financiers and construction companies behind the project. It was the usual gang of speculators, they claimed. BRAL called the Thys EBE study a 'supercherie' – a deceit or a swindle in English – and said it had been forced on Thys in exchange for building permission for the Council of Ministers complex. It was part of a deal with Thys's predecessor, BRAL claimed.

BRAL went to town on Thys. His FB20 million (£330,000) study was 'vaudeville', it said. The double role of architect Vanden Bossche was 'ethically unacceptable'. It suggested that Belgium was moving Parliament's sessions to Brussels by the backdoor: treaty obligations prevented a formal government offer but the private sector was aiming for a sitting before the June 1989 European elections in the new conference centre. BRAL wanted the cards on the table.

The four building companies who would become the owners of the conference and station complex had a well-known track record, BRAL said. The financiers were the Christian Workers Bank, BACOB, and Societe Generale, the largest Belgian holding company. More pointedly it spoke of the firm which will run the centre when it is completed – the Foire International de Bruxelles. This non-profit organisation owned by the Brussels City Council already runs the post Expo-58 exhibition and conference site on the edge of the city, beside the Heysel stadium.

Controversially this company is chaired by Paul Vanden Boeynants, a former Belgian Christian Democrat prime minister, who was convicted of large-scale tax fraud in 1986 and whose three-year suspended sentence was confirmed on appeal in January 1987. The first judge called Vanden Boeynants 'an inveterate fraudster'. This criticism has not stopped him resuscitating his political career by trying to become the mayor of Brussels in the October 1988 municipal election. This would confirm his position as Foire chairman.

So the European Parliament could shortly find itself occupying premises managed by a company chaired by a tax fiddler. Direct control by Vanden Boeynants is mitigated by a large board of directors and some form of democratic check. But the situation is unsavoury at the least. Surprisingly, and to his credit, the Foire chairman does have a better reputation than most for achievements in Belgian and Brussels politics. The company already handles European Commission contracts in the trade promotion field.

The second line of attack made by local residents against the conference centre has been through the courts. Their Association du Quartier Leopold said the ministry had no legal standing to issue the building permission, that the interests of neighbouring households had not been taken into account and that there had been a secret agreement between the minister and the investors. The Belgian government replied, claiming the law had been followed.

The judgement in February was a resounding victory for the residents association. Judge Halsberghe formally ordered the works to stop and put the cost of any further breach at FB500,000 (£8,300) a day. The judge said that Secretary of State Thys had no legal standing to grant planning permission. Under the Belgian constitution he was a minister of the central government and only regional or local governments could approve planning decisions.

Thys, who was re-appointed in the April 1988 government, and the developers expect to get their way with only minor amendments to meet local opposition from residents or communes. This is despite the fact that plans filed in May 1988 boosted the height of the buildings to include two towers of eighteen floors, significantly higher than the surrounding blocks. The local association accepts that the development will take place because much of the area is run down and includes temporary buildings. The fears are that the roads system will not cope. The latest plans boost public transport with a one-kilometre moving walkway from the nearest metro station.

The quarter has become an urban ghetto and fewer people live there. It is a major centre of employment in Brussels with a comparable density of jobs to those in the city centre. But the enormous lunchtime or evening spending power of EC officials on fashionable clothes, fancy food or electronic goods has not been tapped. Shops consist of banks, cafes and restaurants, newsagents, hairdressers and chemists. While some of the housing has been gentrified, much remains Arab-occupied and under threat of expropriation. The squares on the fringes are better preserved.

Much of the architecture comprises plain blocks and will never win any prizes. The Thys EBE study makes comparisons with Washington and New York and there are pictures of well-planted atriums inside buildings and broad pavements with trees. But Brussels compares favourably only on good integration of metro stations into surrounding buildings. The distinctive four-cornered

Commission Berlaymont block is striking, with trees in the front, but acts as a funnel for wind and rain.

The latest claim to grand design is a footbridge high above Rue Belliard to link the Parliament's committee rooms with new office space. Architects and parliament officials say it is symbolic – 'la porte de l'Europe', or gateway to Europe. But it is no more than a glorified gangway.

There is still talk in the study of accommodating the twin goals of increasing office accommodation and making the environment more pleasing. This will be a long-term task as the study also predicts the present works, mainly on the two sites of Council and conference centre, will take fifteen years to complete when putting in the necessary roads and making good is included. This prediction goes hand in hand with rising numbers of EC civil servants in Brussels. It predicts numbers will rise from 13,000 in 1986 to 19,000 at 2.5–4 per cent in the short term and to 21,000 by the year 2000.

The conclusions of the study are rather tame, though the improvement of small specific areas may prove controversial to residents. This is mainly because the study virtually ignores the two main developments: integration of the Council building is not considered because it is not a 'mixed' zone of office and residential. Its only notable mention is its need for a 'quick and reliable evacuation' route out of town to the east. The conference centre development was skimmed over because the plans were being revised.

One thing that Brussels has in its favour as a European centre is its low rates for office rental, though this is beginning to change. The Thys study quotes UK estate agents Jones, Lang, Wootton in 1986 comparing City of London prices of FB30,000 per square metre a year with those in Brussels at FB6,000. In 1988 the rates were moving up smartly. On the 1986 analysis it could claim it was cheaper than London, Paris, Frankfurt, Glasgow, The Hague and Dublin.

But choosing a cheap location does not necessarily mean good value. A major review in 1979 of accommodation by the EC's own financial watchdog, the Court of

Auditors, produced limited reforms. It had queried the way property was nearly always rented. This was due in part to no decision being taken on a permanent location of the EC institutions. The only purchases made by the European Commission had been for external offices in Paris, Montevideo, London (on a 99-year lease), Ottawa and Washington.

Yet at that time, only two out of forty-eight leases the Court examined had been subjected to any comparison of the rental with the capital cost of the building. And in these cases, the calculations had been made by the constructor or the landlord. Its calculations for some of the large buildings made alarming reading. The Court compared the accumulated rentals paid since construction, as indexed to the Belgian consumer price index, with the estimated cost of the construction.

Five buildings, two in Luxemburg, indicated that the rents were so astronomical that it took only between eleven and thirteen years to pay back the cost of the buildings. The Court ignored the interest cost of financing the building, but took a conservative line on other aspects of valuation. It is obvious that where the EC's around, property owners are tapping a rich vein.

The overhaul of the renting policy was the main conclusion from the Court's review. It said that the institutions should consider reducing rentals in future lease negotiations, take up the buy-back written into some leases or remove the indexation in some deals. Another economy that could be introduced was more common planning among the three major institutions, the Council, Commission and Parliament, of their accommodation. Five-year rolling plans, reviewable each year should be made.

Joint planning began in 1981 after the Court's report was backed by governments. Its conclusion was that 'in appropriate cases' property ought to be bought. The Commission has completed just two buildings in this fashion. The first at 121 Rue de la Loi was financed out of its own budget to the tune of FB1.3 billion (£22 million) and comprises 50,000 square metres. This appears immediately to cut the cost. At FB26,000 (£400) a square metre it is under the 1979 court estimate for building of between FB30,000 and FB40,000.

But this first case is slightly artificial because it involved the Commission buying an existing building and land from the Belgian government for a notional one Belgian franc. Only 40,000 square metres are new works. (The Commission offered an ecu, a European currency unit, but the Belgians said they could not accept it.) And the contract allows the Belgians a buy-back option at market price, payment over five years. This development was managed by architects and constructors employed directly by the Commission and began being occupied in 1988.

A second more commercial development has taken place at Rue Breydel/Avenue d'Auderghem. The fixed price contract puts the cost at FB2.3 billion (£35 million) including the land and 50,000 square metres of office space. The capital cost here is the still competitive FB46,000 per square metre. This is not surprisingly above the court's 10-year old figure of FB40,000 but is still good value. According to Ole Bjorn Petersen, Commission official in charge: 'On the rent we are normally paying, it will take up to seven years to get to the break-even point.'

The major new Council block, which has taken so long to get started, is expected to cost FB8.5 billion (£130 million) for 214,000 square metres of space, of which 80,000 square metres is offices, 55,000 square metres conference centre and 75,000 square metres parking. Overall it is a cost of FB40,000 a square metre and on par with the Court of Auditors' 1979 parameters. But take the parking away and the cost rises to FB63,000 a square metre. The land was once again a nominal one franc to the Belgian state.

The Council building is more costly than the two basic office blocks the Commission has just built. This is justified by sophisticated facilities, including interpretation, and a complex infrastructure of roadways. Competitive tendering has been more effective though so far it has not interested many UK companies. One reason was pre-qualification of contractors long before the works were due to start. The fears of an overrun on cost persist but are not yet to the forefront. But in mid-1988 the foundations were only beginning to be laid.

But many buildings are still being expensively rented.

17

By 1988 the Commission will have paid twice over for two major buildings, the Complex Joyeuse Entree and Berlaymont, which it uses in Brussels. (The Berlaymont is the four-sided affair often pictured in publicity photographs.) The Court of Auditors' 1979 figures also predict that the Council will have paid two and a half times over for its Charlemagne building by the time it moves to its new block in 1992. It is expected that the Commission will then take over the Charlemagne.

Both Commission and Council have gone some way to renegotiating better terms on existing rental agreements. The Berlaymont building's rent remains the same, though a five-year plan for 'complete renovations' is being undertaken at the owner's expense. At the Joyeuse Entree complex the Commission has negotiated renovations, possibly worth FB500 million (£8.5 million) and is still discussing rent cuts. It expects to reach a deal that sets rent 'just above half' of the market rate of FB6,500.

One official says: 'If we keep the Berlaymont and Joyeuse Entree for more than twenty years, there is obviously an interest in buying. It should be renovated between its twentieth and twenty-fifth birthday, and we could probably renovate one more time, then have to consider if we can use it any more. Above fifty years, an office building will have lived more than its life cycle. The thing to do is buy from the beginning. I am not saying it is too late, but we have obviously lost.'

Having already paid twice over by renting buildings like the Berlaymont, the Commission now obviously intends to repeat the process. Quite clearly it would have been cheaper to buy these premises years ago. It's small wonder that there are those who express doubts about the EC's use of taxpayers' money.

The Council is critical of the Court of Auditors' 'simplistic' calculations. Its Charlemagne lease was for less than market rates and has since been negotiated 'far below market price'. But the Council eventually accepted that buying was cheaper and is able to spread the cost of its new building over five years from 1988.

If the EC had started life with twelve countries and the policy areas it has today, it would have bought a single green field site and built its own premises. That did not happen. But in coping with its own growth, it could have taken a more critical look at its costs and its efficient running. Too often it attempted to stitch up political deals which did not meet these criteria. In Brussels it has sponsored a quick killing for the property market and neglected the quality of its own neighbourhood. The EC has lost, the taxpayers of several countries have lost – it's only a few Belgians who have gained. No wonder they are all in favour of the EC.

2 STAFF: MONEY FOR OLD ROPE, JOBS FOR THE BOYS

The popular portrait of the European Commission official depicts him, or less likely her, as overpaid, underworked and abroad having a good time. There are stories of the skiving official who leaves a jacket on the back of his chair and a smoking pipe in an ashtray in his Brussels office, but who in reality is sailing his dinghy in Antwerp, thirty-five kilometres away. Another tale cites the official who plays computer chess to while away his day as an adjacent secretary waits anxiously to use the same word processor to type up her day's correspondence.

Other versions tell of a newly-appointed official in town organising his perk of a refund of value-added tax on the purchase of some hi-fi equipment. An inflated price on paper will grant a higher refund of tax and the shop was interested. Elsewhere at an invalidity tribunal, a more experienced official was negotiating his exit from the service. A sickness benefit would still be a handsome income: all he had to do was keep up the pretence of mental instability. Urinating in his boss's ashtray had been a start to a campaign his doctor was backing.

Such stories are dismissed as the myths of being a civil servant in an European Community institution. But the hard evidence reveals more disturbing flaws in recruitment, career development and management of officials. Posting to middle manager jobs is often rigged to make up an illegal national quota or as a political favour. Staff shortages persist in priority areas but overstaffing is rarely tackled. The mixed quality of officials from the UK is improving but recruitment is hampered by an incredible five-year delay in appointments.

A job with the EC is a job for life and the chances of being sacked for incompetence are negligible. Any threat from the management can be countered by appealing to the EC's own Court of Justice in Luxembourg. One official who physically attacked his boss took nearly five years to sack because of court actions. Hundreds of staff cases have clogged up a court designed to deal with multi-million pound legal disputes involving governments and international business.

When the House of Lords' select committee on the EC reported on staff issues in May 1988, it called for widespread reform. On staffing levels, it said some Commission services were 'significantly understaffed'; the recruitment of non-career staff at middle manager level had 'a widespread and seriously adverse effect on staff morale and efficiency'; it called on the UK Government to play a greater role in publicising these careers and to protect promotion rights where UK civil servants join the EC institutions and later wish to re-patriate.

Table 2.1 **Staff employed by EC institutions**

European Commission	15,000
European Parliament	3,100
Council of Ministers	2,000
European Investment Bank	700
Court of Justice	650
Economic and Social Committee	470
Court of Auditors	350
Total	22,270

(Includes vacant posts; the government-owned EIB operates independently from the other EC institutions and has its own more flexible personnel policies)

The size of the Commission has traditionally been a complaint. Comparisons used to be made against the

21

recently abolished Greater London Council. The House of Lords inquiry made loose comparisons with Wandsworth Council in London, the Scottish Office or the Department of Trade and Industry. Clearly the Lords' estimates are out of date. Wandsworth only employs 4,800, the Scottish Office 8,000, and the DTI 12,000. But such comparisons are irrelevant in fixing proper staff numbers to handle the tasks to be undertaken, and merely provide ammunition to pro- or anti-marketeers scoring quick political points.

Detailed staff regulations, with the force of law, lay down the conditions, salaries and perks for civil servants employed by the EC institutions. It has put them into four basic categories, A, B, C, or D depending on whether they are fully-fledged officials making and carrying out policy, their assistants, secretaries or manual workers. In UK civil service terms, an A grade compares to an administrative grade, a B grade to an executive officer. Interpreters or translators are classified in a separate L/A language service grade.

The rules impose rights and obligations on officials. They must work for Europe and 'shall neither seek nor take instructions from any government, organisation or person outside his institution'. It means that an official is not supposed to take bribes or lean towards his or her home-country in policy-making. Equally the blandishments of lobbying groups from either side of industry must be kept at arm's length. With growing pressure from such groups, it calls for the integrity of the official to be of the highest order.

In many ways these regulations mirror those of Whitehall, ensuring that civil servants operate independently. On public elections they may be more relaxed. There are no known cases of officials working concurrently as EuroMPs, but there is an interchange. Several officials from the UK have become MEPs and at least one has returned to the Commission. Taking on jobs, mostly consultancies, straight after leaving is commonplace. There is no Official Secrets Act for EC officials but they are prevented from talking about legal proceedings in which they are involved.

Senior officials are granted semi-diplomatic immunity and the rights that go with it. This puts them on a similar footing to employees of other international organisations, such as the United Nations or the Organisation for Economic Cooperation and Development. Officials are not subject to immigration formalities and gain preferential foreign currency treatment on moving. National taxation is another bugbear removed, though the EC organisations have their own tax regime.

In practice, newly-appointed officials in Belgium can buy furniture, televisions, video recorders, or hi-fi equipment free from VAT during their first year. This is a substitute for the tax-free importation specifically set out in the EC treaty and only one of each item can be claimed VAT-free. Cars are another well-exercised perk. A UK official on only a temporary contract can gain substantially when he takes an expensive model tax-free back to his home country after a two- or three-year stay. First he saves twenty-five per cent car tax in Belgium and then fifteen per cent VAT on returning to the UK.

As the EC moves closer towards economic integration under its plan to remove trade and fiscal barriers by 1992, many of these perks will take some justifying. By then furniture and effects, which have already been liable to VAT in one country, will not be charged again to VAT and no specific right to tax-free status will be needed. The hi-fi 'imports' are a subtle extension of the original treaty to which the same should apply. By 1992 moving across borders within Europe will no longer have the significance it had and some of these diplomatic perks ought to fade away.

The EC is an excellent payer. To secretaries, it is clearly paying over the odds and comparisons are straightforward. Its C-grade secretary salaries vary between FB118,035 (£1,800) a month and FB62,235 depending on seniority. The salary for an average-ability EC secretary, with a minimum of two languages, is rarely less than FB80,000. In the open Brussels market, based on advertised jobs in June 1988, 'a top executive secretary/personal assistant' was being offered FB75,000–85,000. Other multilingual vacancies for secretaries were rarely over FB65,000 and often much less.

It is scarcely surprising that Belgian women have flooded into the Commission to take on the jobs. They have a dominant share amongst the nationalities of C grades, 39 per cent at the last count and way ahead of the next country, Italy, with 15 per cent. The Commission is paying inflated salaries to secretaries compared to the multinational companies around the corner. Its tax and other benefits distort the picture even further. At the C grade, the EC's low tax rate of 20 per cent will even out with allowances, making take-home pay close to gross salary. The non-EC Belgian employee still faces steep taxes.

And the Commission can hardly claim it is offering these high salaries to maintain a geographical balance. It obviously has made little effort to share out posts between nationalities as the statistics indicate. And the need to do so

Table 2.2 **Salary comparison – EC versus national civil services**

(£/year)	A1	A8
EC	81,600	21,600
West Germany	53,500	17,300
Denmark	53,000	21,300
UK	45,300	7,600
Netherlands	40,400	18,500
Luxembourg	38,200	18,700
Belgium	36,300	12,400
Ireland	35,000	9,200
Spain	33,800	8,800
France	31,800	8,200
Italy	26,900	9,400
Portugal	7,000	3,000
Greece	6,800	4,300

(Top A1 step, lowest A8 step, July 1987 currency exchange; the A1 grade is equivalent to a UK permanent secretary, the A8 to an executive officer. The table compares the Commission's A1 grade with top civil servants' pay in national governments.)

is much less important than with policy-making officials. It would do better to go into the open market and cut its salary bill dramatically.

Salaries are based on a complex formula and are reviewed annually to take account of moves in exchange rates and purchasing power in individual countries. The result is a table of salaries for all grades and experience, which is above rates for civil servants in government service in any of the twelve EC countries. The Commission says this is to encourage staff of sufficient quality to work away from their home country with the rigours that entails. No simple comparison between national and European civil service pay rates is possible because of different job descriptions, age and grading structures.

On A grade officials, some conclusions can be drawn which indicate that in the poorest states, Greece and Portugal, the highest Commission salaries are up to ten times better than at home. On the other hand, it is scarcely worth national civil servants from Denmark and West Germany making the move to Brussels. If both husband and wife are already working, it is probably a financial loss to move because one partner would probably not replace their earnings. Spanish pay, above that of France and Italy at higher grades, made EC recruitment difficult when it joined in 1986.

A permanent secretary from Whitehall, the top UK civil service grade, earns up to £50,000 a year before tax and about £35,000 after tax and social security. If a 'perm sec' moved to become a top-ranking A1 Commission official his gross salary could go up to £82,000 depending on the specific posting. Child allowances and an expatriation subsidy of 16 per cent paid in addition to resettlement expenses would increase his gain in take-home pay. But the EC top tax rate of 45 per cent also begins to bite and the oft-used rule that gross pay is close to post-tax pay begins to break down. Despite this a permanent secretary could expect to double his salary with a move to Brussels.

The clear message from comparisons at this and other grades is that a UK civil servant can earn far more with the same skills working for the Commission and this applies to most national civil servants. Whether this draws better or worse staff to Brussels is unclear, though it may attract those seeking high cash rewards rather than those looking for job satisfaction or those who have a sense of public duty. More important is how it competes, especially at the entry level, with alternative careers such as in industry. The UK civil service already suffers from this competition and the EC salaries win on this front.

But surprisingly recruitment of officials from the UK has been patchy in quantity and quality. After the UK entry in 1973, trawls for suitable candidates produced low-quality officials: some from Second World War refugee families who were keen to return to their continental roots. Where strong candidates were found, they often did not stay for long, finding that the Commission environment did not suit them.

Richard Hay, the Commission's Director General for personnel and administration, told the House of Lords inquiry: 'The historical reason is that the enlargement in 1973 was badly managed. I do not mean that as a criticism. It was the first time that the Community had enlarged, and we attempted to do it in one year. We learnt that to try to recruit the volume of people that was in question, in one year, was totally impossible. There were various unfortunate consequences from that: a) we started off with a deficit at the end of the year; b) in the wish to make progress the selection procedures were not always very rigorous.

'Also there was the fact that the British Government then raised a question mark about its continued membership of the Community, which dried up candidates in the period immediately after that initial year, which made it difficult to compensate when we might have been able to do something immediately afterwards. Therafter it became very difficult to make exceptions.'

There are no guaranteed national quotas for officials, except at the highest echelons. Only the European Commissioners, the seventeen politicians appointed by governments to run the Commission, are on a laid down quota: two for a large country, one for a small one. At the A1 and A2 grades of Director General or Director, quotas are in operation though on a less precise basis and after extensive inter-government haggling. This also exists for some A3 posts but not all. For postings below these levels, officials must clamber up the rungs from the A7 or A8 entry level.

Table 2.3 **Nationality of European Commission officials**

	Belgium	Denmark	Germany	Greece	Spain	France	Ireland	Italy	Luxembourg	Netherlands	Portugal	UK	Total
A1	4	1	6	1	5	7	1	7	1	4	1	7	45
A2	11	4	21	4	9	20	5	17	3	9	4	18	125
A3	24	13	48	14	22	54	11	53	10	18	5	43	315
A4	86	14	148	10	7	129	19	142	17	21	4	83	680
A5	75	22	93	21	58	131	18	96	6	28	12	83	643
A6	55	10	55	64	29	61	16	40	6	36	14	63	449
A7	98	6	47	20	60	63	17	29	6	23	26	46	441
A8	12	2	4	3	28	9	2	5	1	5	12	5	348
	365	72	422	137	218	474	89	389	50	144	78	348	2,786

(Source: European Commission, November 1987. At the top levels the UK has its 'share' of jobs. It has 15.5 per cent of A1 posts and 14.5 per cent of A2. This puts it on a par with the other three large countries, Germany, France and Italy. Below this level, the UK begins to slip. At the A3, head of division level, the UK is behind the three large countries with 13.5 per cent of the posts and at A4/A5 levels, where much of the policy is first drafted, it has 12 and 13 per cent respectively. It even slips behind Belgium at the A4 level which has a high share because of its location. UK A6 and A7 shares are 14 and 10 per cent respectively.)

A sign that fifteen years after joining the UK had failed to find career EC officials capable of reaching the top came with the drafting of Geoffrey Fitchew, a Treasury undersecretary appointed in 1986 to head the financial services directorate at the Commission. This had the added attraction of a UK official in a policy area key to future UK interests. In 1987 David Williamson, head of the Cabinet Office's European Secretariat, became the Commission's Secretary General, its chief civil servant, after a complex inter-government haggle. But Williamson had served as a Commission deputy director-general between 1977 and 1983.

A number of Tory EuroMPs have pushed for disclosure of staff figures and better efforts by the Commission to improve the UK share in the mid-range. The Commission replies that if candidates don't come forward for selection, then it is not surprising the UK is at a disadvantage. Recruitment is rightly on merit, though it has to lean towards maintaining the 'broadest geographical basis', as the staff regulations say. Under UK government pressure, the Commission is making greater efforts to publicise recruitment and meet other criticisms of its selection methods. The Government itself is organising seminars.

Witnesses at the House of Lords inquiry listed a catalogue of reasons why UK graduates had been reluctant to seek jobs with the Commission. The Association of Graduate Careers Advisory Services complained that Commission literature about careers was limited and a recent booklet was 'still not attractive or informative by British standards'. The booklet and advertisements concentrated too much on application procedures and not enough on the work which successful applicants would perform. Letters from potential applicants to EC institutions often went unanswered and this gave a bad impression.

Applicants had to have degrees already and could not apply in their last University year, as many did for the UK civil service or industrial jobs. The Commission has traditionally hired staff with some work experience though this is changing slightly. Degrees in law, economics or public administration were often necessary rather than a broader background. Another major obstacle to those who successfully complete the written tests and interview is the delay in being appointed. The EC institutions set up reserve lists and sometimes candidates remain on these for as long as five years.

Because there is no single recruitment office for all the various EC bodies, the smaller institutions such as the Council or the Parliament cannot hold regular selection competitions and vacancies are closed off for many years. According to the House of Lords in May 1988, the Council had not sought A grade candidates since 1984 and the Parliament since 1982. In the Council's case, 5,000 applicants in September 1984 were whittled down to a reserve list of fifty after tests and interviews lasting twenty-two months. The list was expected to be used up over three to four years.

The Lords' report proposed that a joint recruitment service be set up, covering at least the three major EC institutions. This ought to be coupled to annual recruitment exams leading to announcements of reserve lists nine months after the recruitment began. It would avoid the loss of talented recruits who will not wait years to be appointed. It was a sound suggestion to prevent top-quality graduates joining industry or national civil services. There they would end up outsmarting the EC.

The Commission says reforms are underway and believes joint recruiting could be extended to twenty per cent of jobs in five years' time. Specialist competitions for economists or lawyers would be set predictably every two or three years. It aims to cut selection time to a year and 'exploit' the reserve list within two or three months. Hay, the Commission's personnel boss, said: 'Instead of having to wait for three or four, or sometimes five years, a candidate will know where he is within a year and a half, which is a considerable improvement on the present situation.'

The setting of tests and interviews is handled by a selection board including one member nominated by the staff committee, representing employee interests. A large-scale recruitment would typically have a board of five, and three is the minimum. Recruitment is a costly business across the twelve countries and the Commission spent £2.3 million in 1987, or nearly £1,700 for each successful candidate. In very large competitions this can be cut by using national centres for exam-taking. Compared to head-hunting fees of twenty-five per cent of the first year's salary, this is reasonable.

Moving from successful reserve list to a job has proved troublesome for UK candidates. The list is circulated to the heads of each of the twenty-plus Commission director generals so they can pick the staff they want. Directorates from farming to financial services have well-laid down staff numbers in the annual budget, and when a post is vacated by retirement or promotion, they take a name from the reserve list. Their choice is often the result of lobbying by those listed rather than the alphabetically first-named, oldest or other objective criterion.

A graduate careers specialist told the House of Lords: 'Such activities are foreign to British practice – indeed in the public sector are often expressly forbidden! Although the purpose of such contact is to express interest in the work of a particular department rather than to exercise unfair influence, many students find it distasteful.' Other Britons argue that UK applicants should change their attitude and make their claim to the jobs better known.

The obstacles to becoming the chief civil servant in the European Commission don't end with recruitment – they only begin. The national rivalries, the political differences and the personal jealousies emerge quickly. The paper shuffling up the hierarchy and back again begins. The trade-offs with officials in other directorates or with national administrations are planned. The backstop position on negotiations is fixed. The finessing of documents, the staple fodder for all civil servants, is underway. In a high-priority policy sector the work will be stimulating; in others a stagnant and depressing backwater.

And moving from one directorate to another is no easy task. Commission officials too often become specialists, not all-purpose civil servants in the British model. Some continental officials prefer making their life's work mastering the intricacy of some arcane farming regulation. Whether this is healthy for their own development is for them to decide. It must be doubtful if it injects the most imaginative ideas into EC policy or is the most efficient use of resources. The continental tradition has made it accepted management and personnel policy for this to continue.

Hay claims mobility is rising and that ten per cent of A grade officials will change jobs each year. He does not expect it to rise as high as 20 per cent because of the many specialised services in the Commission such as nuclear reactor inspectors, vets and doctors. In 1986, 35 per cent of new staffing needs were covered by people moving within directorates to priority areas. He says: 'You have to persuade each director general that it is a good thing to do. Some of them are better at it and it is becoming more of a habit in the house. Only by preaching can you make people do it.'

In the Commission, when posts below the A2 level become vacant, they must be advertised internally before other applicants can be considered. The staff regulations spell out three ways to fill vacancies. The first is by promotion or transfer within the institution, the second is to hold an internal recruitment, and the third is to consider transfer applications from officials of other EC institutions. In practice these sideways and upward moves are not always handled so straightforwardly. Particularly at the A3 level, they can prove highly controversial with the national quota re-emerging.

At the lower echelons, a division head will often appoint the candidate he has lined up for the post. Unless there is an outcry from the trade unions or staff committee, most of these empty posts are filled quickly and efficiently. But many of the vacancy notices for these posts are geared specifically to favoured candidates and their experience or skills. It is another bar to mobility. The staff committee in Brussels deals with about one complaint a fortnight. As the level of grade rises to A4/A5 or A3 the appointments become more controversial with serious claims of rigging on geographical or political grounds.

The charge is a long-standing one. When a high level review body examined the staffing of the Commission in 1979 it said: 'Appointments at A3 are frequently influenced by political or geographical considerations and, at this level, staff inevitably have to be recruited from outside. As there are no special rules like those for grades A1 and A2, these recruitments are made by devious procedures, the appointee being brought in on a temporary contract and subsequently established as a full official by means of an internal competition at which because of his special experience, he is sure of being successful.

'A similar procedure also operates for appointment of outsiders at A5/A4 which has a generally disruptive effect on career prospects. These purely formal competitions – the so-called 'rigged competitions' (*concours-bidons* in French) – are understandably unpopular with staff; and they do not even provide a guarantee that the Commission will select the best possible candidate.'

Often on these occasions, high-quality staff are recruited, though one can guess that there have also been mistakes. That is not directly the problem. The unions and staff side complain about its disruptive effect and this is not surprising either, since it is their job prospects that are at risk. The national interests of officials on temporary contracts can also be overplayed – it is just as much a fault of full-time officials. The real problem is that the procedure is underhand. The motives of those carrying out this pantomime are not genuine. In many cases, their choice is already made.

One Commission official involved in personnel policy says: 'The policy is that we want to follow the staff regulations but we also want some freedom to nominate those people who are good. We will not give up the freedom of acting in that way.' This is a sensible course and one that the rules ought to allow. Changing the staff regulations is regarded as taboo but one which the Commission ought to face up to. It would prevent the farce that exists today – searching out loopholes in the rules.

An early 1980s' case involved an A3 appointment in the Luxembourg-based nuclear safeguards directorate. The Director General at the time was Christopher Audland, a British official who after retiring, advised the House of Lords on their personnel inquiry in 1988. Audland had begun discussions in 1982 with the French Atomic Energy Commission to find a replacement for the existing French A3 division chief. He believed he had found a suitable candidate who could be appointed under a staff regulation for A1 or A2 officials or 'in exceptional cases, also for recruitment to posts which require special qualifications'.

But the Commission had trained up its own experts and Dutchman Erik van der Stijl had been covering for the existing French official, who was ill for a long time before leaving in March 1983. By June, nine officials from the Commission had presented themselves for the vacancy, including van der Stijl. The consultative committee for A2 and A3 appointments shortlisted three of the candidates and one was judged to be very competent and fully qualified for the post. None of the internal candidates was French.

Bernard Math, the better of two energy authority Frenchmen, was appointed by the Commission at its meeting on July 27, 1983 with effect from the end of September. During October, van der Stijl lodged a complaint against being passed over but it had no effect and the Commission president confirmed the decision in November. Audland later told the Court of Justice that the qualifications of the best internal candidate were 'equivalent although different' to Math. The Commission's decisions were cancelled by the Court in October 1985 and Math briefly stepped down.

Math was later reappointed and van der Stijl launched a further two court challenges, including a claim for compensation, before he retired in 1987. At one point during 1987, there were eight legal actions outstanding involving Math's job after others intervened. The Commission ought to have had the rules changed to allow it to manage better but instead it preferred to break the ones it did not like.

Another long-running dispute involves the sharing of jobs between nationalities in the directorate for competition policy. Once again, the Commission never came clean on what it was up to. The sordid story had to be revealed in legal proceedings.

In March 1984 the Commission reorganised the running of its competition directorate of several hundred officials, executive officers and secretaries. One aim was to introduce more coordination within the various aspects of the anti-trust and subsidy scrutiny. It was not universally popular and morale suffered in the short term after the shake-up by Frans Andriessen, the competition policy commissioner at the time. But it was the allocation of the reorganised posts that brought the row to a head. Internal recruitment was following a pre-planned pattern, claimed the officials who had lost out.

Early in March the Director General had to circulate a statement to his staff that copies of a 'new organisation chart' had no validity, and that the nationalities assigned to the posts were premature. But at the end of May, Dutchman Paul Waterschoot was duly appointed to the 'Dutch' post to head a team curbing the monopoly power of state utilities. The appointment was challenged by a German and a British official who together with Waterschoot had been among sixteen candidates for the post. The Commission re-ran the recruitment once again as a series of postings were held up. This second appointment prompted a full court challenge.

After the Court of Justice ruled against the Commission management in July 1987 the vacancy was re-advertised and Waterschoot appointed for the third time. Legal proceedings were launched in 1988 by rival candidates. Doubts that the Dutchman had the correct university qualifications and experience for the post may have been overtaken. Waterschoot may well be the best qualified candidate now but the Commission has not made it easy for this version of events to emerge. The case makes it look as if it set the nationality criterion above that of merit.

Andrew Moat, the president of the staff committee in Brussels told his colleagues in 1988: 'We can only hope they (who challenged the appointment) win again, and that the Commission will take account of the effect of its actions both on the morale of those staff whose candidatures are, apparently, not treated seriously, and on the moral of the favoured who find their appointments attacked and annulled in this way.'

The Commission chiefs say picking staff is their job – let the managers manage! (The court has no right to pick a new candidate for the post and it can only cancel the previous appointment.) Hay says that in 'the multinational context, appointments can include an element of nationality, but not at the expense of quality'. If the choice at A3 level and above was solely on merit, the larger countries would probably gain. Choice on a strict geographical basis would undermine quality. The Commission must make up its mind which it wants and make it crystal clear to its staff where they stand.

In the long term the aim must be choice on merit alone through a stricter application of the system of search inside the Commission first before a wider advertisement. Officials ambitious enough to reach the top are only going to join the Commission if they know they stand a chance of achieving their goal. If they see obstacles, such as infusions at the higher levels barring promotion or the imposition of national quotas, they will be put off applying in the first place.

But it is 'parachutage' of officials from Commissioners' cabinets, or private offices, into the full-time services that is most controversial. Parachutage goes beyond hiring national experts from outside or fixing geographical quotas. It leads to charges of personal favouritism at the highest level. Unions and staff committees detailed a series of cases in spring 1988 as the four-year Commission entered its last year and the parachutage season began.

It is a by-product of the stronger continental private office system. Handled well this can sharpen policy and ginger up full-time officials. It surrounds a political chief, such as a government minister or commissioner, with a handpicked and highly-motivated team. Through them the commissioner wields his power. It doesn't mean top civil servants are cut out of decision-making but plans become more clearly focussed. The UK minister's private office often suffers from being too small and too rigidly civil service. Outside experts are only slowly breaking this down.

The cabinet system has its dangers too. EC worthies from politicians to top civil servants reckon they rate a cabinet, when all they really need is a personal assistant, a researcher or a secretary. In these cases it can add unnecessary hangers-on employed under suspect arrangements. Where the politician carries real clout it can be a useful organisation.

Many cabinet officials are high flyers picked by the commissioners for their proven track record, political skills and ability to work long hours. Some are drawn from national civil services, others are already full-time Commission officials; some are political party hacks. Most were in mid-career and sought out their next posting as their master's contract came to a close at the end of 1988. Would they return to their home country and resume work there or would they continue in Brussels which they had come to enjoy? It was a big temptation to exchange their temporary contract with the Commission for a permanent one.

Parachutage does not involve a large number of posts but when it occurs, it brings charges of nepotism against the commissioners involved. Such complaints have never been proved and it would be difficult to do so. Figures covering the five years to 1986, spanning the end of the four-year Commission in December 1984, revealed that only eight A3 posts were filled by former cabinet officials. But as proportions of overall A3 posts, the four who filled 1985 vacancies were a third of all that year's vacancies.

Parachutage involved only one A3 post in the other four years and three A2 posts over the five-year period.

Liam Hourican, a former Irish television and radio journalist, prompted an outcry and threats of court action when he landed a full-time Commission post in the 1984/85 season. He was first hired in January 1977 to join the cabinet of Richard Burke, the Irish commissioner. A number of the cabinet staff came from outside the Commission and the civil service and included Alan Dukes, who in 1988 was the leader of the Fine Gael, the Irish political party. By the end of 1980, Burke's four years were over and Hourican was back in Dublin, first as a press spokesman for Fine Gael and then in the Government's press service.

It took the Irish general election of February 1982 to send him back to Brussels. Burke's successor as European Commissioner, Michael O'Kennedy, had returned to Irish politics after only fourteen months and Burke was appointed in his place ironically with responsibility for personnel issues. This brought Hourican back as the head of his private office (chef de cabinet). During 1984, he spotted an internally advertised full-time A3 vacancy in the office of the Commission's secretary general. He believed that his generalist skills and seven years at the Commission would bring him the post. They duly did.

The full Commission backed his appointment at one of their last meetings in December 1984. But Hourican took up his new post to a clamour of complaint from a group of Irish officials, with some backing from the unions. A threat of European court action led to the appointment being cancelled in April by the new Commission. After being re-advertised, a selection board was set up to assess the candidates, including Hourican. In the meantime he had become deputy chief in the office of Peter Sutherland, the new Irish commissioner, taking the social affairs brief for a year.

Vicious and personal propaganda circulated in Brussels and Dublin as up to fifteen candidates were assessed for the full-time post in the Secretary General's office before Hourican won and took up the post in October 1986. Full-time Irish officials in the Commission have traditionally had difficulty in promotion to the A3 level, and many careers were blocked in the 1970s. An attempted parachutage from the O'Kennedy cabinet at A3 was halted in 1981 after Irish officials complained. When Burke took on the personnel brief in the early 1980s, there was some A4 to A3 promotion. The Hourican case raised the same anger but has since been settled.

Hourican had fought the hard way for his job and succeeded. He genuinely wanted a Commission post and after a year's probation, was given permanent status. He is responsible for coordinating the activities of the Commission's information offices and makes regular visits to check on their performance.

In April 1988, the European public service union alleged three cases of parachutage, two from commissioners' private offices, the third by a Danish official from the European Court of Auditors for an A5/4 Commission post to monitor food aid finances. It coyly referred to a mysterious 'SB' in the cabinet of Lord Cockfield, and claimed that internal candidates for an A3 job were being turned down and that the post would be advertised externally. SB is Cockfield's deputy chief, Sebastian Birch, who is on secondment from the UK's Department of Trade and Industry.

In Autumn 1988, it was widely assumed that Birch was on a shortlist of seven leading candidates for the job. Birch himself refused to confirm this. Applications had had to be in by the beginning of July, advertisements in newspapers had said. The post involves the 'elimination of fiscal frontiers and a system of compensation for VAT' and tackles an important part of Commissioner Cockfield's programme for a single economic market in Europe. Colleagues say Birch's present work would suit him ideally to the new post. The appointment is likely to be made in December by Cockfield and Christophersen, the Commissioner in charge of personnel.

In the European Parliament, parachutage is threatening on a large scale as the life of the Parliament draws to a close in June 1989. Full-time officials from the adminstration and committee services feared that temporary staff from the political groups would try to parachute into full-time posts. This would limit the scope for promotion by career officials. Political staff who had joined since 1979 were barred from applying when posts were advertised internally but a change was afoot. If they had served ten or only five years, perhaps they could compete.

At the top A1 and A2 levels, appointments were already made by the political groups. The appointment of a Dutch socialist to an A2 post looking after the Parliament's buildings had provoked one row in 1988. The fear is that staff at lower levels will increasingly become political appointments. Selection boards will arbitrate between political choices instead of those of merit and experience with the two largest groups, the Socialists and the Christian Democrats, carving up the jobs. An independent service for all parliamentarians is at risk.

Politics influences nearly all the prestigious jobs. The appointment of a new head of the Commission's London office in 1986 aroused clear political friction. The outgoing chief, George Scott, was a former journalist and associated with the UK Liberal Party. But the Tory government in London wanted their own man, John Drew. He was an expert on European business and had strong links with Touche Ross, an accountancy firm which handles a number of top Tories. The job was advertised twice and the procedures gone through again but the result was inevitable. Drew may have been the best candidate but the impression was left that he got the job because he was a Tory.

In Lisbon, the centre-right government of Anibal Cavaco Silva has not got its way with the Commission office in the Portuguese capital. The Commission had appointed Antonio Menezes, a former head of the BBC's Portuguese service who speaks fluent English. Cavaco Silva wants to appoint his own man and has cold-shouldered Menezes. One Commission official involved says: 'The Portuguese said this guy is politically wrong and the Commission say they must stick with that decision.'

The politicisation of a civil service is not a phenomenon well understood by the British. In the UK, a government changes overnight from Labour to Tory and the civil service will swing behind with its loyalty – the political colours of civil servants are not well advertised. At the upper reaches loyalties develop, though many of these are still non-party political. It is no secret that Sir Robert

Armstrong, the Cabinet Secretary and top UK civil servant before the 1987 general election, would have been sacked if Labour had got in. It didn't and Armstrong got a peerage instead.

But the politics don't run deep in the British civil service, whereas in many EC countries and in the Commission they do. The top seventeen European Commissioners are, in the main, politicians with ministerial experience. Many of the officials in their cabinets are of the same ilk. Too often jobs are handed out because people are 'one of us' whereas what is needed is an efficient manager. The demarcation between political and non-political jobs is too hazy and many could safely be pulled off the political list.

The recourse for many unhappy officials is not to the politicians but the European Court of Justice in Luxembourg. A rising tide of staff cases has overwhelmed the court, forcing it to expand its facilities to deal with the commercial cases on EC law which are its *raison d'être*. About 20 per cent of the court's 400 cases in 1987 involved staff. Some are serious and the way jobs are handed out in breach of staff regulations is often cynical law-breaking by the Commission. The cases involving Math and Waterschoot were clear abuses but even there, the remedy ought to lie not with the court but with a reform of the regulations.

Many of the cases coming before the court are frivolous and vexatious. One British translator took his drunken story to Luxembourg, well before UK entry in 1973. In 1962 he claimed FB5 million (£75,000 in today's money) for being dismissed for chucking four or five empty glasses from the ninth floor onto a crowd of journalists. About twenty empty whisky and brandy bottles were found in his office after he left.

In court, the translator said he enjoyed 'a drink with a colleague' when he had to stay late to translate documents for ministerial meetings. He said finding work with another international organisation would be difficult. The court slapped down the claim but noted that it was the first opportunity the translator had been given to put his defence and told the Council of Ministers to pay four-fifths of the costs.

Another discipline case in 1984 went further towards supporting the rights of staff. A Frenchman from Corsica, working in the Commission, had been seconded to the French Ministry of Cooperation and Development under an exchange scheme. A month after his arrival in France in July 1982, the official put himself up for election to the Corsican Assembly and was duly voted in. The Commission's Director General for personnel, Hay's predecessor Jean-Claude Morel, was only notified a month after the vote and in breach of the staff regulations.

The Commission was slow to respond and the official requested an interview for 6 October. This meeting ended in disagreement and violence with Morel punched in the face and kicked in the stomach. One witness suggested an ashtray was thrown at Morel. Two psychiatrists who examined the Corsican later said account ought to be taken of his 'neurotic personality characterised, in particular, by an inability to contain frustration and of his Mediterranean temperament'.

The affair was not settled quickly. A disciplinary board proposed in March 1983 only to downgrade him from A5 to A6 but this was overruled in April by Richard Burke, the Commissioner for personnel. He wanted him removed from the post but without withdrawal of pension rights. In January 1985 the European Court of Justice backed the official's claim that the Commission's decision should be set aside. The court said tht Burke ought to have gone over the evidence again and taken the mitigating circumstances – lack of premeditation – into account. He had not justified his more severe penalty.

Many people in private sector employment will find such a saga ludicrous. A junior manager from a multinational corporation would never have been posted abroad on such a loose rein. Striking the managing director may have led to a police assault charge, would certainly have prompted an immediate escort to the factory gate and his cards sent in the post the same day. Even for the public sector, the treatment was gracious. The onus should have been put on the official to justify his return to work – instead the employer had faced all the questions.

In May 1985 the Commission again sacked the culprit. This time the action was more successful and the formalities properly observed. But it didn't stop another appeal through the court and calls for three new witnesses to appear, including the Corsican's father. The court chucked out the claim 'in its entirety' in February 1987. It had taken four and a half years to sack the man. The case is an appalling comment on the Commission's ability to manage its staff. With the delays in appointing staff it means that it takes the Commission five years to hire staff and nearly the same time to fire them.

Table 2.4 **Breakdown of subject matter of staff cases**

	1985	1986	1987
Compensation	14	9	5
Pensions and illness	3	6	5
Recruitment and promotion	13	17	17
Discipline and downgrading	3	–	1
Other	5	4	10
	38	36	38

(Based on court judgements from all institutions. The mix is likely to remain much the same over the next two or three years. The 79 complaints filed by staff in 1987 comprised compensation issues (22 cases), recruitment and promotion (24), pensions and illness (7), discipline and downgrading (6), others (14). The nature of six other cases was unknown.)

Other cases dealt with by the court find a number of employees on temporary contracts disputing their status. Many have come to regard themselves as full-time and expect the rights that go with that status. This problem has touched most institutions and staff from language tutors to Third World aid workers. The use of short-term contracts is a two-edged sword: it offers the employer the benefit of much-needed flexibility, and puts the more vulnerable employee on his mettle to perform better or not get his contract renewed.

Unfortunately the EC has used neither factor to its advantage. The contracts just ran and ran and the staff expected the same. There were those who felt discriminated against when they didn't get the full-time staff terms. When the Commission didn't agree, it all too often ducked the issue and tried to dump the dispute on Belgian courts. Contract labour could be an effective way of managing staff resources to match needs but the Commission fears the governments would hijack the operation. Some coordination and straight talking would improve efficiency.

Another rigidity only now being removed will allow the high-quality EC interpreters to move from their specialism to policy areas. The formidable Rene Van Hoof is the only woman at the top of the EC civil service as head of its joint interpretation and conference service. She told the House of Lords inquiry: 'One of our interpreters is head of our information office in Cardiff and has just left us. There is another going to China in the delegation, in Beijing, and one in the cabinet of Mr Christophersen, and there is another one with the Director General for transport.

'I kick them out as soon as they get another offer. I do not think interpreting is a lifetime's work. It is a fantastic way of knowing how to negotiate, and to learn in all the meetings, whether heads of state or of technical experts. I do not want them to remain interpreters for their whole life. There have been terrible obstacles. For the first time, the first *concours* (recruitment advertisement) has been published to move an official from (grades) LA to A.'

Unions had blocked earlier moves to allow LA to A transfers in court. Van Hoof then persuaded Commission personnel chiefs to set up the advertisement-recruitment system. Unions believed it was a further threat to their members' career prospects, in the same way as parachutage and temporary contracts. They pressed for the setting up of a new joint committee to oversee appointments from the linguistic service. Commissioner Christophersen resisted this move but agreed to informal contacts with union representatives. He said he did not want to make 'further concessions' as the plan took hold.

Many of the staff cases reaching Europe's premier

court could be dealt with by an independent industrial tribunal, yet the only reforms being planned will put a further burden on the court. A European Court of First Instance is being planned to deal with some types of commercial cases and those involving staff. The new court will be more involved in fact-finding and allow the main court, which will still hear appeals, to handle major cases involving governments and business. The judges have done little to cut staff cases from their burden apart from spelling out time limits for claims.

One frivolous case never to reach the court in Luxembourg involved claims of alleged sexual harassment by Sir Roy Denman, the head of the Commission's delegation in Washington. In US district court proceedings his former secretary, who was fighting an unfair dismissal claim, failed to persuade the Commission to lift Denman's diplomatic immunity. Her allegations had first emerged in a Commission inquiry into her professional conduct. Clearly there was nothing in the allegations and the European court's time has not been wasted on this case.

Latest plans to 'modernise' the Commission go further than previous efforts but have a restricted mandate. Commissioner Christophersen and Director General Hay have a five-point strategy: the introduction of new technologies, such as word processing, computerised databases and electronic mail; simplification of day-to-day procedures and their decentralisation; a review of staff policy covering recruitment, mobility and middle management; more training; and better management of resources to policy priorities.

Middle management plans have already run into union opposition. The aim of the Commission is to extend management further into the ranks and allow greater horizontal flexibility. High flyers will get the chance of regular moves to make them the talented all rounder that will get to the top. Instead of management being solely in the hands of A3 division chiefs and above, the lower grades of A4 and A5 grades will be expected to manager where they are clearly in charge of a team. It could be a radical move going well beyond ideas practised in the UK civil service.

At the same time, these posts will be advertised automatically and a committee of top management given a greater role in the appointments. One fear of the unions is that the staff will spend all their time on the move between jobs and miss out on promotion. The management proposal says that promotion will only be attained by those who have gained management experience. The system will boost those keen and competent officials who perform well. At the same time it brings an end to promotions which some union members believe are theirs by right.

Plans have already been unveiled to discriminate in favour of women in A grades, where they only hold 10 per cent of the posts. At the top level it is as few as 3 per cent (A3) or 4 per cent (A4/5). The Commission wants to push the figure up to between 14 and 17 per cent by 1990, by giving women more responsible jobs when they emerge, and promoting women who are not eligible where no other candidates present themselves. They will gain preference for training and secretaries will be able to apply for official-grade posts.

Hay explains his plans for training: 'In the public service as a whole, training is not seen as having the importance which the private sector recognizes for it. In the Commission – which is a microcosm of the public service – rather than looking for profits, people looked for efficiency and devotion to work which was of a largely political kind. At the senior level, it was linked to European construction. In these cases, motivation was seen largely in that aim, and people did not consider there was a technique which could be imported by training that could be useful.

'Language training was important because it was linked to the European ideal. I suppose there was also budget austerity. The third point which distinguishes us from the public services in some member states has been to recruit with professional training. They came to us ready-trained.'

Training is expanding to cover management and skills for information technology. Officials have been sent to INSEAD, the business school outside Paris, or attended seminars at the European Institute of Public Administration in Maastricht in the Netherlands. But the main effort, and more than half of the £2.7 million training budget, is going on two-day courses that bring all the staff of one directorate together. At FB7,300 (£110) a head the courses are 'slightly cheaper than our ad hoc tailor-made programme. It is not expensive per head but obviously expensive', says Hay. Turnout has been in the 80–90 per cent region.

The programme was intended to be completed by the end of 1988 but has run into criticism. The choice of Danish firm Time Manager International to handle the assignment led to the predictable, but mostly private, claims that Commissioner Christophersen from Denmark had steered the contract to his mother country. Even Hay was sensitive about the contract, which had been properly advertised. He said: 'I was not in the group which decided on them but it included staff representatives. My impression was that choice narrowed itself down to two and was then quite an easy choice.'

The two-day seminar is a cross between a Billy Graham evangelical meeting and a television game show. Its charismatic host, Claus Moeller, was compared with Bob Hope by one official. His style is mid-Atlantic, full of humour and anecdotes about his wife. The content is 'universal, well packaged common sense'. It is aimed at generating team spirit and management by objectives. It falls into two clear parts: one tackling the psychology of management and interpersonal relationships, the other learning how to use a Filofax-style time manager. Each employee leaves the course with one of these.

The seminars have attracted cynicism. Some would have preferred the crisp British Army style to the jargon of 'transactional psychology versus winners and losers' and the idea of 'stroking' colleagues' feelings. But reaction in the seminars has generally been favourable with few objections to taking two days away from the office. Outside commentators tagged it the 'charm school'. One of the Commission's trade unions asked its members their reactions, and found that the overwhelming majority had found no change in attitude from their superiors and that three-quarters had no intention of using their time-managers.

Table 2.5 **Factors helping career progression in the Commission**

	%
The right connections	72
Seniority	69
Luck	64
The right nationality	61
Service in a 'cabinet'	53
The will to succeed	50
Ability	48
Qualifications	48
Knowing when to keep quiet	47
Producing results	44
Hard work	38

(Three years into its 'modernisation' programme, the Commission asked its staff what they believed influenced their promotion prospects. The percentages are those who 'fully agree' or 'tend to agree' with the factors, out of 7,400 who answered the poll. The Commission claims the results mirror similar polls of private sector employees showing that 50 per cent believe 'the right connections' help them progress in their company. But this ignores the finding that 80 per cent of these employees believe 'producing results' is the best route to the top.)

The approach may be an expensive mistake. And in a similar but cheaper vein, the Commission has conducted an opinion poll of staff attitudes to a variety of workplace issues. The Commission management is attacking real problems of lack of motivation, work satisfaction and good humour. But the solutions are scratching the surface, and a far more radical approach needs to be taken.

Root and branch reforms were proposed in 1979 after a review by a team led by Ambassador Dirk Spierenberg and including Dick Taverne, the former centrist MP. It called for reforms at all levels with a slimming down of the 'college' of European Commissioners themselves to just one per country. This would have cut the number to twelve. It said there were not enough portfolios to hand out to keep so many Commissioners fully occupied. In the seventeen-man 1988 Commission, some claimed that the small business and culture policy were two briefs which did not provide enough work.

Some governments, including at times the UK, have warmed to the idea but it stands little chance of gaining EC governmental agreement. Most can't stand the idea of having only the same clout as tiny Luxembourg. If the EC expands in the 1990s with new countries, then the need to streamline its executive will become compelling. As governments finalised their nominations for the 1989–92 Commission, the only innovations were the renewal of president Delors' term, though only for two years, and the possibility of an industrialist as the UK's number two Commissioner.

The Labour Party, which expects the second Commissioner spot as of right, would have been furious. In July 1988, Labour eventually put up the name of Bruce Millan to accompany Leon Brittan, the former Cabinet minister, who had taken the number one spot. Millan, an ex-Scottish Secretary and chartered accountant, is reckoned to be a colourless choice.

The appointment of Sir John Harvey-Jones, the ex-ICI chief, or the more widely tipped Bill Poeton, a successful and influential small businessman, would have breathed the real world into the stuffy Commission. And apart from shaking up the internal workings it would have given industry a key voice in Europe's economic community. The other leading choice of Sir Michael Butler, former head of the UK's EC delegation in Brussels and now a banker and company director, would also have injected new ideas.

The Spierenberg review tackled the structure below the Commissioners and their cabinets. It wanted to group four of the directorates covering personnel and finance under the president himself. This would leave the directorates dealing with external policy issues under the Commissioners responsible. But only minor efforts have been made to carry out this reform. Giving the personnel directorate overall control of personnel policy would be a major improvement. It would end the present squabbles where too often, other director generals wield enough power to make their own personnel policy.

The only other major review of EC staff policy was completed by the House of Lords select committee. It also proposed cutting the number of commissioners, noting that it 'would allow a substantial reduction in the large number of staff employed in cabinets'. It made a half-hearted recommendation that the 'incidence of parachutage be reduced' and left its best comments to criticising the lengthy recruitment procedures and 'multiplicity' of unions. It called for more joint services and the joint Commission/Parliament offices in capitals.

On staffing levels, it said that governments should listen more closely to pleas from the Commission for extra staff. Often the new resources did not meet the demands of policy agreed by the governments in the first place. The scope for redeployment had been extensively used already. Their Lordships had hoped to discuss with the Court of Auditors the Committee's proposal for an independent review body to monitor staff allocations but were rejected. The Committee had thought the Court might perform a greater scrutiny of staff levels as part of its audit of sound financial management.

The Court turned down the Committee's invitation to provide any help beyond a one-page reply to the question-naire sent to all EC institutions. It was the second time in the space of a year the Court had treated the Committee brusquely. This second snub was less surprising and followed the roasting which the House of Lords select committee had given the Court's own performance a year before (see Chapter 4). The Court has its own personnel problems and is scarcely in a position to tell others how to handle theirs.

The charmed life of the EC civil servant continues: officials are not going to draft policy that will withdraw their own perks. But the time will have to come when the glorified diplomats become more like national civil servants; when they too have to deal with Belgian or Luxembourg social security, taxes and inscription at the local town hall; when the hard-working officials, of whom there are many, stop supporting their duff colleagues. With the EC plan to bring business practices into line, a suitable date for putting EC civil servants on a similar footing to national ones should be 1992 – but it is unlikely to be.

3 PARLIAMENT: SPENDTHRIFT OFFICIALS SNUB THE POLITICIANS

When film makers came to the European Parliament's session in Strasbourg to shoot a thriller about the arms trade, the fictional plot of *Trouble in Paradise* was only marginally more *risqué* than the real-life exploits of Euro-MPs. The fictional Jean Pierre Miro's campaign against the arms trade, his affair with the chief Dutch interpreter and his murder at the hands of hired killers were only a little over-the-top for an MEP. In real life they campaign for, and against, just about everything under the sun, go on lavish trips, eat £350-dinners for two and have affairs with their research assistants.

If voters don't like the way their MEP has carried out his or her mandate, then in the June 1989 European elections, they can throw them out of office. But making the Parliament's own staff accountable follows very different rules. In 1982 £50,000 was discovered missing from the members' cash office. It was only six years later that Henri de Compte, former head of the Parliament's treasury and accounts department, was demoted for his responsibility in the affair. No criminal charges were brought and de Compte continued to draw a substantial salary for six years. The £50,000 has never been recovered and insurers refuse to pay any claim.

In 1987 a series of spending decisions by Jean Feidt, the Parliament's Director General for administration, and his staff, were queried by a financial controller brought in specifically to toughen up controls. Rental figures approved for a warehouse were nearly three times the actual cost; estimates for the cost of the gas supply at the same site was overestimated ten times; a sale of old typewriters was confined to people linked to the Parliament, whereas it should have been public; and cash was committed to spending on flooring and lighting in the Rome information office before the lease had been signed. The list went on.

Members of the Parliament often accept its abuses and inefficiencies. Even those in the Parliament's budgetary control committee, which scrutinises EC spending, seem loth to look at their own finances. Only the British MEPs Peter Price, Tory for London south east, John Tomlinson, Labour for Birmingham West and Dutch Socialist, Piet Dankert, have been prepared to persist. Even they may decline to vet the way political parties spent £10 million in 1987 and £19 million in 1988 on a 'European Information Campaign' and how much, illegally, goes on political campaigning for those June 1989 elections.

But back to the early 1980s and the Parliament's former head of treasury and accounts, de Compte. He was the accounting officer responsible for the members' cash office at the Parliament. His office paid MEPs for travel, subsistence and secretarial allowances in bank transfers, cheques or cash. From a Luxembourg base, travelling cashiers visited the Parliament's offices in Brussels and Strasbourg. To handle MEPs' demands for different sums, the office used what are called 'imprest accounts', though it later said it intended to drop this for the more fixed amounts paid to secretaries and assistants.

Imprest accounts, with a fixed float, are often used for petty cash by an organisation so that the risk of major losses can be reduced and operations better managed. An office manager might maintain an imprest account for tea, biscuits and small supplies with a float of £25. Each time he sends the office boy out for groceries the boy comes back, fills out a voucher and gets the money he spent reimbursed. When the manager runs short of petty cash, he goes along to the company cashier, hands over the vouchers or has his books checked, and gets cash to top up his float to £25. It is a simple system and widely used.

With de Compte in charge and because of the need to pay hefty expenses to many more MEPs, the imprest accounts handled more than just tea and biscuits. Direct elections in 1979 boosted the number of members from 198 to 410 and a further 24 Greeks arrived in January 1981. According to the European Court of Auditors, who began scrutinising Parliament's accounting systems in July 1981, the balance on the imprest accounts at the end of December 1981 was £4.4 million, way above the maximum balance authorised on that date of £70,000. In addition, December saw the opening of eight new bank accounts to fund the system.

£21 million in twenty-two different currencies was swilling through the cash office each year with controls presenting 'a large number of irregularities', said the Court. Supporting documentation was not the basis for payments as it ought to have been; members' travel and subsistence was mixed up with their assistants' allowances in the accounts. Signed blank cheques, cheque books and stubs were floating around uncontrolled. Those handling payments did not check each other's work and there were no surprise checks on the funds. One result was that £1.7 million ended up in the accounts of 1980 when it should have been in those for 1981.

The financial management was 'unsatisfactory', said the Court. Some bank accounts were in credit while others were overdrawn; too much cash, £310,000, including US$93,000 in travellers' cheques was being held. Where members had been overpaid, recoveries were not being properly pursued. Until March 1981, payments in pounds sterling and Irish pounds were made from the same bank account. For several years, allowances made out in Irish pounds were paid in higher value pounds sterling. (An Irish pound is worth about 90p.) In 1980 and 1981, this happened on eighty occasions covering £10,500. No effort was made to recover these overpayments until the Court pointed them out.

The most serious allegation that the Court made concerned an account kept at the Midland Bank in London on which cheques for £35,177 and £17,189 were cashed in September and November 1981. The two cheques were exchanged for a mixture of French and Belgian francs and Deutsche Marks at a Luxembourg bank seemingly in readiness for use in paying MEPs' expenses. De Compte claims that the cash was passed to Parliament's cashiers on the same day. Later disciplinary charges against de Compte suggest 'on the basis of the documents available, this interpretation is not obligatory'.

Investigations have never clearly pinpointed the ultimate destination of this cash though the Parliament officially records it as a 'shortfall to be recovered'. De Compte claims it disappeared into a fog of inefficiency. Some facts have been ascertained. First, the two cheques were signed by different members of the Parliament's cash office and both countersigned by de Compte. Second, the cheques were originally drawn on an undisclosed Midland deposit account but because the bank does not allow this form of deposit withdrawal they were cashed on an allied current account.

Further inquiries showed that despite being cashed in autumn 1981, the cheques were not recorded in the Parliament's books until February 1982. This in itself was irregular. De Compte later justified the transactions as 'treasury operations' to give 'a better presentation' of the accounts at the end of 1981. By March 1982 the paperwork still did not satisfy investigators who dug deeper. But it took extensive inquiries and some luck before a more alarming possibility emerged. This suggested that interest earned on the deposit account could have covered up the £50,000 loss.

Even at this stage a cash count had failed to uncover the shortfall, though the continuing questions prompted de Compte to send a memo at the end of March 1982 to Piet Dankert, the Parliament's socialist president from The Netherlands. According to investigators he told Dankert that 'due to serious administrative problems, transactions amounting to a net value of FB4 million (£50,000) had not been brought to account. He sought approval to make a global entry in the accounts to regularise the situation'. It hinted that paperwork rather than cash was missing.

Dankert and his advisers were nonplussed by the request and its manner. It was unorthodox for a civil servant to write directly to the president. The more usual route would have been via his superiors and the Secretary General, who heads the Parliament's civil service.

Inquiries during April 1982 led investigators part of the way to explaining why the shortfall did not at first show up. These were based on the discovery of the deposit

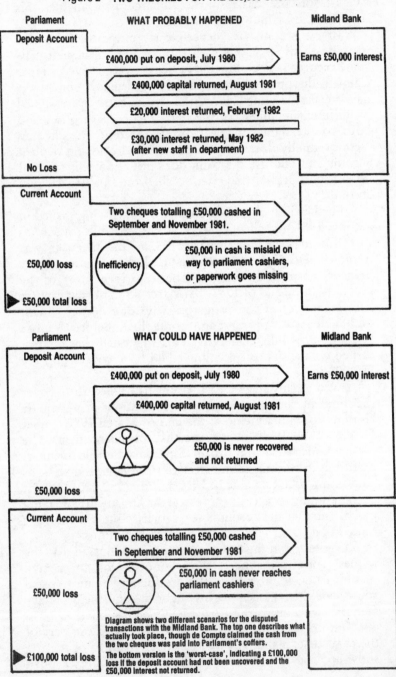

Figure 2 TWO THEORIES FOR THE £50,000 SHORTFALL

WHAT PROBABLY HAPPENED

Parliament — Midland Bank

Deposit Account — Earns £50,000 interest

£400,000 put on deposit, July 1980

£400,000 capital returned, August 1981

£20,000 interest returned, February 1982

£30,000 interest returned, May 1982 (after new staff in department)

No Loss

Current Account

Two cheques totalling £50,000 cashed in September and November 1981.

Inefficiency — £50,000 in cash is mislaid on way to parliament cashiers, or paperwork goes missing

£50,000 loss

£50,000 total loss

WHAT COULD HAVE HAPPENED

Parliament — Midland Bank

Deposit Account — Earns £50,000 interest

£400,000 put on deposit, July 1980

£400,000 capital returned, August 1981

£50,000 is never recovered and not returned

£50,000 loss

Current Account

Two cheques totalling £50,000 cashed in September and November 1981

£50,000 in cash never reaches parliament cashiers

£50,000 loss

£100,000 total loss

Diagram shows two different scenarios for the disputed transactions with the Midland Bank. The top one describes what actually took place, though de Compte claimed the cash from the two cheques was paid into Parliament's coffers.

The bottom version is the 'worst-case', indicating a £100,000 loss if the deposit account had not been uncovered and the £50,000 interest not returned.

account with the Midland Bank in London which was found to contain £50,347. It had never featured in the Parliament's books or accounts and had been out of sight to auditors. It represented interest on £400,000 transferred for a year from the Midland current account held by the Parliament. Interest rates up to 16 per cent had prompted the bank to suggest in 1980 that the Parliament put some money on deposit.

It is questionable if the investigations would have uncovered the deposit account if UK banking practice was different. And if the two cheques had not had to pass through the current account then it is also questionable whether the investigation would have found a cash shortfall at all. All the ingredients for a straightforward fraud were present. The capital had already been safely returned. If the interest had been more cleanly removed and the account closed, no one would have been the wiser. It would have been a case of making a nice turn on someone else's money: moonlighting with the Parliament's money.

The Court of Auditors comes close to this conclusion. It says: 'As the deposit account was not recorded in the Parliament's books, these facts raise questions as to the responsibilities of the officials concerned. The attempt to conceal the deficit by manipulation runs counter to any regular financial management. At the time of the Court's audit, the irregularities amounted to FB4.1 million, but this does not rule out the possibility of deficits in other areas which were not subject to examination.'

By the end of April 1981, Dankert had appointed Moret and Limperg, an outside firm of accountants, to confirm these findings, as the Court of Auditors stood aside. On 1 May, de Compte and his deputy were transferred to other posts by Dankert. Disciplinary measures were in the offing, though proving them was another matter. The affair quickly moved out of the purely technical one involving the entries in the books. The £50,000 was definitely identified as a shortfall now that the deposit interest had been uncovered and repaid. But the complexity of the accounting made it a difficult message to get across. Politics soon entered the argument.

Dankert had been elected as the Parliament's president with the aim of ending its reputation as a 'gravy train'.

Overseas jaunts with bottles of champagne waiting at the MEPs' next top-class hotel were to be curbed. Critics dubbed Dankert's stance as Dutch Calvinism, but he was keen to make the Parliament appear more hardworking, enjoying a well-earned drink after the work was completed. Because the de Compte affair was internal to the administration that Dankert had taken over in January, he found it confusing and embarrassing. But he tackled it as a technical issue without the wider political proportions it quickly assumed.

De Compte attracted a lobby on his behalf as the disciplinary proceedings got underway. Staff were already facing reorganisation by Dankert and this offered an opportunity to attack him. A lobby based on nationality, ideology, politics and freemasonry moved behind de Compte. Jean Feidt, the French Director General of the Parliament's administration, has been a long-time de Compte supporter and is a leading light in the Parliament's masonic lodge of members and officials. The disciplinary boards were infected by the lobby and often did not bother to study the detailed accounting reports.

Armed with the technical report from the Moret firm of accountants, Dankert laid disciplinary charges against de Compte at the end of September 1982. They alleged that he had repeatedly exceeded his responsibility and had breached sound financial management of his department. It prompted the first of a series of challenges by de Compte to the European Court of Justice. He claimed that he hadn't had an opportunity to put his case or that demotion would cause him financial hardship so that he would not be able to repay the loans on the various apartments and house he owned.

Dankert was forced to start disciplinary proceedings again in January 1983. More legal challenges meant the disciplinary board did not reach its decision to reprimand de Compte until February 1984 and then only by three votes to two. The voters against wanted to dismiss the charges. And then president Dankert dithered over how to carry out the sentence. At first he wanted to remove de Compte from his A3 post before changing his mind and demoting him to grade A7. The rethink followed the full Parliament's vote to approve de Compte's 1981 accounts.

This in turn led to the Court of Justice overturning the demotion.

By June 1985 the Parliament was four years down the track from the Court of Auditors' first investigations and no nearer pinning the blame on those responsible for the £50,000 shortfall. De Compte and his supporters had run rings around Dankert, the Parliament's president. Partly it was the generous system of appeals granted to staff disputes. But the members were also to blame for approving their accounts and letting politics affect their judgement on issues of financial management. Not calling the police in was another mistake – the Parliament's legal service could not decide which had jurisdiction, France, Belgium or Luxembourg.

Since then the affair has dragged on, with many MEPs saying it is past history and ought to be forgotten. Many had less persistence than de Compte who continued to thrive on his A3 salary of about FB240,000 (£4,000) a month. It is a gross salary on a par with the top Whitehall grade of permanent secretary. De Compte's take-home pay was probably a similar figure: extra allowances and EC tax tend to compensate for each other. And he was ready to take up legal cudgels if a new attack was mounted.

Evidence that the Parliament's insurance company lived in a more commercial and realistic world emerged. Royal Belge, the Belgian insurers, had refused to pay out for the loss, taking the view that 'a serious offence' had been committed and that there had been 'intentional violation' of the regulations. It refused to pay under the terms of its policy.

The EuroMPs budget control committee has concentrated its efforts on recovering the £50,000 loss. It delayed the discharge of Parliament's 1982 accounts until the Court of Auditors filed their second unpublished report in November 1985, pinning the blame on de Compte but not naming him. After a good deal of behind-the-scenes efforts, British MEPs from all parties insisted on a recommendation that no discharge was to be granted to de Compte 'in respect of his stewardship of funds up to 30 April, 1982' when he was transferred. The rest of the 1982 accounts were approved.

Some MEPs became alarmed at the way their colleagues tried to sweep the affair under the carpet. Terry Pitt, a Labour MEP on the budget control committee, claimed that freemasonry was at work. Masonic brothers of de Compte were trying to cover up his failings, he said. De Compte says he is not a mason and only claims 'very good relations' with Parliament's lodge. Pitt's claim was ignored by some colleagues who said 'let's stick to the financial facts and pursue it that way'.

The fear that masons look after their own ahead of the law is never easy to prove. Thorough independent scrutiny of judicial-type decisions ought to show up any bias. Disclosure by masons of their allegiances is another aid. Masonic influence in the European Parliament came to the fore. Les Huckfield, the Labour MEP for Merseyside East, tried to set up a register of MEPs' masonic links along the lines of councillors in some UK left-wing councils but failed to gain support from the wider Socialist group, of which the British Labour Group is part.

Continental women members were particularly vocal opponents of Huckfield's plan. In the different UK masonic tradition, women are not normally admitted to the brotherhood. Huckfield says: 'They said you could be good socialists and freemasons. It was needed to counteract the church. At the local level, freemasons were quite radical, they said. I did not get support from the BLG. I got in a shouting match with Rudi Arndt (the Socialist leader from Germany) at a press conference. He said there was just a feeling against freemasonry. The Socialist group just buried my resolution.'

By mid-1988, the 1981 cash shortfall had still not been decisively resolved and required continued pressure from John Tomlinson, Labour MEP for Birmingham West, who had become responsible for scrutinising Parliament's detailed spending. The private office of Lord Plumb, who became the Parliament's president in 1987, was also making progress. Plumb, a UK Tory MEP, had come in with a brief to clean up the Parliament's internal administration. Some reforms had taken place since Dankert's time more than two years before and Enrico Vinci was a more decisive Secretary General than his predecessor in charge of the Parliament's civil service.

Plumb launched disciplinary proceedings against de

Compte and on the unanimous recommendation of a disciplinary board, downgraded the former chief of the members' cash office in early 1988 from A3 to A7. It was the second attempt in six years and there was greater confidence that the decision would stick. But the timescale and delays were hardly a resounding vindication that the disciplinary system operated quickly and efficiently for either management or staff. The system clearly needed a thorough overhaul.

De Compte, who works as a junior administrator in the personnel division, again resorted to internal and Court of Justice appeals but failed to gain the immediate suspension of demotion he had achieved earlier. Plumb was expected to reject the internal appeal in June 1988. De Compte was already preparing to fight on and filed a sheaf of papers with the Court. The case will drag on into 1989 before reaching a conclusive resolution. The demotion is financially tougher than dismissal from the Parliament since de Compte loses his right to an A3 pension which is higher than an A7 salary. Dismissal without pension is very rarely invoked.

It was never clear who was directly responsible for the missing £50,000 or where the cash ended up. De Compte had taken a share of the responsibility for the overall management and had been disciplined but there was no evidence to suggest that he had committed a criminal offence. It is surprising that many are prepared to accept that the cash disappeared into a fog of inefficiency. It leaves many unanswered questions which only a more thorough investigation can unravel.

But if the abuses in the members' cash office had begun to be cleaned up, there was still a long way to go in other areas of the Parliament's financial accountability. Plumb had begun to take on the task but without letting it bog him down in a political row or distracting him from his mainstream goals. His straight, if occasionally naive, attitude brought results, whereas Dankert had possibly been ahead of his time. In the early 1980s it was easy to put Parliament's inefficiency down to growing pains after the first direct elections, as parts of the administration and de Compte regularly did. But the reforms still had some way to go and a new scandal pushed along the process.

The events in 1987 were never as dramatic – no cash went missing – but larger sums were at stake. The two senior officials, de Compte and Feidt, were buddies but there the connection between the two incidents ended. The latest discoveries were also a result of efforts put in train to improve financial controls.

A range of administrative spending came under scrutiny as British MEPs once again pressed for the facts. A measure of doubtful spending can be determined from the number of times that the Parliament's financial controller refused to sanction proposed spending because it did not meet financial regulations. These only come to light when he is in turn overruled by the Parliament's president. This overruling is normally on grounds of urgency or political pragmatism. In 1983 the number of refusals overridden was three (though one was subsequently modified), in 1984 none, in 1985 one, and in 1986 on ten occasions.

In September 1986, Irishman Eoghan O'Hannrachain was appointed as financial controller of the Parliament by its French president Pierre Pflimlin. O'Hannrachain had moved from researching and drafting reports for members of the Parliament's budgetary control committee to putting its beliefs into practice. In 1987 he refused thirty-two times to add his approval to demands from officials – authorising officers – who wanted to spend their budgets. On at least fifteen occasions, he was overruled by either president Plumb or Enrico Vinci, the Italian Secretary General.

Accountants in commerce or industry might find that some of the EC's financial regulations are highly restrictive. For instance, a private sector accountant would allocate expenditure for goods delivered and contracted in year one to that same year even if they were not paid for until year two. In the public sector, spending is more closely allocated to when the money was actually spent. This follows from the public sector's decision not to distinguish capital spending from short-term spending. It is also because the public sector has to remember that it is spending taxpayers' money, where stricter legal controls are required.

O'Hannrachain began his 1987 refusals on 15 January by refusing to approve FF20,000 (£2,000) for architects' fees because they related to the 1986 financial year. He completed his 1987 refusals on 21 December by refusing to sanction an advance of FB29 million (£500,000) covering renovations to an office block in Luxemburg which were behind schedule. The return on the advance was 'lower than the minimum acceptable'. It ended a busy year, one where his scrutiny had uncovered financial mismanagement in all shapes and sizes.

In February, the financial controller blocked spending of £3,500 for five freelance television technicians because their fees exceeded previous estimates that had been authorised. In April the Parliament's 50 per cent contribution of 32.5 million lira (£10,000) spending on alterations at the Rome information office came up for the controller's approval again. It had been refused once in 1986. In October, the controller challenged the maintenance cost of the Parliament's electronic voting system run by the Italian computer company, Olivetti.

O'Hannrachain really came into his own with his challenge to seven requests to approve spending on a warehouse to be rented at Zaventum, near the Brussels airport. It was part of a plan to improve documentation for Parliament's committees in Brussels with a print shop and to concentrate more facilities in the city. Both required more storage and it was decided in early 1986 to look for space to rent. Feidt and his staff were in charge of contacting a number of estate agents and received three offers between April and September 1986, including one from Brixton Estates' Belgian subsidiary, Brixton Belgium, which was chosen.

At the end of June, the financial controller refused to approve £60,000 spending on rent, water, electric, gas and service charges. He noted that the Parliament itself had said that decisions should be backed by statements of their implications. He said 'principles of economy and sound financial management' were not being respected. This was easy to conclude since the Zaventum warehouse did not represent the least economical of the three options put to the consultative committee on purchases and contracts. Yet Secretary General Vinci urged president Plumb to overrule O'Hannrachain.

Plumb was not to be rushed into a decision and on 10 July asked the quaestors, the senior MEPs who handle housekeeping-type issues, to examine 'a number of difficulties' which had arisen over the warehouse rental. The president was under some pressure to act quickly as Brixton Belgium, the arm of the UK property company, had complained. The contract Feidt had negotiated bound the Parliament to pay rent from January 1987 and it was already July. Plumb decided to pay the 1987 rent but wanted Vinci to check if the Parliament had to pay prior to occupation and ordered that no interest be paid on the late rent.

With summer holidays looming, the issue was not picked again up by the quaestors until September. They appointed one of their number, Jimmy Provan, Tory MEP for North East Scotland, to report back. The no-nonsense Scot questioned Vinci, Feidt, O'Hannrachain, lawyers and other officials. He also spoke to Brixton. He concluded that although it was only a small warehouse the problems were 'significant' and the financial controller should be 'congratulated' for pursuing it. Provan blamed the affair on two factors: 'serious failings' by the administration and 'inadequate preparation of dossiers' presented to the bureau and quaestors.

Provan, in a clear swipe at Feidt, said: 'I am surprised that the Directorate General has not carried out an internal inquiry to find the solutions.'

The dossiers were inadequate because they did not provide full information on the three competing warehouse proposals; contained a 'gross error' in the rental figure and failed to break down rent from associated charges; lacked a 'proper explanation' of a drop in the estimated rent from FB2.5 million a year to FB2.5 million for three years, neither corresponding to the first year's rent of FB961,944; and included 'incomplete and contradictory' details of other costs. Estimates were 'at best cavalier'. It gave the impression of 'slap-dash' management. Provan singled out the gas bill which started at FB1 million, slid to FB600,000 and then FB60,000.

But the Parliament was stuck with the warehouse, and Provan recommended paying rent from January, despite legal opinion saying this was not necessary. Brixton had not been well treated and he feared litigation. There was a lack of coordination between the Director General for administration and the financial controller, concluded Provan. Feidt differed with O'Hannrachain over his interpretation of the financial regulations. Feidt said it was not up to O'Hannrachain to consider alternative options such as whether a warehouse was the best way of managing paper and office supplies. Such necessity or suitability were for him alone to decide.

It was not the first time that Plumb had had to deal with Feidt. During the October 1987 parliamentary session in Strasbourg, he acted swiftly to prevent the Parliament from being carpeted in the press over a Feidt plan to install contraceptive machines in the Brussels and Luxembourg offices. The fast-footed Labour group had condemned the plan as 'bonkers' and made quick political capital. One of their MEPs was quoted as saying: 'The scheme will give people the impression that we are all sex-mad instead of knuckling down to our work. I am all in favour of responsible action against AIDS, including the provision of condoms, but the officials have blown the problem out of all proportion.'

Feidt had been put up to the plan by a company called Ladeja, which proposed free installation and ten per cent off the maintenance of the 'automatic distributors'. He said the nearest chemists were too far from the Parliament's offices in the two locations and the move responded to concern over the spread of AIDS. In France, a further legal study was required before installation. The press made hay with the story: The Daily Star's newsdesk asked its reporter if '"automatic" meant that you put your penis in and it automatically rolled it on'. Plumb quickly dashed the idea with a statement at the end of the afternoon.

Plumb told the MEPs in the chamber: 'First, the suggestion originated with a commercial firm who wished to install such machines. It was not a suggestion from any Parliament source. Second, there is absolutely no question of this suggestion being taken up by Parliament's administration. It has also been rejected by the staff committee. I regard the matter as closed.'

By the beginning of 1988 Secretary General Vinci had got down to overhauling the system. There had never been any question of officials pilfering cash but there must be doubts about whether the warehouse was good value for money, though it is understood the estimates for the alternative warehouses have since proved faulty. The other danger was contracts being handed out to friends and then kickbacks. Provan, who investigated the case, says there is no suggestion that these contracts were the subject of such connivance and corruption.

Vinci said he hoped in future, differences between the controller and authorising officers could be ironed out at an early stage. Refusals submitted to himself and the president had already become a *fait accompli* and he wanted to catch bad spending at an earlier stage. He said: 'In practice, any difference of view in this sphere should be resolved by both the financial controller and the authorising officer being flexible and communicative in their approach.'

The Parliament's top civil servant said that he had proposed that if a controller refused his approval, then the final decision to override now rested with the president on his, Vinci's, proposal. Previously Vinci had taken these decisions himself. He wrote: 'This (proposal) was accepted and represents in my view a more correct interpretation of the financial regulation'. In the Court of Auditors' report published in December 1987, the Court complained about Vinci carrying out this task and said the financial regulation 'expressly lays down that this type of decision may not be delegated by the institution'.

The Parliament told the Court that it changed this practice in December 1986, 'in advance' of the criticism, and that it provided the Court with details of new internal rules in February 1987. The Court also complained that the ten 1986 refusals were supplied on 22 May 1987 after 'several reminders'. They should be supplied quarterly in the month following the end of the quarter.

With new procedures, better organisation and a change in staff, the Parliament was hoping to put its latest financial scandal behind it. Feidt, who was never held directly responsible for his mismanagement, had followed de Compte and the members' cash office. While the two were in no way similar, both suggested a common malaise. MEPs, such as the Tory Andrew Pearce from Cheshire West, linked the two and brought the issue onto the Parliament's floor. He said it was distracting Parliament from its proper job and required tough action with the police being called in.

Plumb's staff and members such as Tomlinson preferred a behind-the-scenes effort before going public when, much later, the cases were resolved. The opposition to the Pearce method was twofold: the Parliament got bad publicity and lobbies built up against an investigation. Whenever public passions flowed over the de Compte affair, the problems became political and no longer technical. Few members mastered the technicalities of what had happened. The same argument could be applied to Feidt. But the legitimate fear was that in dealing behind the scenes the incidents would be covered up.

The next potential scandal lurking in the Parliament's finances is over funds for the 'European Information Campaign' in the run-up to the June 1989 elections for EuroMPs. It could well become the most embarrassing for the politicians themselves, and is likely to lead to the strongest claims of 'cover-up'. In a bid to meet halfway the differing traditions of funding election campaigns, the European Parliament has set aside substantial sums for alerting voters to the European Community, the Parliament and its members. Tough controls and guidelines are supposed to prevent cash being diverted into national political parties.

It is not full political party funding as found on the Continent, and cannot be used for electoral campaigning or literature urging a vote for a particular candidate. It goes against UK traditions, which have been against direct political party funding. But there are strong arguments that the MEPs are better placed than Parliament itself to inform the European public about the EC. The funding is designed to boost interest and voting levels in the Parliament, which attracted only a 33 per cent turnout in the UK in 1984.

Loose rules at the last 1984 elections prompted the European Court of Justice to declare void the £30 million expenditure during the campaign in 1982, 1983 and 1984. The French party of ecologists, Les Verts, challenged October 1982 guidelines set by the parliamentary authorities allocating 62 per cent of the cash between the political groups, non-attached members and a reserve for 1984. The split was based on the number of members in each group elected at the previous 1979 election. The remaining 31 per cent reserve was to be handed out to all political groupings who contested the 1984 elections and gained more than five per cent of valid votes in one country or one per cent in three or more countries.

The rules were worked out by the chairman of the political groups, who said that no more than 25 per cent was to be spent on administrative expenditure for office staff and rental of equipment. Money was to be kept in a separate bank account and spending was to be accounted for separately between administrative, meetings and publications and publicity. Reports were to be provided to the Parliament president on spending, which had to end forty days before the date of the elections. Further rules in October 1983 set down how the smaller parties were to claim funds in advance of gaining their five or one per cent of votes. Various returns had to be made.

Les Verts complained to the court on seven different grounds why it felt the 1983 guidelines were illegal. Citizens were not being eqully treated, it said, and the money was allocated in order to ensure the re-election of the members elected in 1979. Specifically Les Verts, which received nearly £60,000 from the Parliament, challenged the reserving of 69 per cent of the money to existing groups. The court ruled in 1986 that the spending was flat-rate reimbursement of election campaign expenses and not an information campaign. It was therefore void under the treaty.

Les Verts later claimed a share in the cash but was turned down by the court in 1988. The clear message was that the money was gone and would not come back. Next time the Parliament would have to make sure the cash was better controlled. The Court of Auditors would come along and vet the spending afterwards, something they had not reported on in 1982, 1983 and 1984.

Labour MEP Tomlinson took on the task of overseeing the spending and ensuring that auditors would be employed who would be able to make a report afterwards. He told his budget control committee colleagues in early 1988: 'We can't be in the position that the bureau lays down rules and the groups adopt their own rule in some way.' He began a round of consultation with the groups in order to set up a common system of accounting for the money. The large sums were seen by the groups as important means to secure the re-election of their members. Whatever the rules might say, many regarded it as electoral campaign expenses.

Despite guidelines, there were claims in 1988 that UK spending was breaking the rules. Both Labour and Tory European Parliament groups were under fire from each other. Up to £6 million was available to political groups from the UK with the Tories of the European Democratic Group receiving £2.4 million. It had to be spent before a deadline ninety days before the 15 June 1989 UK election date. The British Labour Group had already rejected a complaint from Christopher Prout, the EDG leader, over literature issued at a glitzy campaign launch in 1988 attended by Neil Kinnock, Labour's UK leader.

Prout explained to Rudi Arndt, the leader of the Socialists' umbrella group in the European Parliament, that the campaign could include information on the work of the Parliament, its groups and by individual members. This included their speeches in the Parliament attacking the UK Government. But Prout was angry that Labour literature repeated these attacks. He said: 'What I object to is the fact that some of the Labour literature carries on that attack on the Government. That is not what the campaign is about. It is perfectly legitimate to say that they are fighting the UK Tory members of the European Parliament.'

Arndt rejected the complaint and there may be little more Prout can do until the three years' expenditure is vetted after the campaign by the Court of Auditors and the Parliament's own budget control committee. Less formal complaints had criticised the Labour European pensions campaign and the Tory campaign in Scotland. A vice-chairman of the Conservative Party in the UK was chairing a committee on spending the EDG money but did not receive cash himself. Prout says the EDG can call on anyone for advice, paid or otherwise. Labour for instance was paying an advertising agency £750,000.

The three-year campaign will spend £34 million across the twelve EC states and split between the nine political groupings in the Parliament. The largest shares have gone to the Socialists with £10.5 million, followed by the centre-right European Peoples Party £7 million, and the European Democratic Group £4 million covering the British, Spanish and Danish Tories. All spending has to be within the political guidelines and backed by valid invoices. It cannot include any equipment, land or buildings. It will prove a sound test of the Parliament's keenness to monitor its spending and whether voters can take it seriously as part of the EC set-up.

4 FINANCIAL WATCHDOG: THE COURT WHERE THINGS DON'T ADD UP

The Court of Auditors, the European Community's financial watchdog based in Luxembourg, ought to have stopped the mismanagement and waste that has blighted the EC's internal operations and its external spending. It could not have done it all on its own but it should have made significant progress. Instead, the Court has been sidetracked from scrutinising the EC's £20 billion annual spending. Its top-heavy management structure, the political role its chiefs have chosen for themselves and the personal favouritism exercised in appointing staff have made it a laughing stock. Its cock-ups extend from the way it pays its pensions to the way it treats its chauffeurs.

The Court is a good example of how not to set up an international organisation and a warning to any future EC institution, such as the European Trademark Office now being considered. It has failed to gain the cleaner-than-clean reputation essential to an independent financial watchdog, where its bosses should be forced to give up outside work barred under the Treaty of Rome. In 1987 the UK's House of Lords select committee for the EC said: 'The time is ripe for an extensive review of its own organisation, methods and role in the Community'. In 1988 the Court grudgingly appointed an external firm of accountants to audit its own annual accounts, though insisting on the final word.

Many people – including some who carry it out – believe auditing is dull and not worthwhile. They argue that checking the finances after the money is spent is an academic exercise. It's not. It may not carry the glamour that a fraud investigation does, but its impact for future spending and fraud prevention can be just as profound. Auditing involves vetting the year's financial transactions to make sure that money has been spent soundly on what it was intended for. The latest computer techniques make the job better-targeted and less tedious to carry out. Less paperwork is selected for routine checking and instead areas are highlighted which require in-depth investigation.

Done well and promptly, it provides an important input in keeping an organisation on the financial straight and narrow. Contrary to popular belief, many of the detailed checks are carried out only days or months after the transactions themselves. This means that improvements can be proposed and put in place well before any final report is published for wider consumption. But auditing done badly corrupts those who carry it out and is unhelpful to those who pay for the service.

One of the few factors in the Court's favour is its youth: it is only ten years old. Treaty of Rome amendments in 1975 which gave the European Parliament a greater say in budgetary issues resulted in the Court being set up in October 1977. It took over from the Audit Board, which according to a future Court member 'was not performing adequately', and the smaller auditor to the Luxembourg-based European Coal and Steel Community. The Court began with the latter's six staff and drew on those among the twenty-five Audit Board staff who were prepared to move from Brussels.

But the die had already been cast. The 1975 Treaty set down an EC audit court with one Court member from each country. Under that were the staff to carry out the detailed financial checking. It was closer to the continental audit court than the more 'autocratic' National Audit Office in the UK with a single comptroller and auditor general at its head. It did not mirror exactly the French Cour des Comptes with 250 magistrates led by a premier president and seven *presidents de chambre* at the top. Sir Norman Price, the Court's first UK member, has called its style 'a bit of a *melange*'.

There was also the issue of to whom the Court should report. In the UK, the comptroller and auditor general reports to Parliament via the public accounts committee. In countries where the public auditor plays a more judicial role, he sometimes has the right to fine a civil servant who has mishandled public money. The EC Court reports to both the Council of Ministers, in effect the twelve governments, and the European Parliament. Armed with the Court's annual report the Parliament can refuse 'discharge', or approval, to the EC institutions, particularly the European Commission, and their annual spending until improvements are made.

An alternative set-up, taking the UK's more autocratic style and the continental power to fine civil servants, would have been far more effective. It would have been quicker and certainly more fearsome. The Court could have celebrated its tenth anniversary in 1988 by counting the fines levied and holding a bumper bash.

National audit authorities also make different choices of expertise at the top level and in the ranks. In some countries top appointments are political. In the UK the comptroller is usually an ex-Treasury official 'appointed by the Crown on a proposal from Parliament'. In other national audit offices, the top officials are often career auditors. Staff in the more legalistic continental-style audit offices are lawyers rather than the accountants who are more numerous in the UK. Most audit bodies also employ a number of economists.

In a bid to tackle the two traditions of public auditing, the scope of the Court's work was to include checks on the legal regularity of transactions and 'whether the financial management has been sound'. The modern value-for-money audit, which takes a step towards questioning the underlying policy of spending, was to be included. According to Eunan O'Halpin, a Dublin Business School lecturer who has studied the Court: 'Broadly speaking, the treaty produced a body with a Southern European structure and a Northern European remit. It was not a happy combination.'

The 1975 Treaty said there must be nine members of equal ranking normally serving a six-year term, one of whom would become the president for three years. When new countries joined the EC, the number would rise accordingly – one member per country was the rule. Former UK member Price told the House of Lords committee investigating the Court: 'I have heard that, at the time, the Dutch negotiators were in favour of a top management team of four, but the passion of member states for equality of treatment which I came to know only too well, insisted on parallel representation.

'This was a pity. From four it would have been possible to build up had that number proved inadequate. From nine, still more twelve, it was impossible to plane down.

'When the Court met in those closing weeks of 1977 to discuss its future, there was a choice between two courses. Either the members could withdraw themselves from the heat of the battle, so to speak, allowing the officials recruited to carry out the substantive work of audit and administration, bringing the results to the Court acting as a joint tribunal to approve or disapprove. The national audit bodies of some members states tend to work in such a way. Or the members could take an active part in the work as leaders of teams, and then discuss the outcome of these operations jointly before delivering opinions to the waiting world.'

To their credit, and in the absence of supporting staff, the Court members rolled up their sleeves and each took on an area of EC spending to audit. They were a motley bunch of lawyers, politicians and civil servants appointed because of their experience as auditors or at a high level in the field of finance. The Belgian, Pierre Gaudy, was the previous EC Coal and Steel Community auditor and member of the Audit Board; the Dane had also been an Audit Board member and done time with the NATO audit authority, based in Brussels, as had the Italian; the last were both lawyers.

The remaining six, all new to Euro-auditing, came from a similar mix of backgrounds. In Luxembourg's case, Marcel Mart had also headed the European Commission's New York office. The French member was Pierre Lelong, a former minister in a Pompidou government and member of the Cour des Comptes. The West German had been chairman of the Bundestag's (parliament) budget commit-tee; the Irishman, Michael Murphy, was a career civil servant who rose to permanent secretary in the Ministry of Finance and took on the Court's presidency; the Dutchman, Andre Middelhoek, was an economist in a senior position in the civil service.

The first British member, Price, had been Chairman of the Inland Revenue, a civil service posting. His had been a last-minute appointment by the UK government: he was nearly two years into retirement but proved a stalwart Court member. His life-long career in the squeaky-clean Revenue, his personnel skills and a post-retirement period with Price Waterhouse, the international firm of accountants, proved invaluable.

Taken together, the first nine Court members show that each government had made their appointments for completely different reasons. For some it was because the member was already doing a similar job, in other cases it was their political credentials or their knowledge of public finance. But only one or two had the qualifications or experience of digging in government books as a career auditor.

Since the beginning of the 1980s, the organisation of audit work has been into groups of three members. With twelve EC countries the twelve Court members broke into groups of four. The management roles were first undertaken by just three members, and by 1988 had become the sole responsibility of the Court president. Putting right a management structure plucked from the air by governments was evidently taking its time. It was like putting a square peg into a round hole.

This latest organisation is tacit acceptance that a nine- or twelve-man Court is not the form for an effective auditing force and has more to do with pacifying national claims through the EC Treaty. The Court has created three 'mini-courts', as some members call them. These examine in detail the reports of the audit areas of the three (or later four) individual members in the group. Each group takes policy areas that link together and most farm spending is in one group. The full Court only deals with the most important points in an audit report. This procedure is not binding and the member responsible for working methods has attended all groups of three meetings.

Groups also chose in the main to use the English, French and German languages and most of the basic audit work chooses one of these languages to work in. Cutting down on languages and with it the need to use local freelance interpreters allowed the members in the groups of three to be less reticent and vent their criticisms. Price said: 'Luxembourg is a tight community and stories of rifts when harmony ought to prevail could do some damage to the Court. With no interpreters present, one could be reasonably outspoken and effect improvements which a softer approach could not obtain.'

According to Price, the quality of draft audit reports for scrutiny by the full Court improved and the work of the groups of three was extended to vetting work programmes before the audits began and as they went along. Price was less successful in making the staff of one member available to the (then) two other members of the group. But since 1985, audit staff have been divided between the three groups rather than by particular member. Interchange between the groups, subject to negotiation and with the president's approval, is limited as members protect their fiefdom. Resources are not matched to audit demands.

By the time Price left the Court in October 1983, total staff had reached the 300 figure, though the number of actual auditors was substantially lower – between two-fifths and a half. He told the House of Lords: 'Through the jaundiced eyes of a former UK civil servant who has witnessed many post-war economy drives, there appear to be too many secretarial and messenger staff in all EEC institutions. Some of this is avoidable, some is not. The avoidable element arises mainly from prestige reasons – "I must have 'my' secretary"; "I must have instant messenger services available" even if it means that the secretary or messenger is underemployed.

'The Court has tried to do something in its audits to cure this but, I am afraid, is handicapped by its own beams. The non-avoidable element again arises from language problems. If there are margins of a typist's time available from her own work, it is more difficult to utilise them for excesses elsewhere if the excesses are not in a compatible language. Thus typing pools etc are more difficult to set up, particularly in a small institution. These factors (including a staff of 70–80 translators) lead to a higher percentage of non-effective "audit staff" than might be guessed though (the language cost is) more significant in figures.'

What Price did not tell their lordships was that each Court member also has his own private office or cabinet. It copies the European Commissioner with his own cabinet but on a smaller scale. It contributes to the fuzzy image of Court members: are they quasi-politicians or are they auditors? In December 1987 and excluding the twelve members, the staff in post were 68 translators (including an estimate of 30 B-grade staff), private offices of two assistants, secretary and chauffeur totalled 48, secretarial and messengers, 87. It left only 130 active auditors, or 39 per cent of the 333 total staff.

The private offices are an area where staff ought to be cut or re-allocated and were savagely attacked by O'Halpin in his study in 1987. The personal assistants are the sole appointment of the member and usually come from outside the Court. Some are from national audit offices but the appointments are 'effectively debarred' to permanent staff and this blocks their promotion. This effect is magnified by parachutage when assistants from the cabinets wish to join the Court's permanent staff when their member's term is completed. It is a personnel problem which this new institution could have avoided.

O'Halpin queries the role of the cabinets in a small organisation where members are directly involved in the day-to-day audit work organised by the permanent staff managers. The government and public administration academic says: 'Some members use their personal assistants as supplementary auditors. In other cases, they exist mainly as a co-ordinating mechanism between the members. Some personal assistants become part of the chain of command between a member and the permanent audit staff, others do not. One personal assistant has written that the cabinets are now without any obvious role. One person interviewed commented that in his experience they simply "created and then solved problems".

'While it is important to co-ordinate the activities of the members, it is hardly necessary to have such a staff attached to each member to do it. Furthermore, if co-ordination is their main purpose, it would make far more sense to give each member a private secretary, making this a promotion post to be drawn from the permanent staff. The co-ordinating function could be much better performed by people who already knew the Court than by neophytes. The freeing-up of a number of vacancies for promotion, albeit temporary ones, would surely improve staff morale.

'The argument that members would be lowering their status in the Community if they forswore some of the more ostentatious trappings due to them is, to an outsider, hard to comprehend. The members are on a par with commissioners, but they have very different tasks to perform and they have a very different scale of organisation to run. The Court might find it easier to preach sound financial management if it voluntarily dispensed with some of the peripheral benefits which its members currently enjoy, and which some Commission officials take an understandable pleasure in ridiculing.'

The straight-talking O'Halpin also suggests the cabinets ought to be filled by secondees from national audit offices, partly to improve their links with the Court which are not generally strong. The 1975 Treaty specifically encouraged these links. O'Halpin says the internal management difficulties affect the way the workload is divided with each member taking on a segment of EC spending. He says that until 1983, only two members dealt with agricultural spending, even though it was 70 per cent of the EC budget. This has changed and at least four members, plus the president, are currently responsible for this area.

Early mistakes have taken years to rectify and many remain. There was little attempt to assess the audit work that needed to be done and then match resources against it. Price, who became responsible for staff issues, says he tried to introduce such a measure in 1981 but it never got off the ground. Under this plan if EC cash was being wasted in the farm sector, then major parts of the Court's resources should have been devoted to tracking it down and finding a remedy. Instead members spent their time bitching at each other and increasing their own staff and prestige.

Two early mistakes were made in hiring staff and have led to long-term problems in creating a sensible career progression, according to Price. First, Court members were allowed to put their own assessment on the number and grading of staff in their sectors. Secondly new recruits from outside the EC institutions were only to be offered temporary posts until they proved themselves. This recruitment was 'perfunctory and mostly on the basis of paper qualifications', says Price who, with hindsight, is highly critical of some of his colleagues. He blames them for 'their inability to select good staff' with relevant qualifications.

The top tier of management under the members proved difficult to put in place. The heads of audit teams who reported to members were normally to be of the A3 grade, but there were to be a small number of more senior A2 appointments. One A2 official from the old Audit Board who had joined the Court had to be 'hidden' as head of the audit sector, according to Price. 'Some animosity' had developed between him and one of the Court members who had been on the Audit Board. It would have been 'awkward' to appoint him in his former role as a director general. It would have been better to have cleared out the deadwood.

A French A2 was successfully hired from the Cours des Comptes to head the common agriculture policy audit sector under Lelong; Peter Keemer came from the UK's National Audit Office to be responsible for work methods, and a West German civil servant joined to handle personnel matters. Price told the House of Lords that while Keemer was 'an excellent choice', the German was 'much less successful. He was compulsorily retired in 1981'. Keemer returned to the NAO in 1986. His interest in European public sector auditing led to an external Master's degree thesis at Bath University.

Price's colleagues pressed for A2s to cover each audit area but he said it was not justified on 'work performance grounds. If the member's overall control of his audit allocation was properly carried out and if the A3 was effective in day-to-day terms, there was no room for an A2 in a sector other than the CAP. The Council did not take kindly to the proposal to increase when granting the Court's 1983 and 1984 budgets, and I suspect that the ambitions of the Court are now modified.' Governments saw through the Court's grandiose scheme.

Auditors at the lower A grades and in the B executive

officer grades were recruited from other EC institutions, national audit offices, government departments and the private sector. Those from other institutions were either lawyers or looking for a fresh start and only two or three were successful. National public sector auditors were better. Price also took on qualified UK or French chartered accountants from private Luxembourg firms who were 'excellent'.

But not all Price's private sector efforts bore fruit: 'We had some awful flops. There are two Italian (accounting qualifications), one very estimable, the other for not-so-glorified book-keepers. We took the wrong ones.'

There was also a long-term solution which Price developed. He ran a publicly advertised recruitment for qualified graduate accountants at the lowest professional A7 grade. It would introduce a career structure and end the hotch-potch recruitment to date. It was 'an uneasy compromise', Price admits. The recruitment, along best UK Civil Service Commission lines, whittled down 750 candidates, by written test to 100 for interview, before 30 were offered jobs, of which most took them up. The aim was to bring in a high-quality auditor who could develop common skills, apply them consistently and work his way up the organisation.

In 1987, Price declared the compromise had not been very successful. He said: 'If one is designing a career for a good 30-year-old, one must ensure that he can see his way to the top. This implies some policy about age-ranging in the higher ranks. But by recruiting people from other institutions at 35 to 45 to fill posts in the next three grades up, initiative is likely to be destroyed. I hear with some sadness that a number of my brighter recruiting prospects have now moved elsewhere out of a sense of frustration.

'I have no doubt that the policy of the "second" school is the right one and that the recruitment of higher graded officers should have regard to the provision of a proper career for the young entrant.'

Since Price's brave attempts to create an effective auditing force, staff/management relations have deteriorated. Court president Marcel Mart has gained a stronger external reputation for the Court but failed to grapple with personnel issues since he took them on in 1985. Morale among the middle- and lower-ranking staff appears low and no reforms either to retire or counsel staff to leave has been made. Instead a war of attrition has ensued. The prospects for promotion or a career path continue to be slim as commitment to long-term recruitment is further threatened by secondment from national audit offices.

The pressure on promotions has led to complaints and legal actions where Court members promoted favoured candidates and internal recruitment was rigged. In the early 1980s when individual members had more scope to act in their own right, complaints were regular. In the mid-1980s, more A4 and A5 posts were created which eased some of the tension, but by 1988 these had been filled. The new fear among some staff is that the few A4 positions falling vacant will be taken up by national experts. One staff activist says: 'We want a proper staff policy defined by management – medium- and long-term.'

Mart (who declined to be interviewed) states his policy through Henri Marty-Gauquie, the head of his private office, who says career possibilities are 'decided not by the Court but by the budgetary authority (governments and the Parliament). If someone is promoted, it makes room for people to be promoted. It is the same if someone leaves the Court. But if these possibilities don't exist, we can't promote people. We try but the system is blocked. We try to have people interested in their work. We try to organise it that people change their sector every four years. Also you interest someone more in his work by changing his work than by an extra FB2,000 each month.'

Marty-Gauquie is dismissive of the high number of cases where the audit court has been taken by its staff to the European Court of Justice. He says that they are not numerous compared to the number of staff and that the Court is a small institution and numbers therefore likely to be proportionately higher. He blames troublemakers for the high number of cases. He says: 'From the record you will see that it is mostly the same people. You will notice that there have been three officials who brought four cases each to the Court of Justice and another who brought three, another two. What else can we do?'

Table 4.1 **Comparison of EC institutions' major staff disputes**

	1985	1986	1987	Average employees	Actions a year/ thousand 'ees
Court of Auditors	4	6	3	330	13.0
Economic and Social C'tee	2	3	2	470	5.0
Council of Ministers	6	3	4	1,900	2.3
European Commission	26	22	26	15,000	1.7
European Parliament	4	2	5	3,100	1.2
Court of Justice	–	1	–	600	0.6
	42	37	40	21,400	1.9

(Based on cases decided by the Court of Justice)

The Court of Justice's record partly backs Marty-Gauquie's stance though the level remains alarmingly high and ten new complaints were filed in 1987, more than the Council, Court of Justice and ESC put together. Even against the much larger Parliament, staff only filed thirteen complaints. The rise is even more surprising since the audit court has tried to choke off legal claims by being tougher on legal costs with its staff. Most other institutions leave it to the judges to award costs, but the audit court always asks for staff to pay costs if they lose.

Marty-Gauquie is correct in his claim that the names of Calvin Williams, Charles Lux and Henri Maurissen appear more than once in legal disputes with the Court. But a reading of the hearings and the judgements does little to enhance confidence in the personnel management of the Court of Auditors. Many of these cases were brought for sound reasons and upheld by the judges. They also confirm Price's doubts over staff and recruitment policy.

Calvin Williams graduated from the London School of Economics with an accounting degree in 1963. Internal audit and financial controller jobs with a series of US multinationals led to location in Brussels where he gained employment with the EC's Audit Board in 1974. A permanent posting at A7 grade came in June 1977 and after transfer to the new Court of Auditors, he was promoted to A6 in May 1979, backdated to July 1977. Williams in May 1980 complained to the Court members that those recently appointed to A6 grade had ten years' less experience and could they 'do anything to correct this anomaly?'

Members agreed it was the case but since Williams had accepted his classification, decided to do nothing about it. Williams reacted in January 1981 with a FB1 million (£15,000) claim for regrading. He said that temporary staff were being promoted to 'generous' full-time grades. An internal memo from the Court president, Murphy, had regretted that new recruits included a number of poorly-qualified people. Williams criticised an internal recruitment to 'regularise' the status of temporary staff which had not asked for a knowledge of accountancy. The recruitment produced 91.66 per cent – 11 out of 12 – success rate.

In October 1982 the Court of Justice backed Williams, forcing the Court of Auditors to pay the additional salary. Williams twice went back to court, unsuccessfully, to extend the effect of the ruling back to 1974, the date when he joined the Audit Board. The courtroom career of auditor Williams was only just beginning and his most famous victory was yet to come. He was sure that job vacancies were rigged to suit favoured candidates and he set out to prove it. In October 1982 an internal vacancy was announced for an A5/A4 posting to carry out advisory duties relating to the Court's own administration and budget.

Written tests for this vacancy and five more for other posts were fixed for 17 November 1982. Each applicant required a relevant degree plus six years' professional experience; a non-graduate required ten years' experience. Williams was so confident that all six vacancy notices were 'shams' that the day before the tests he deposited with a Luxemburg lawyer his predictions of the six winners. As the judgement later recorded: 'It is common ground that Mr Williams's predictions all proved correct.'

In Williams's own vacancy he came second to Hartmut Schwiering who was the favoured candidate. Schwiering was the private office chief of German Court member, Albert Leicht, and had served as his personal assistant when Leicht was the chairman of the German parliament's budget committee in the mid-1970s. Schwiering claimed professional experience of three years and eleven months at the Bundestag and five years at the Court, a total of less than nine years. In order to qualify for the vacancy, he also claimed his twenty-seven months at Bonn University where he had failed to complete a legal studies degree.

The audit court members ignored Schwiering's lack of experience for the post and duly appointed him. The Court's financial controller, a stopgap on many occasions against abuse, thought otherwise and refused to accept the appointment. The full Court tried again in February 1983 and was similarly rebuffed by the controller who repeated that Schwiering did not have sufficient qualifications to apply for the vacancy. In March the Court overruled their financial controller.

Respect for EC rules in the financial arena is supposed to be the Court's hallmark but this incident sets a pretty poor example. One of the Court's roles in scrutinising EC expenditure is to vet all cases where financial controller's refusals are overruled. The Court is very often critical of these decisions when taken by the European Commission, for instance on farm spending. According to the Court's annual report on 1983, it was one of two occasions when the Court's controller was overruled. It evidently was not the first time it broke the rules in its own backyard.

At first the audit court told its financial controller that Schwiering's nine years of professional experience together with his twenty-seven months at university amounted to ten years of professional experience. Then it argued that because of the way legal studies were organised in Germany and to make them comparable with other EC countries, Schwiering ought to be given credit for the equivalent of a bachelor's degree. In this way he had a degree plus more than six years' professional experience. Neither explanation satisfied Williams, the controller or the Court of Justice where Williams took his action.

Williams told the Court of Justice that Schwiering was a subject of favouritism in high places at the audit court and that he, Williams, was *persona non grata* after his previous October 1982 legal victory. He said the audit court's interpretation of uncompleted studies as equivalent to years of professional experience was 'both novel and inconsistent and would encourage all kinds of favouritism'. The audit court replied that it had accepted its selection board's view of Schwiering's experience. It also added that Williams's claim was too late and that he had 'no interest in bringing the proceedings'.

The Court of Auditors was made to squirm as the bench of judges got down to detailed questioning. They wanted to know exactly how Schwiering had met the terms of the competition set by the Court's selection board. The answer is one straight out of a creative accountancy handbook. Schwiering's five university terms and good intermediate certificates together with twenty-one months out of his experience at the Bundestag were sufficient to meet the university degree or equivalent condition, it claimed. By adding the remainder of this political experience to that at the Court, the six years' professional experience was also satisfied.

The Court also admitted that this was not the first time it had taken this 'fairly flexible' attitude to professional experience and qualifications. Uncompleted studies were often taken into account, it said, and promptly produced five other postings where candidates' professional experience was insufficient. It was continuing a long-established practice, it said.

The Court of Justice's Advocate General, Marc Darmon, ripped into the audit court's argument. In doing so, he accused it of 'retreating' behind a statement drafted in April 1984 by Marcel Mart, the selection board chairman and new audit court president. Darmon said that Mart's explanations 'flew in the face' of the notice of the vacancy. 'For an occupation described as "normally requiring a university diploma" cannot by definition be made to include an activity which takes the form of studies and is undertaken as a means of obtaining that very diploma.'

The full bench of judges agreed and said Schwiering was wrongly admitted to the tests in the vacancy. It told the Court of Auditors not to re-appoint him on the basis of the results of the contested vacancy. It would either have to hold a new recruitment contest or appoint another candidate. While Williams had gained 'full satisfaction', it was still the audit court's decision whether to appoint him or not.

Two days after the judgement of October 1984, Williams replaced Schwiering in the administrator's job which the latter had held since April 1983. Schwiering lost his A5 grading and was offered a temporary post at the A7 level. His boss, Leicht, had left his membership of the Court in October 1983 and there was no cabinet job available. His lawyer attempted an 'amicable settlement', asking the Court to give him a temporary A5 post and to arrange an internal vacancy to make this a permanent position. In return Schwiering would drop his legal actions.

But the audit court was taking no chances this time. The Court of Justice quickly slapped down Schwiering when he took up his legal threat against the audit court. The judges, pointing out that Schwiering had already earned extra salary for eighteen months, said that taking any of the steps he proposed would infringe the EC's staff regulations. They were clearly becoming tired of dealing with the audit court's 'jobs-for-the-boys' approach to personnel management.

Charles Lux is another to have made more than one legal claim against the audit court. In December 1984, Lux's first claim was successful but in the meantime had been overtaken by a further legal case challenging his transfer to different work in the Court. Lux, a lawyer, had joined the Court from the Commission's legal department and worked in the Court's legal department until March 1983. Then he was transferred to the audit sector dealing with EC staff and operational expenditure and this prompted his complaint.

The case reveals the mistake in appointing lawyers who did not have the skills for the Court's work. Lux told the Court of Justice that he had only worked one out of his first six months in the new job, spending one month on holiday and four months without being given any work. He said this backed up statements made by Leicht, the Court member in charge of the audit area, and by the head of the audit division that they needed an auditor, not a lawyer. Lux added that the head of division had told him there were no legal subjects planned for the 1984 audit work programme.

When the Court of Justice ruled against Lux in June 1984, it accepted the audit court's contention that it needed auditors and lawyers in its staff. It noted that Lux 'initially failed to show in his work the willingness and enthusiasm with an institution is entitled to expect from a responsible official'. But it said it was not its role to interfere in the Court of Auditors' internal organisation and how it allocated jobs. It did not become embroiled in Lux's argument that Marty-Gauquie, temporary lawyer and future presidential aide, had taken over his old post, a claim which had been denied.

The final member of the litigious threesome is Henri Maurissen, though five others made legal complaints against the way the same 1985 internal recruitment was held to appoint an A7/A6 official to manage the Court's administration department. Judges in February 1987 told the audit court that its selection board should have been more assiduous. It should have looked after officials' well-being as well as the interests of the service. The second legal case over this 1985 vacancy was brought by two candidates excluded because of their knowledge of a second language.

Schwiering, who had 'won' and then lost the earlier rigged job contest against Williams, also brought a case over the same 1985 vacancy. The boot was on the other foot when the Court of Justice ruled he ought to have been admitted to the tests. Schwiering's 'mistake' had been to send photocopies of 'attesting' documents. The selection board said these had to be originals or certified copies, not mere photocopies. Schwiering was never told of this necessity and the Court of Auditors claims it considered stepping in to change the board. It ended up supporting Schwiering's action.

This extraordinary saga did not end when the Court of Auditors decided after a resumption to continue the recruitment with only the four who had taken it success- fully to the Court of Justice. Two more officials stepped up in 1987 to claim that as far as they were aware, their candidatures had never been rejected and that they ought to be evaluated in the latest round of tests. They said it was their impression that previous judgements meant a full re-run from scratch, not just for those who might challenge it further in the law courts.

The points raised in these disputes are petty in the main: whether a 'financial analyst associate' was a 'financial analyst', when to test a knowledge of French, and telling applicants that documents could not be photocopies. Yet the Court and its selection boards could not manage these simple tasks. The question whether these litigants were better for the posts being advertised is not the issue. Price's high-flying graduate career auditors would have sailed through anyway – if they had still been there. The issue is that selection boards were manipulating recruitment and the Court chiefs were letting it continue.

Table 4.2 Court of Auditors – management record on staff disputes

	Number of cases	Cases won	Success rate (%)
1985	4	3	75
1986	6	3	50
1987	3	2	67
	13	8	62

(Based on Court of Justice judgements)

More recently the Court of Auditors has won a number of actions brought by its staff but the suspicions linger on. In 1987 Jean-Pierre Kerzmann, a Luxembourg-origin official began an action against the audit court over the appointment of Edouard Ruppert, another Luxem-bourger as the Court's secretary in 1986. Kerzmann claimed that Court president Mart had 'used (his) powers to promote an individual interest rather than the general interest'. There were signs of Grand Duchy intrigue and

Kerzmann argued that Ruppert did not have the experience for the job, which includes relations with outside organisations.

Relations between Mart and the Court's staff committee reached a low in early 1987 with the mass resignation of five of the committee's eight members and two acrimonious legal actions involving Williams and Maurissen. It came at the height of the House of Lords' wide-ranging inquiry into the Court's workings and effectiveness. Further serious allegations concerning the members themselves emerged, which questioned public confidence in the Court. 1987 proved a watershed and led to reforms: many said enough was enough; it was time the auditors sorted themselves out.

The importance and influence of the staff committee, with representatives from EC trade unions, is difficult to determine. Mart, the Court president, claims through Marty-Gauquie that 'as the appointing authority (for jobs) he makes every effort to discuss complaints. When fifty per cent of the committee resigns it is not his concern and if you refer to the minutes of this trade union, these people have been censored by the majority of the board of their trade union'. The role of staff committee nominees on selection boards has sometimes been questioned in the same way that Court members have been accused of favouritism.

The support which the staff committee has is uncertain and quorums at some crucial staff meetings have been difficult to muster. The higher levels of staff, including those on temporary contracts, can see their careers ahead and are unconcerned by the rows. Mart's colleagues, who praise him for his leadership and commitment to a quality audit product, admit they would like to see a stronger central personnel policy. Others whose careers may be blocked are less restrained. Their frustration boiled over with the staff committee resignations of February 1987.

Williams was quick to link the mass resignation to the appearance by Jo Carey, the UK Court member since 1983, before a hearing of the Lords' committee in London. Carey is a former Treasury undersecretary, and though less experienced than Price, has proved himself a straight-talking and tough Court member. He also brought experience from a stint in the UK's delegation to the EC in Brussels as its top Treasury counsellor. He has taken on important farming briefs at the Court. Mart had turned down giving evidence, 'because of constraints of his timetable', but Carey was keen that the Court made an appearance.

Williams fired off a rousing telex to Carey in London, care of the Lords' committee office. It began by referring to the resignations: 'Reasons given various but all boil down to fact that trying to run a personnel policy with Marcel Mart is akin to signing a non-aggression pact with Joachim von Ribbentrop'. The telex went on to make five serious allegations against Mart, the Belgian (twice), French and Dutch members of the court. In flamboyant style, Williams went on to tell Carey he was copying the telex to Margaret Thatcher and if he wanted to 'see fur fly' he should join him the following week at his luncheon club where Mart was giving a talk.

The allegations require examination because, as a former Williams colleague says, there is always 'a scintilla of truth in what he says'. The allegation against Mart links him to the Luxlait scandal in Luxembourg's dairy sector (see Chapter 8). Williams said that Mart, as the Grand Duchy's minister for economic affairs to 1977, bore a collective responsibility for allowing the tax and accounting abuses to continue. A study of the scandal indicates that his Liberal/Socialist government did more than its predecessors to uncover the problems.

The two allegations against Paul Gaudy, the Belgian member, over a pension to a former colleague and a car are rejected by Court chiefs. Jacques Planchard, Gaudy's personal assistant from his time as auditor of the Coal and Steel Community, retired on a pension because governments agreed to reduce the number of posts at that senior grading and his job disappeared. Planchard had become governor of the province of Luxembourg, in Belgium, in July 1976 and according to a provincial aide left EC auditing at the same time. He says the new job is 'as a governor in the US' – not quite full-time.

According to Williams, Planchard still ought to have been working for the Court. At fifty-seven years old he was too young to qualify for normal retirement pension and his job did not disappear until the end of 1978. (The Court's 1979 budget is the first to indicate that the number of A2 director posts was cut from five to four and with it Planchard's post. The number of director posts has since been raised again.) Despite the Court's denial that any regulations were broken, Planchard's 'retirement' left a director's post empty for two and a half years.

Frenchman Pierre Lelong's outside appointment as mayor at the small Brittany town of Treflez only ended after the European Parliament's budget control committee got wind of it. Lelong had been re-elected mayor but stood down before vetting by the Parliament on re-appointment in 1983. The population of the town is less than 2,000 and the job part-time only. The Court says there was no conflict of interest but it was sufficiently embarrassing for Lelong to duck going to the Parliament to justify the appointment.

The Court confirms the final allegation that Dutch Court member Andre Middelhoek and British director, Peter Keemer, took Concorde to a value-for-money auditing conference in Washington in the United States. This may well have been the most efficient route on price and because it allowed the two to be fresh for their conference. The two claim they checked beforehand that Concorde via London was cheaper than via Frankfurt, Amsterdam or Paris by jumbo. But an Icelandair flight was said to be cheaper. Flying Concorde to a value-for-money conference was not the most tactful choice.

The response to the allegations from Court president Mart was the suspension of Williams on half pay. Predictably the Court of Justice became involved as Williams appealed against Mart's suspension. He said fifty per cent was too harsh, because he had to pay for his son's studies in the United States, expensive medical attention for his American wife and for his own health. Responsibility for the defamatory telex was diminished by this last factor. In April the salary cut was reduced to twenty-five per cent by the Court of Justice and in June, Williams began a year's sick leave after a medical examination.

The audit court hoped Williams wouldn't come back, although he was determined to do so. He began a year's business school course in Brussels but did not complete it.

By the spring of 1988, he was back standing for the two-yearly staff committee elections. He came fourth out of the eight candidates elected. He scored 106 votes and would probably have done better if it had not been for the late entry of two secretaries in the running. It is believed about 220 of the 330 staff voted. There was clearly widespread sympathy for Williams' criticisms at the way the Court was run.

The House of Lords select committee produced its conclusions on the Court in March 1987. It said major strides had been made in ten years but that 'considerable problems remain. The Court has recently been enlarged by three members, complicating still further the difficulties of language and differences of approach. There have been major developments in audit practice and there is continuing debate about the Court's objectives and techniques.' It recommended an external audit and a more extensive review of the Court's organisation, methods and relationships with the other institutions.

It said that the UK's National Audit Office was extensively audited each year by an outside firm of accountants and the European Court of Auditors ought to face the same scrutiny. Other recommendations included further developments to the three audit groups to improve staff mobility and work planning 'to bring all the audit work up to the standards of the best'. Career planning and promotion prospects should be improved though the committee at the same time said that secondments from national bodies should continue. More accountants and improved training were also required.

The report was no whitewash but it never tackled the sleazy areas of rigged job recruitment or other matters. Getting the Court to change its ways was another matter. It had never felt easy about the inquiry at all. As a supranational body, it did not see itself accountable to a national parliament. Mart had only entertained peers informally in Luxembourg. The pressure for the external audit became overwhelming during 1987 as Labour MEP Tomlinson met Mart. Once again he soothed fears and said that private sector firms of accountants from Luxembourg would be asked to bid for the contract to audit the 1987 accounts.

When the contract details were sent to about ten local

and international firms, there was surprise over the wide scope of the audit and the limited funds to do the task. While it was a prestige EC assignment for the firms, some didn't bid because the fee was just too unrealistic. The audit covers only the basic accounts of the Court along company accounting lines. Early contract details suggested that the internal systems were to be checked but the contract does not include a value-for-money audit as carried out on the UK's NAO.

The price for the contract is £5,600 and prompted one firm to ask if a nought had been left off the price. A more sensible estimate put the time needed by auditors to carry out the task at 200 to 300 hours, which at charge-out rates of only £50 an hour (a rock-bottom rate for such detailed work) comes to a minimum of £10,000. Price Waterhouse and its German affiliate Treuarbeit put in a successful joint bid, though it is unclear if the Court realised they were from the same stable. The Court still refuses to confirm that PW has won the assignment. But it is unlikely that the firm's opinion of the Court's accounts, the most essential part of any audit, will ever be published.

Marty-Gauquie, president Mart's aide, says defensively: 'They will report on the truth and fairness of the accounts to the Court and then the Court will have to take the necessary measures and report in its annual report (on the accounts of all the EC institutions). There is no reason for publication. Why the hell should he publicise our draft documents? It is totally transparent. Either the Community has confidence in its external auditors or not. They should have confidence in its report. It is also a matter of public confidence. If you don't trust a public body what else can you do.'

After the criticism and period of unease, the Court's best option would have been to publish and be damned – if that is what PW says. The Court says adverse comments will be published in its annual report on EC finances and that the Parliament's *rapporteur* may have access to PW's opinion. This method only creates distrust which the Court ought to be dispelling. The idea that this method is transparent – the EC buzzword for full disclosure – is ridiculous. Critics will merely say they can see straight through the Court's plan (if not through its machinations).

The choice of PW was surprising in one respect, because of a dispute the Court has with the European Investment Bank, the EC's government-owned long-term finance house based in Luxembourg. This is audited by PW. The Court has had difficulties in getting access to some EIB loan documents where it manages the EC's own loans, and its interest subsidies are involved. The conflict of interest between PW acting as the EIB's auditor and PW as auditor of the Court's own accounts is being dismissed as negligible. PW is unlikely to be tackling the Court's operating role and direct conflict does not arise.

The Court's most recent annual report on 1986 spending brought confirmation of another restriction on its auditing. A number of governments are blocking access to their VAT records so that the Court cannot confirm that the share paid over to Brussels is correct. Italy and Luxembourg refused to provide tax statistics and France will not give details of its collection system. Germany, France, Italy and Luxembourg refused to let the Court carry out checks to see that VAT collection was as the governments described them. At one point, the UK had wavered over access by the Court too.

The Court's inquiry touched the sensitive area of national fiscal policy as well as the main chunk of the EC resources. The Court said that in 1985 and 1986, it had been 'unable to discharge its responsibilities in full' to audit £15 billion revenue a year. The Court had merely 'drawn the attention' of governments and the Parliament to these audit limitations. If the Court continues to be refused access by these governments, then it ought to consider taking them to the Court of Justice. But one suspects that such a move would be too tough for the 'political' Court to take. There would inevitably be questions over whether the Court of Auditors had the right to take governments or anyone else to the Court of Justice, but at least it would prove it had some teeth. Instead the Court has restricted itself to words rather than deeds and plays a game of lobbying and politicking behind the scenes.

In October 1987 a new round of Court members was appointed after vetting by the Parliament's budgetary control committee. This committee and the full Parliament had the opportunity to say 'yes' or 'no' but could not put up its own candidates. This was the governments' prerogative. There were six candidates, though only one new appointment. This was the replacement of the first Belgian Court member, Paul Gaudy, by Fernand Hebette. The candidacy prompted complaints by Belgian Socialist EuroMPs that Hebette's wife worked as an A-grade official in the Commission's budget directorate. The Commission claimed it was a junior post.

The twelve Court members in 1988 are the same mix of politicians, civil servants and public auditors as the first nine were in 1977. And four of the originals still remain: Mart, the president, Aldo Angioi, the Italian, Lelong, and Middelhoek. Mart and Lelong had led political lives at some point in their career. Angioi was a career public sector auditor. Out of the five of the latest six appointments excluding Angioi, three were career public sector auditors and two were politicians.

The Spanish politician and ex-journalist Subirats had been elected a counsellor of his country's court of auditors and president of its tax chamber. The Irishman, Ryan, was a former finance minister and had sat on the European Parliament's budget and budgetary control committees. Neither the Court nor governments have a consistent idea of what sort of people they want in charge of the Court. None of this conferred clear leadership on the Court's job in rooting out waste.

And how good had the Court been at uncovering financial mismanagement – what was the quality of its output in the form of special and annual reports? Certaintly the reports were full of criticism, but then it would be difficult not to fall over foul-ups everywhere in the EC set-up. Some spelt out clearly how farming subsidies were wasted. Its solutions were often quite radical. Recent reports on milk, wine and tobacco went straight to the heart of the matter. But too many criticisms were superficial or relied excessively on the Court's systems-based approach to produce something that had little to do with reality.

Criticism of the quality of the Court's work has been muted. The Commission or governments are not going to say they are not audited properly and those bits which the Court gets wrong are edited out well before the reports are published. The obvious 'user' is the Parliament's budgetary control committee but it too has said little. Partly this is because the Court is its main, if not only, basis for its deliberations. Also Heinrich Aigner, the German Christian Democrat chairman of the committee, did much to set up the Court in the mid-1970s and it is claimed the two organisations had an unofficial agreement not to criticise each other.

A senior official of the Court provided the author with a copy of the Court's annual report, in which he pointed out areas of good and bad auditing. Only the main farming subsidy areas and regional aid earned good marks. These were awarded where large-scale abuses were identified and firm figures were put on their effect. Here the criticism was from the hip and told the Commission that it was quite clearly breaking its financial regulations. The chapters on structural measures in the farm sector, the social fund, staff and administrative spending and Third World development earned a bad mark. And it was easy to see why.

The black marks were mostly against sections where the Court apologised for not doing its job properly. 'No satisfactory explanation' had been obtained, but it was not said who was to blame for this; auditing was 'made more difficult' because of the way the Commission kept its books; legal conditions covering grants were 'complex' and 'not easy to audit'. The scope of on-the-spot visits was minimal. Only one cooperative and one Italian wine distillery were visited, the Court said. Statements such as 'some decisions contain mistakes as regards the amount approved' were not backed up.

It was fairly clear who was responsible for the chapters involved, though changes have since been made to the responsibilities of Court members. The former Belgian member Gaudy was responsible for the farming structural measures and the social fund, the Italian Angioi for the development fund and the Greek Court member Stergios Vallas for the staff and operational side. The Court decided not to publish a chapter on the 1986 social fund spending, published in its annual report in December 1987, the year that Gaudy left the Court.

The Court's attitude to its job and its skills in

managing its organisation is best summed up in the continuing saga of the chauffeurs for the twelve Court members. A car and a driver has often seemed to be a member's key priority, a perk he can't afford to be without. The first incident between Dutch Court member Middelhoek and his chauffeur ought to have been warning enough that outside observers would link the members' control over perks such as chauffeurs to their wider role in scrutinising EC spending.

Four questions in 1983 from Richard Caborn, then a Socialist EuroMP and in 1988 Labour MP for Sheffield Central, made the connection. Middelhoek's extensive use of his chauffeur and official car for private use had attracted attention. So too had the chauffeur's role as butler and garden handyman. Were Court employees being taken advantage of and was the job in line with the terms of the members' appointment, asked Caborn?

He wanted to know if the Court had any external auditor and added: 'Given the heavy responsibilities entrusted to the members of the Court of Auditors, the treaties not unexpectedly provide that "they shall refrain from any activity incompatible with their duties" and "when entering upon their duties they shall give a solemn undertaking, that both during and after their term of office, they shall respect the obligation arising therefrom"'. Middlehoek cut back his demands on the driver, who retains the post, but the warning to cut down on perks was not heeded.

Another row erupted in 1983 when Pierre Lelong, the Court's president up to October 1983 and still a member in 1988, tried to appoint a head driver. It soon became clear that fixing job vacancies extended to appointing drivers too. After an interview in March 1983, Lelong promised one of the existing drivers, Maurice Pauvert, the job though he had not applied for the vacancy and another driver had been recommended by the Court's director of personnel. In order that Pauvert got the job and the promotion that went with it, Lelong had to replace the first notice with a new one.

Predictably the dispute soon involved lawyers and the panoply of the European Court of Justice. Top briefs were soon pronouncing on this unseemly squabble. Sir Gordon

Slynn, the legal court's advocate general, said: 'It seems that the reason why this second notice was published, which was said to cancel the first notice of 16 February 1983, was to enable Mr Pauvert to qualify as a candidate.'

The second notice changed the requirement for fifteen years' driving experience to one of fifteen years' work experience, of which eight were to be as a driver. Pauvert had only eleven years' driving experience whereas the other candidate had more than fifteen. In May 1984 Marcel Mart, the new president from Luxemburg, held an internal test for the post. There were further candidates, some of whom had not applied for either vacancy previously. The audit court made one of its few sensible decisions in making no appointment as head driver. Pauvert complained to the Court of Justice but lost. He was told he had had every opportunity to pitch for the job.

Why the Court of Auditors should have needed a head driver is unclear. Perhaps he would have been in charge of keeping the cars spruce and shipshape, or making sure his driver colleagues brushed their shoes in the morning and perfected their driving etiquette. Perhaps he would lead the Court's motorcade when the members descended on the Commission for a major fraud investigation. No, the reasons are clear: president Lelong wanted Pauvert to get promotion and tried to fix it for him.

More widespread friction between the top auditors and their drivers led to another dispute in 1985 when president Mart reorganised the administration, so that he alone became responsible for drivers and they ceased to be allocated to individual members. Eight of the drivers complained about this decision because they believed it no longer guaranteed their fixed overtime allowance of one-third of their salary. In 1988 the Court of Justice agreed and cancelled their transfer. Their employment contracts had been broken. Another dispute had been mishandled by the Court's bosses. It is hard to have any sympathy for either side.

The most recent incident to prompt staff-side questions over the employment of chauffeurs involved Ryan, the Irish Court member and a former finance minister and EuroMP. He has declined to give his version of this petty late-night accident. He had enjoyed a pleasant evening at the theatre in Luxembourg Ville and had arranged for his driver to meet him at 11.30 p.m. But the driver was slightly late. When he arrived, Ryan asked him to get out of the car and said he intended to drive himself. As the driver went to get his coat, the car door swung back knocking him sharply.

Ryan drove off leaving his driver, who lives over the border in France, stranded in Luxembourg for the night. Three weeks later at the beginning of March 1988, the driver was still off work. X-rays showed no serious damage but rest was prescribed. The court's staff committee took an interest though no formal complaint was made. Neither party appeared blameless but without Ryan's side of the story it was not possible to be sure.

The lengthening list of conflicts between Court members and their drivers ought to be brought to an end. It is a list which also includes claims that Josep Subirats, the Spanish member, is on his third driver in three years. It is understood that Carey, the UK member, has given up his chauffeur and drives himself. The other members ought to do the same. The only difficulty with such a plan is the cost and means of making the drivers redundant.

If the Court members had been swanning around Brussels under the scrutiny of EuroMPs and the large corps of journalists, these excesses would have ended years ago. Putting themselves on a par with European Commissioners and government ministers is bound to have influenced their attitude as auditors – and not for the better.

And the Court has trouble getting its own sums right – perhaps a case for watching the (Court's) pennies and the (EC's) ecus will look after themselves. In its annual report released at the end of 1987, it admitted over-paying £20,000 in pensions to its former staff between 1983 and 1985. The Court is considering legal action to recover the sums. According to one senior official: 'It is part-comedy, part-tragedy and part balls-up. It was an elementary boob.' Some Court members are also surprised Sir Norman Price, former UK member, put forward his name in a series of legal test cases challenging EC pension levels because of adverse exchange rates.

The Court of Auditors has failed to generate the

confidence that a financial watchdog requires. Nor does it show much sign of putting its house in order. Marcel Mart, its president, is rated as one of the few Luxembourgers who can hold his own with the rest of Europe's leaders. But he has failed to handle its personnel or carry out the much-needed reforms. Professional training, despite regular consultants' reports, is not underway. A single central building with computers was one grandiose achievement in 1988. An alternative – such as an international firm of professional auditors – may be needed.

Section 2
AGRICULTURE

5 FARM FRAUD: THE £BILLION A YEAR RIP-OFF

Swindling the European Community's agricultural subsidies is big business. Klaus Tiedemann, West German professor in economic crime, says: 'The common agricultural policy is the greatest incentive to crime in Europe today.' He believes that between ten and twenty per cent of subsidies are being ripped off. The European Commission, which manages the EC farm policy, believes the figure is under one per cent. The twelve governments believe it is lower still. Not agreeing on the scale of the problem is one obstacle preventing a clamp-down on the fraudsters.

As EC officials, auditors and governments tinker with their leaky financial controls, an inventive industry has dipped into European taxpayers' pockets to the tune of billions of pounds. Ingenious schemes have taken advantage of weak and overly-complex regulations. In particular the subsidised trade between EC countries and the rest of the world has been wide open to abuse. Trade in agricultural products between countries has offered a smaller margin, but one the unscrupulous have found still worth exploiting. Subsidies to support prices or buy in excess stocks have suffered the same way.

Of the £55 spent on behalf of the European citizen each year to support farming, at least £5 lines the pocket of the fraudster. It is probably more than most people give to charity each year. All countries are involved: northern European traders play the sophisticated international version, while poorer southern cooperative farmers over-bid their claims to make up for being paid late.

Tiedemann blames a system which does not offer 'something in exchange' for the handout, the 'artificial' EC control system and the lack of 'a social control' or conscience by the perpetrators. These factors are exaggerated in this supranational set-up because loyalties to Europe don't exist and market forces don't operate to check on cheats. Tiedemann says it has led to the features of Eastern Bloc planned economies, such as the black market. He says: 'I have been working with colleagues from Hungary and Poland, and what you see are patterns of fraud and cheating that are known from planned economies.

'This factor and pattern of criminality and illegal behaviour is lacking in national systems in Germany and UK. With my colleagues I said "let's look at what happens when Spain enters the EC (in 1986)". I said, these things are going to happen again. Two months after entering, the same patterns emerged and now they have put forward a law concerning EC fraud. It reads like a textbook of criminality.'

Tiedemann's claim of more than ten per cent of fraud amounts to £1.5 billion each year. And though not all is wilful fraud proven in court, it is a better estimate of how much breaches the rules than official figures. It is a claim accepted by many EuroMPs and one beginning to be taken seriously by the Court of Auditors, the EC's own financial watchdog. Hard data from the detailed scrutiny of actual grant payments and 'soft' data from monitoring trade flows indicates that anecdotal evidence from official investigations is just the tip of a multi-billion pound iceberg.

Export refunds are the biggest single subsidy scheme for European farmers and the food industry and one of the most abused. In 1987, £6.4 billion or 40 per cent of the EC's budget for subsidising the price of produce was spent on refunds. In 1986 the figures on refunds were £5.2 billion or 34 per cent of the budget. Each time agricultural commodities are exported from the EC, the exporter receives a refund to make up the shortfall between the lower world market price and the guaranteed higher price he would have expected inside the twelve countries. When imports are made, the reverse process occurs.

The aim is to discourage imports of food or agricultural feedstuff to the EC by charging an importer a levy. This lifts his cost up to the level of EC prices. Exports are

Figure 3

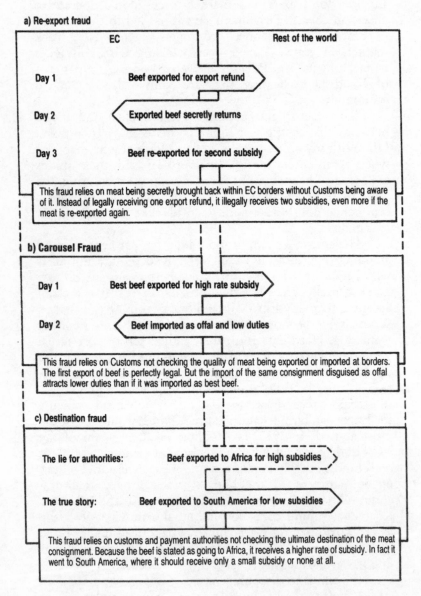

a) Re-export fraud

EC — Rest of the world

Day 1 — Beef exported for export refund

Day 2 — Exported beef secretly returns

Day 3 — Beef re-exported for second subsidy

This fraud relies on meat being secretly brought back within EC borders without Customs being aware of it. Instead of legally receiving one export refund, it illegally receives two subsidies, even more if the meat is re-exported again.

b) Carousel Fraud

Day 1 — Best beef exported for high rate subsidy

Day 2 — Beef imported as offal and low duties

This fraud relies on Customs not checking the quality of meat being exported or imported at borders. The first export of beef is perfectly legal. But the import of the same consignment disguised as offal attracts lower duties than if it was imported as best beef.

c) Destination fraud

The lie for authorities: — Beef exported to Africa for high subsidies

The true story: — Beef exported to South America for low subsidies

This fraud relies on customs and payment authorities not checking the ultimate destination of the meat consignment. Because the beef is stated as going to Africa, it receives a higher rate of subsidy. In fact it went to South America, where it should receive only a small subsidy or none at all.

encouraged by refunds. The European plateau of prices, like those of the US, Japan and some other countries lies above the lower world open market price. In theory, it provides a living for European farmers, encourages a stable market and production. In the early- to mid-1980s the stocks bought in by the authorities, to keep prices up, rose dramatically and with it the incentive to export.

The real-life stories point up the endless imagination of the agricultural and food processing industries. In 1985, frozen beef from Northern Ireland was licensed by the UK authorities for export to Egypt but ended up in the Caribbean. Documentation showed the beef was received in Egypt, gaining a higher rate of refund. Another UK trader told the UK Intervention Board for Agricultural Produce, which pays out EC refunds, that he had exported beef to Yugoslavia. The beef had been diverted to The Netherlands and the trader was successfully prosecuted for £150,000 of fraudulent claims.

The largest single documented fraud case involved £12.3 million of export refunds for beef declared for export to Egypt but shipped to Brazil from Le Havre. The EC offers no refunds for exports to Brazil because it is a major producer of beef and doesn't need subsidised imports. Along with the US and Japan it receives a nil rate export refund. Highest rates of subsidy in 1988 were Western Africa at £1.50 a kilo and Northern Africa at £1.60. Middle East Gulf states also qualified for over £1 in refunds per kilo. International traders took advantage of short-term demand to take up the EC funds.

The Egypt rip-off was half the size of the UK's largest robbery, the £25 million Brinks-Mat gold bullion heist at Heathrow Airport but is treated as if it was a theft from the petty cash tin rather than a huge organised swindle. Four years after it took place the French company involved denies responsibility and the alleged culprit remains beyond the EC's grasp in Switzerland. In 1988 the Commission was still dithering over whether to make the French government pay or bear the cost itself.

Fraud on EC funds is a crime of less seriousness than robbery in many states and does not even attract criminal proceedings. Yet the effect is the same – money ends up in the hands of someone who has no right to it. And in this case the money is contributed by European taxpayers.

Beef has been a big area for fraud and another case had customs officials from North America scurrying to Brussels during 1986. Their aim was to crack down on a beef/veal 'merry-go-round' that cost £1.8 million in subsidies. It was a complex scheme with meat from the EC going to the US, staying there in transit and then coming back again, this time declared to the authorities as offal. Then, taking advantage of the EC transit regime which allows containers to move freely between the twelve countries, swaps were made with containers containing genuine offal. Import levies and export refunds had been successfully manipulated.

Meat frauds have been widespread in Germany. In one case high-quality beef was shipped in from South America as offal. Despite veterinary certificates at approved abattoirs in the exporting countries and sampling in Germany, the beef only paid low-import levies. The same organisation tried the scam in reverse by exporting offal as high-quality beef for the Third World and claiming the export refunds. Altogether up to £10 million was defrauded before the criminal courts got their hands on the culprits.

The plan only succeeded with bribes, corrupt customs officials, friendly freight agencies and negligent vets. But it proved that the checks were so ineffective that a well-organised team could take on the EC and win. It also backed Tiedemann's belief that loyalty to Europe was thin on the ground.

Other recent cases involving fraudulent or irregular export refund claims cover exports of beef by six EC countries, including the UK, to Zimbabwe. The declared destination of South Africa offered exporters £3 million in fraudulent export refunds. Because Zimbabwe exports beef to the EC, no subsidies are available for exports there. The subsidies for trade with the apartheid regime angered Labour EuroMPs, who prefer to scale down trading and impose further sanctions rather than offer financial incentives. But foreign policy and farm policy are not in tune.

Customs authorities in a number of countries in northern Europe, the US, Canada and the Caribbean are even now piecing together a trade in cheese. One strand involved cheese from outside the EC, imported through an EC country and then on to the US and Canada. The American authorities queried the EC origin and reduced import duties were at stake. The cheese was coming from Austria, Switzerland, Poland, Czechoslovakia and Hungary and took advantage of the £1.20 per kilogramme EC subsidy because of its supposed exportation to the Bahamas.

The Eastern European cheese had become a major economic problem by 1986 with 15,000 tonnes out of the EC's 60,000 tonne quota to the US not coming from within its own boundaries. The effect was not helped by the second strand to the investigation. This was the cheese declared for export to the Caribbean, such as the Bahamas freeport, but in fact ending up in North America – Florida in many cases. EC export refunds were only available on trade to the Caribbean. Recovery for £530,000 has begun against four Danish companies and investigations have been extended to cheese declared for end-use in Sweden.

Every country in the EC is affected by farm fraud. A recent Belgian/Italian case uncovered twelve containers of veal exported from Belgium, supposedly to Beirut, which were imported at Trieste in Italy as if they had come from the Yugoslav port of Koper. The Italian authorities have taken the importers to court. In early 1988 the Belgian authorities were still examining false Lebanese certificates of delivery which permitted the payment of export refunds. Clearly the Lebanese civil war was no bar to fraud.

These examples show that checks over origin or destination are evaded or are ineffective. All the cases were discovered but have required the authorities to recover funds. Other cases involve the quality of products not being checked by the authorities. A Belgian court hearing in 1988 was expected to hear how butter was put on the market containing up to 45 per cent of Italian pig fat. The suspicion was that the Italians had claimed refunds or monetary compensation amounts (MCAs) for exports claiming to be good quality butter. The case enraged various ethnic communities who don't eat pig products. Not even religion can stop the determined fraudster.

Quality was at stake when trainloads of French butter were exported to Yugoslavia, a trade which may be exploiting a loophole in the detailed code of the EC regulations. Two weeks of exports alone collared up to Dm30 million (£10 million) in refunds. In Yugoslavia, salt, eggs and water were added. The 'diet mayonnaise' was imported into West Germany and paid only low duties. The mayonnaise was inedible and was re-processed in a factory near the East German border. The eggs and salt (pepper had been excluded because it was difficult to extract) were extracted and the butter was re-exported for more subsidies.

This carousel technique was repeated a number of times before the quality became too degraded. Detailed criteria, or recipes, for the contents and quality of exports are often interpreted legalistically even though the product may be inedible. For instance, meat offal was made into sausages for export to Yugoslavia and Bulgaria for prisons. They were so 'disgusting', said EC officials later, that prisoners refused to eat them. The products still gained export refunds because there was no definition of what a sausage should contain and they qualified under a different heading.

This is a snapshot of real cases, all well known to national authorities and reported to the Commission under an 1972 agreement with governments to supply information on 'irregularities'. It is the officially acknowledged tip of the fraud iceberg, the part that has been uncovered and is being investigated by the national authorities. 'Irregularity' was used in the 1972 regulation instead of 'fraud' to prompt as much reporting to the Commission as possible. It is not fraud established by a judge but is based on 'primary administrative or judicial findings of fact'. Reports are still patchy.

According to these figures, fraud is dramatically on the rise, reaching an official level of 0.4 per cent of farm spending in 1987. And this is certainly just the small portion that has been uncovered. The Commission believes that the 1987 figures are a more complete picture than earlier versions and is the result of a drive to get better reporting by governments. In the past, Germany had reported too many frauds, 35 per cent of 1986 cases, and

Table 5.1 Irregularities reported – the official figures

	1985		1986		1987	
	value in £m	number of cases	value in £m	number of cases	value in £m	number of cases
Belgium	0.6	10	2.8	24	1.8	13
Denmark	0.3	17	0.3	19	0.1	12
West Germany	3.2	116	0.8	124	0.3	52
Greece	–	–	–	–	–	1
Spain			–	–	–	–
France	0.4	28	1.6	57	2.6	75
Ireland	–	–	3.7	3	1.3	8
Italy	3.2	40	10.5	50	52.6	131
Luxembourg	–	–	–	–	–	–
Netherlands	–	–	–	13	–	–
Portugal			–	–	–	–
United Kingdom	0.6	40	0.3	21	2.4	93
	8.2	230	20.0	311	61.1	385

(Source: European Commission)

the UK and Italy not enough. The Commission believes that in some cases the Germans have been over-enthusiastic, reporting cases where traders made genuine mistakes and subsidies were subsequently paid back.

The smaller EC states are hit more sporadically. Belgium was badly hit by a £3.3 million total in 1980 but reported levels well under £1 million until 1986 when one case alone amounted to £1.7 million. Denmark and The Netherlands, where efficient administration is the watchword, have reported levels of under £300,000 a year throughout the 1980s and in many years much less. The Commission believes the Dutch are 'not keen' on reporting. Their coordination was good on paper but reporting was below what was expected from a country with so much agricultural activity.

There were also gaps because states had not supplied any information. Spain and Portugal were regarded as too new to be ticked off about this, though they had no special dispensation. Greece was also living off its 'new boy' status though it had joined the EC club in 1981. Greece supplied just the one irregularity in its wine sector in 1987. Either the Greeks were holding back on the data or had not prosecuted any fraud. It is very unlikely, given the poor rural economy and administration, that fraud is not occurring. Commission anti-fraud officials were planning a trip to Athens to discuss the issue.

The Commission accepted Luxemburg's claim to have a higher degree of control than bigger states. The scope for fiddling with a 20,000 tonne shipload of meat is limited in the Grand Duchy, it believed. So its anti-fraud unit was 'astonished' to hear of the events outlined in Chapter 9. It waited to be notified when the investigating magistrate had completed his inquiries and the impact on EC funds could be established more accurately. It was barred from making its own inquiries because the case was under judicial inquiry. But it was an example that the Commission's intelligence network was seriously fallible even over a range of 200 kilometres.

The 1972 rules also require governments to supply data on new fraudulent practices or ones affecting other countries. This led to eight new sightings in 1986, although half were uncovered by the Commission itself. These affected meat, milk, and wine sectors in Belgium, Germany, Denmark and the UK. In earlier years, Greece reported five irregularities under this heading. These presumably relate to other countries since Greece has only admitted one EC fraud within its borders.

It is not really surprising that the reporting system works so badly: there is a positive disincentive for governments to give a full reply. Under EC accounting, governments pay out the subsidies to their farmers and claim the cash back from the Commission in Brussels. When subsidies are defrauded, national authorities must recover them and report quarterly under the 1972 regulation on what progress has been made. Where a government abandons its recovery efforts, then the Commission wants to know why. If a government has been negligent, then the

Commission can refuse to pay the sum out of the EC budget.

Table 5.2 Fraud clear-up rates – recoveries by European governments (£ millions)

	1971 – 1986			1987		
	defrauded	recovered	%	defrauded	recovered	%
Belgium	8.2	0.3	4%	1.8	–	0%
Denmark	1.7	1.3	74%	0.1	–	57%
Germany	49.1	21.2	43%	0.3	0.1	49%
Greece	(no fraud declared)			–	–	0%
Spain	(no fraud declared)			(no fraud declared)		
France	6.0	1.6	26%	2.6	0.6	23%
Ireland	4.5	0.8	18%	1.3	–	0%
Italy	35.7	1.2	3%	52.6	–	0%
Luxembourg	(no fraud declared)			(no fraud declared)		
Netherlands	2.9	2.1	70%	–	–	–
Portugal	(no fraud declared)			(no fraud declared)		
United Kingdom	6.5	2.3	36%	2.4	0.1	5%
	114.6	29.8	26%	61.1	0.8	1%

Proving negligence is embarrassing to a government and may involve it bearing the cost of the lost subsidy itself. And if it doesn't have a provision in its budget, it must go to its parliament's budget committee, confess to being defrauded and make a plea for funds. In practice, the Commission is lenient in applying this sanction, though there is no legal reason why it should be. Over the last few years it has encouraged states to supply better data and the 1987 figures show some success in this. Before these arrived, the Commission had called for a more 'rigorous and homogenous' set of reports.

It had said of the much lower 1986 figures: 'The figures do sustain the "tradition" of uneven distribution, so often regretted by the Commission in recent years, as regards the number of cases of irregularities notified and their financial implications, and corroborate the fact, already mentioned by the Commission, that the intensity of fraud in any given member state cannot be measured only on the basis of the number of cases of irregularities notified.'

The 1987 total of £61 million irregularities was inflated by large fruit and vegetable frauds in Italy. Taking that away made the figures modest. The Commission pointed to a higher level of reporting from most countries when it compared their 1987 totals against their average for the three previous years. Apart from Germany, where it wanted less rigorous reporting, only The Netherlands showed a decline. Four countries were still not supplying realistic data. And while the upward trend now covered five years, the 1982 figure had outstripped every year, except 1987, with its £23 million total.

Analysis of the particular produce hit by fraud backs up the anecdotal evidence of the sectors at risk. In 1986, fruit and vegetables were the top sector with £7 million of frauds, virtually all in Italy and covering twenty-two cases. In 1987 the number of Italian cases had risen to fifty-eight and involved £48 million or 79 per cent of all reported EC farm 'irregularities'. The overall spending on fruit and vegetables had declined to a steady £650 million a year in 1987, putting the level of fraud at 7 per cent plus. Given the parlous state of the sector it was scarcely surprising that some farmers had turned to fraud.

Demand and supply were hopelessly out of line and large surpluses of fruit and vegetables were being bought up by the authorities. In 1986, 10 per cent of tomato production was withdrawn, 10 per cent of the orange crop, 17 per cent of peaches and 90 per cent of mandarins. The cost to the EC of these purchases was £200 million. 93 per cent of the tomatoes and oranges and 95 per cent of the mandarins were later destroyed. One complaint was that marketing of Mediterranean crops in Northern Europe was poor. The economics of this strategy are not easy but the EC efforts have been feeble: exports outside Europe are growing faster than those within its borders.

With no prospect of decent prices in the market,

farmers turned in their droves to EC subsidies to bail them out. There were few checks to prevent fraudulent claims, even though 1985 rules had introduced tighter inspections to check on the quality of produce claiming export refunds, withdrawal and processing subsidies. The Commission was to oversee national efforts and mount its own inspections. But it claimed a lack of staff in 1986 prevented this from being carried out. By 1987 it was too late and fraudulent claims had reached massive proportions. It had not been the first farm sector to suffer in this way.

Official statistics for 1986 showed that beef/veal frauds amounted to £4.5 million with the majority, £3.7 million, involving Ireland and caused by rustling across the border with Northern Ireland. In 1987 meat was the second in the league of shame after fruit and vegetables with £4.7 million at stake. France scored eleven meat frauds of £1.9 million in value followed by Ireland with eight cases worth £1.3 million and the UK eighty-nine cases covering £0.9 million. One of the surprising figures was the nil wine fraud in Italy in 1986 and 1987 (see Chapter 6).

Sectors are hit in phases as their economics change. In the early 1980s wine was a major Italian, French and German intervention rip-off as surpluses soared. It remains the most common fraud in France with thirty-eight cases costing £500,000 in 1987. Meat subsidies were the target in 1986 because the refund rates for exports to Africa were so high. Italian fruit and vegetables followed in 1987 because there was no open market outlet. The next Italian sector being hit is intervention subsidies for hard durum wheat. Export refunds for other cereals may offer North European producers a rip-off opportunity after the 1988 US drought.

The Court of Auditors has increasingly queried the government statistics. In its annual report published at the end of 1984, it said the figures should be treated 'with some circumspection' and noted that countries have a different conception of fraud and irregularity. A year later it said governments had a 'certain indifference' to the financial interests of the EC and generally refrained from reporting attempted frauds to the Commission. These would have helped efforts to counter future crime and allowed counter-measures to be taken before frauds took place.

In December 1986 the Court returned to the 'high concentrations of irregularities' in some countries and 'regretted' the delay in introducing IRENE, the Commission's computerised database. In its report on the 1986 accounts, filed in December 1987, the Court decided to devote a separate chapter on efforts against fraud on farm funding. It analysed a sample of the 1986 figures and found that 25 per cent of cases involved export refunds or MCAs. Most cases involved 'well-known techniques, eg inaccurate declarations of nomenclature, quantities, weight etc, and adulteration of products'.

It said that information was often too vague and because names were usually omitted, it was impossible to detect frauds repeated several times by the same culprit and where aid could continue to be paid. It also noted that in Italy, several fraud cases were only detected by the tax authorities after the recipient had gone bankrupt and not by those directly responsible. The Luxembourg-based Court also accepted at face value the Grand Duchy's own statistics. It went so far as to commend them to other states. The Court evidently does not read its local newspapers, otherwise it would have known about the Luxembourg milk sector.

But – and this is the key point – the official figures only record detected irregularities – a fraction of all fraudulent cases and 0.4 per cent of the overall EC farm budget of £15 billion. Even for official statistics, they appear too low. In 1987 Guy Guermeur, a French EuroMP and fraud expert, compared the lower 1986 statistics to the reported figures of detected tax fraud in France and Germany, which he put at 2 and 1.45 per cent respectively. Guermeur then put a 0.7 per cent, or £105 million a year, figure on fraud on EC farm spending because he said checks are tougher than those on income declared to the taxman.

The figure is still too low and does not answer the key question of how much fraud goes undiscovered, nor how many claims there are where quality and quantity are overstated by a significant enough margin to make them fraudulent. It is estimates of these factors that make Tiedemann's much higher figures of between 10 and 20 per cent appear realistic. It is based on both 'soft' and 'hard' data. Soft data comes in the form of trade statistics which prove a commensense check of the level of subsidies. It predicts the wine production from the known number of vines and compares it to the volume of wine coming onto the market. It then asks why there is such a mismatch.

According to Tiedemann, soft data checks would have queried why Germany was one of Europe's largest exporters of rice and Belgium a major sheep exporter. It would have told the bureaucrats that the Rhine is not lined by paddy fields and that the Ardennes are not populated by sheep. Comparison of an importing and an exporting country ought to reveal similar inconsistences. French researchers have compared French corn exports to the non-EC Austria with Austrian figures for imports from France. Tiedemann says there were 'tremendous differences' indicating that EC exports were inflated by fraudulent claims for refunds.

He says: 'Products that left France never arrived in Austria or Switzerland, according to the subsidies. I expect that whole streams of exportation are faked and only exist on paper. The whole export is faked or it is not to a non-member state. With other means it has led to this estimation that fraud may go up to 10 per cent of the EC budget. It is only an estimate, because in cereals and meat our findings are quite exact. We have not been able to find statistics concerning all sectors of agricultural products. In many sectors it is 10–20 per cent and this leads us to the conclusion there might be an average of 10 per cent.'

The Commission's agricultural anti-fraud unit dismisses the idea of these economic studies as 'looks easier than it is'. Statistics from third countries are not always reliable and use different descriptions of particular commodities. They claim that despite common customs systems, one country might describe pigs as 'pigs' whereas another will separate them into umpteen categories by age and sex. Officials have done several studies on EC and Swiss and Austrian trade but it is complicated because transit statistics are almost impossible to get hold of. Splitting out real exports from those only passing through has not always been possible.

Concrete results are few and far between, though the anti-fraud unit receives fortnightly reports on suspicious market trends from other agricultural divisions in the Commission. These are either fraud or a bad application of the regulations. For instance, harvest forecasts may prove wildly out of line. Information also goes in the opposite direction, warning officials when inquiries have unearthed anomalies in prices for commodities or export refunds. One anomaly was the large quantities of butter exported to the Vatican state, which turned out to be for down-and-out visitors. It prompted changes to a re-export form.

Tiedemann has proposed a more thorough soft data exercise along the lines of Scandinavian research, which revealed up to 50 per cent of irregularities, 'although this included trivial offences'. These countries also pay refunds when farm produce is exported though the study covered a single week's trade in all goods. It was a 'total investigation' of every transaction and involved customs officials, police, research workers and temporary staff. Organised by the National Swedish Council for Crime Prevention and the Finnish Research Institute for Legal Policy, this expensive exercise drew protests from those moving goods.

Tiedemann says: 'A huge group stopped all trains and cars with exported goods and investigated to what extent the quantity and quality that was declared compared to the paperwork. The amount of quasi-criminality was 50 per cent. A half of all the quantity and quality differed with the paperwork, many with very fine differences. The final report said that, if you ignore the trifling amounts, there is 30 per cent of serious differences where there is some degree of criminality. I proposed to the European Parliament's budgetary control committee that such an experiment should be repeated in the EC.

'Yes, it would be an enormous exercise, but you could do it. You can't control all export streams for one week, but for each country to make one main export station examine all goods. This would give a quite secure basis for estimation.'

Commission fraud experts dismiss the Swedish study because it included 'even the slightest error in statistical origin or destination which did not have financial consequences for the Swedish fisc (tax authority)'. They say it included trader error which gave a higher tariff rating and that overall the irregularities, according to the EC definition, amounted to 'two or three, or a maximum of 6 per cent'. Conducting such a study in Europe would be virtually impossible and even at one port, such as Rotterdam, would be an enormous task. Such a plan would also require national authorities' agreement.

The reaction from the Commission to most bright-sounding ideas is a dash of cold water. There then follows a complaint about being understaffed and not being able to cope with the work in hand. Morale in the anti-fraud unit comes over as higher than other deadbeat agricultural divisions where most could do with a big shake-up in work practices and organisation. Despite the EC's abysmal record on farm policy from food mountains to fraud, such radical solutions rarely see the light of day.

Hard data on the level of abuse comes from specific studies of EC spending, says Tiedemann. He quotes a 1950s study of subsidies paid by the European Coal and Steel Community for scrap. This found that 20 per cent of all compensatory payments were gained fraudulently. The beef slaughtering campaign in the middle of the 1970s produced further evidence in Germany. A study of the first 10,000 of 80,000 slaughter records by the Dusseldorf tax authority led to more than 1,000 fines being imposed for incorrect slaughter premiums in the 1975/6 financial year. He says this is a proven crime rate of 10 per cent.

Tiedemann's own Institute for Criminology and Economic Crime at Freiburg University, which was set up in the early 1970s, has tackled hard data. Financed by the German Ministry of Justice and the Federal Bureau of Police, it works closely with both. He says: 'EC criminality is just one of our research topics. About twelve years ago I was asked by the Federal Ministry of Justice to investigate this type of criminality, and then had a similar request from the European Parliament's budgetary control committee. That was how I came to investigate this type of crime and how I got access to material.

'I normally get files from criminal justice and administrative agencies in cases where subsidies, in the broadest sense, have been revoked. I try to investigate not only those cases that proved to be criminal, but also those cases that turned out to be illegal practices – illegal enough to revoke subsidies that have been granted. The material covered almost 2,000 cases and a bit more than half came from the Federal Republic where we had quicker and better access to material. Others came from France, Belgium, a small part from The Netherlands, a big part from Italy and very recently from Spain.'

Tiedemann has built up an unparalleled expertise and knowledge of Eurofraud from his base in the southern German university city by the Rhine. The soft and hard data from his studies are the basis for claims that fraud on EC intervention and export subsidies is mounting, and presents problems similar to those of planned economies in East Europe. The Commission won't accept his claims that 10 per cent-plus of subsidies are being ripped off. They say he can't prove it scientifically. One of their fraud experts says: 'I agree even three per cent would be too much. The known cases are not all the cases that occur – that is for sure.'

Yet national authorities, the Court of Auditors and the Commission all have a clear idea of the real levels from their own studies. Tiedemann says government studies in France in the early 1980s showed that 0.7 per cent of EC farming subsidies to France were irregular and that German finance ministry estimates in 1985 came close to one per cent. The levels reported to the Commission in 1987 were only 0.06 and 0.01 per cent respectively of their share of that year's subsidies. Tiedemann says the higher levels tally well with recorded economic crime, for instance by German private companies. Even the best-reporting Germans have toned down their filings to the Commission.

A 1988 National Audit Office study in the UK suggests a higher level of export refund irregularities in 1986 than the two cases valued at £340,000 reported to the Commission. (This is below the UK annual average on number of cases but comparable on value.) The report notes that a special Customs CAP evaluation and liaison team set up between November 1985 and March 1987 investigated fifty-one cases of possible fraud just in the Port of London. It said: 'In many instances, the amounts involved were small and caused by clerical errors made by traders, but in two cases under further investigation, the possible irregularity exceeds £1 million.'

Separate verification of export refunds by the UK's Intervention Board for Agricultural Produce, which handles payments to farmers, involved visiting 250 traders a year between 1983 and 1986 and identified 700 errors or other queries involving £500,000. Checking by IBAP and Customs and Excise covered only a sample of claims. The proportion of payment paperwork scrutinised was up to 17 per cent in some respects but chemical testing of quality by customs was often below one per cent. The evidence suggested that incorrect claims went far beyond the handful notified by the Commission and where prosecution was underway.

Other recent studies of EC farm spending reveal higher levels of irregularities. A Court of Auditors special report on the olive oil sector found that £70 million of annual subsidy claims, out of a £200 million plus total, disappeared when a minimal amount of local scrutiny was introduced. This would suggest 35 per cent had previously been fictitious. Even this level may be too low. The wine sector suffers similarly inflated subsidy claims mainly for distillation aid. Chapter 6 indicates rates towards 50 per cent and the audit court specifically queried 100 per cent of France's distillation aid in the late 1970s.

But many of the Court's special reports suffer from not putting a figure on the scale of fraud. The clear official message that fraud is a large-scale problem costing billions of pounds is not put across to governments, MEPs and the public. The Court, like Tiedemann, may not have scientific proof but at least its testing is up to date, covered the EC and is reasonably sound. The samples of transactions it has tested ought to have made sensible predictions possible. Yet too often it is besotted by its 'system-based audit'. This meant it has concentrated on how the bookkeeping has broken down but not by how much.

Any private sector auditor could have told it that system-based audit has to be put to one side if the system of controls has broken down so badly that they are no longer reliable. When this happens in a private company, an auditor has to rely on large-scale testing of transactions and other commonsense quantitative checks. Only with that data can he report confidently if the accounts are correct or, if not, by how much they are out. Without doing that, the auditor would risk a negligence suit. This possibility has never faced the Court.

Even the Court's special report on olive oil in 1985 comes close to not quantifying the extent of rip-offs. It goes into great depth on where individual breakdowns in the system have occurred. It comes up with useful tips on improvements, including the national control agencies which have since been introduced successfully, but it failed to put a hard figure on abuse. Because it did not conduct economic or aerial reconnaissance studies, it could not say how many trees did not exist but on which aid had been claimed. It made a grand comparison of the conflicting sets of statistics without a clear conclusion, and hid it in an annexe.

One of the Court's worst examples of the systems approach was its August 1985 report on export refunds which went so far as to describe typical types of fraud, diagrams of accounting systems and the risks. Visits to four countries' customs and payment agencies led to a short-list of missing cross-checks in two unnamed states. It pointed out that only Germany had 'an optimum system' to inspect goods leaving and match them for quantity and quality with the refund claim by the exporter. It said there was a need to eliminate the risk of roundabouts and fictitious export transactions in the other states.

But it was not a comprehensive comparison country-by-country with an idealised system, nor was there any indication of the financial impact. Was export refund fraud costing the EC billions or was it just a few bob? It was the sort of report that a newly-qualified accountant from an international firm could have knocked off in a couple of weeks. It is the Court's job to point out financial mismanagement in the EC, yet it failed to get the correct message across that here was the major abuse of the 1980s.

Henri Marty-Gauquie, aide to the Court president Marcel Mart, dismisses Tiedemann-type estimates of 10–20 per cent fraud levels as 'foolish'. He says: 'The Court was wise enough to consider fraud from the systems side. The Court describes in its annual report how the legislative system works up to now, and says how with this type of legislation you get nowhere, and this is something that the

Council of Ministers recognises. But if you bang on with the figures, they always say the figures are not true. It is not the proper way of getting the member states to discuss the topic'.

The Commission itself has data on the scale of fraud from 'clearing' the claims that governments make on EC coffers for the agricultural subsidies they have paid. Governments pay out the subsidy claims and receive 100 per cent in advance on account from the Commission. It is good for their cashflow and the final settlement of the account takes place a number of years later. Clearance tests that subsidy payments have been made within the regulations in a legal way and that there are controls against the wrong people getting the cash.

This clearance operation in the Commission is separate from its anti-fraud unit, though both are in the agriculture directorate. The civil service logic of this is that each is applying separate parts of the EC rulebook. The clearance section vets the government claims worth £15 billion a year, while the anti-fraud unit collects the numbers of 'irregularities' reported, and mounts investigations into known areas of abuse. A third arm of the Commission which vets agricultural spending is the financial control (internal audit) directorate.

All this could be better organised. It would make a lot of sense if the three groups' work was better coordinated. Fraudulent subsidies could be denied reimbursement when governments filed accounts for them; repeated fraud behaviour could be quickly stamped on across the board; and the anti-fraud unit could be freed to target areas before they are hit by fraudsters and to prepare counter-measures.

In practice there is limited liaison between these different operations. In 1986 the clearance section inspectors, milk sector officials, the financial controllers and to a lesser extent the Court of Auditors cooperated on a special study of the management and control by governments over the milk levy system. This penalises farmers exceeding their set production. The study found that the levy was not paid by farmers within time-limits, quota registers had not been adapted for a new system and there were no quality checks on fat content.

The volume of abuse appeared to be widespread but

exact levels are not available. Governments bore the blame for not putting the EC rules in place. The Commission began legal action against Italy for not applying the rules at all and against Germany, The Netherlands, Denmark and France for only applying them in part. The claims were more than technical with Italy, Germany and The Netherlands breaching quota limits. The actions against all except Italy were dropped in March 1987 though the Commission retained the right to refuse clearance to the accounts later.

The Court of Auditors, in one of its better efforts, criticised the Commission for dropping these actions and for not mounting a further one against the UK over the Milk Marketing Board's quota leasing scheme which 'negates the purpose of the Community regulations'. It also looked at how national authorities had tackled 'fraudulent circumvention' of the rules such as milk smuggling across the Irish and Belgium/Netherlands borders, unrecorded milk sales completely outside the UK quota system and other transfers to ease the effect of quotas. It said the abuse was 'limited' and prompt action had been taken.

The distinction between governments not complying with EC rules and farmers or traders defrauding the system is not a clear one but the loser is the same: the European taxpayer. Some government breaches involve the detailed interpretation of law. But in many cases, clearances of accounts are refused by the Commission because a government kept no control over the way subsidies were handed out. Farmers were allowed to put in claims breaching the rules on quantity or quality. It raises the question of who intended to defraud whom.

The work of the twenty-six officials in the Commission's agricultural clearance section is an audit plus the targeting of specific sectors. It cannot check in depth all claims for expenditure either on paperwork sent to Brussels or at national authorities during on-the-spot checks. In 1986, 74 such visits were made comprising 918 working days. It verifies that national subsidies are not paid at the same time as EC ones. This led to £25 million in export refunds being denied to the Greeks on their 1982 accounts. The Greek government is still disputing this case in the Court of Justice.

Table 5.3 **Clearance of accounts – amounts disallowed by the Commission**
(latest statistics available)

(£ millions)	1982		1983	
	disallowed	total subsidies	disallowed	total subsidies
Belgium	1.3	370.3	0.4	451.3
Denmark	3.4	390.7	4.8	486.9
Germany	0.1	1,530.0	0.4	2,322.9
Greece	45.1	235.3	6.7	380.7
France	4.8	1,908.9	8.9	2,493.3
Ireland	0.8	336.0	0.6	395.9
Italy	10.6	1,559.6	7.0	1,876.8
Luxembourg	–	1.8	0.3	3.2
Netherlands	11.7	1,061.2	11.5	1,292.7
United Kingdom	9.7	819.1	21.1	941.7
	87.5	8,212.9	61.7	10,645.4

(This excludes scaling-down of national claims in negotiation with the Commission and amounts where the Commission overruled its own financial controller. This is impossible to quantify but may run into hundreds of millions of pounds a year. In one case alone, £70 million was involved. It is another example of the figures telling only half the story.)

This Commission scrutiny of farm spending has until recently been many years behind. It has not ensured that governments breaking EC regulations, or frauds by farmers, are picked up early so counter-measures can be instituted. Work has been brought up to date by Henning Christophersen, the Commissioner responsible since 1985, after years of neglect. During 1986, the Commission also employed a private firm of international auditors to devise more up-to-date methods for its inspectors.

The Court of Auditors has urged the Commission to expand its systems-based audits from export refunds and MCAs at paying agencies to other farming subsidies. It also said the Commission's expertise in computer audit appeared to be 'rather limited'. Much of this accounting is computerised and the scope for computer fraud may be huge. There was clearly still a long way to go.

Table 5.4 **Clearing the accounts – 1980s backlog**

Year of accounts	when cleared
1980	August 1985
1981	August 1985
1982	June 1986
1983	May 1987
1984	July 1987
1986	(projected September 1988)

Most of the clearances are subject to court judgements on issues such as the Greek grain, overfishing of quotas by six states including the UK and The Netherlands, additional national subsidies in Italy, The Netherlands and Ireland. The Commission lost all the cases covering 1980 and 1981 apart from one against Italy over £600,000 and £1.5 million of subsidies for olive oil. The Court of Justice ruled that the Italian authorities did not make the necessary checks and supplied the Commission with 'insufficiently precise information'. The Commission did not have to pay out on what was only a small part of olive oil fraud.

Christophersen ruled out further speeding-up and said he backed a move to extend the time limit, laid down in regulations, from eighteen months to two years. 'Experience shows that there are serious technical problems because some states are slower than others.' Delays in claims from governments and following up discrepancies takes a long time. Bringing the process up-to-date allowed officials to begin verifying 1986 spending on-the-spot in May 1987. Systems auditing could bring the testing even further forward, making it more alert to fraud and mismanagement.

But it is questionable if the clearance will overturn fraudulent payments to Italian olive oil producers in 1982 and 1983, despite the clear evidence that millions were paid out for non-existent olive trees. Commission fraud experts draw 'a clear distinction' between irregularities – known prosecuted frauds – and disallowance of subsidy claims on clearance where governments have not applied regulations. National authorities are in the clear if they have carried out their task of prosecuting the known irregularity cases and undertaken a fixed level of checking of claims of about five or ten per cent.

It is baffling to the ordinary European taxpayer that when £100 million has been paid on fraudulent claims that the Commission is not querying this amount of Italian subsidy claims. The Commission says it would disallow all the expenditure if the 5 per cent checking had not been carried out. A first glance judgement would suggest that either the Italians chose an extraordinarily 'pure' sample of claims or the Commission hasn't probed deep enough. In practice a more unusual deal appears to have been struck as part of an overall package for much tougher policing by the Italians in the future.

The Commission insisted on the completion of checking of subsidy claims by the Italian authorities. At the end of 1985, 188,000 cases from 1981/82 and 680,000 from the 1982/83 campaign had still to be checked. According to the Commission, the results of this would have no financial impact on the clearance though it retained a 'general reserve'. It had insisted on a specific check by national officials 'independently' of the clearance, it told auditors. It was also closely monitoring the setting-up of a tougher regime which it would part-finance.

Clearance, anti-fraud measures and better financial management at national level also ought to be linked more closely. At the moment, the measures to counter fraud consist of the Commission's anti-fraud unit mounting specific inquiries and monitoring national authorities' own procedures to check and prosecute offenders. The only EC-wide rules are the monitoring and recovery rules set down in 1972 analysed earlier; a 1977 directive requiring national authorities to audit certain levels of subsidy claims; and an 1980 regulation giving Commission officials scope to mount their own inquiries in countries.

The 1977 directive obliges governments to carry out 'regular and systematic' checks on companies receiving large amounts of EC farm funding. It was introduced because national authorities were already uncovering most frauds in this way and it was felt that a common system across Europe would uncover or deter more. The scrutiny each year has to cover half of the firms which receive more than £70,000 in EC farm subsidies. These checks were intended to be in addition to existing inspections. The Commission failed to introduce guidelines explaining this.

Impact of the directive was initially restricted when only two countries, Germany and UK, implemented it on time in 1979. Most did not introduce it until 1981 and it was only in 1983 that all countries had implemented the measure. Even then, some had only adopted it in part. During 1987 the Commission was still discussing with governments its 'views on a number of questions relating to the interpretation of certain aspects of the directive'. It was finding it difficult to understand the way the checking systems operated in some countries.

Introduction of the essential detailed checking of subsidy applications across Europe has not proved successful. As in many areas of activity, governments just did not apply the directives they agreed to in Brussels. And there was no mandatory level of physical inspection of the goods. This was a major gap in the legislation that meant offal continued to be exported past customs as best-quality sirloin (attracting a hefty subsidy). Rules requiring national authorities to check the quality of 5 per cent of exports were not proposed until 1987 and then faced opposition from governments.

Specific inquiries by the Commission's eighteen-man agricultural anti-fraud unit, including those under the 1980 regulations, are more time-consuming and often offload the donkey-work onto national officials. They are prompted by reported irregularities or tip-offs from the clearance section. The twenty inquiries carried out in 1986 cover eleven countries, excluding Luxembourg. Five were in Italy, three covering wine including the methanol scandal and the unexplained extra production (see Chapter 6). Three were in The Netherlands covering milk products, processed fruit and vegetables, and oilseeds.

'Special checks' in 1986 amounted to twenty-six and were spread across the EC countries, including a ten-state quality test on cereals sold from intervention stocks. In these checks, the Commission takes a leading role and on cereals, sent samples to its own choice of commercial laboratories. Checks on French producers' organisations in the fruit and vegetable sector prompted a FF74 million (£7 million) disallowance in the accounts clearance covering 1973–84. Checks on pig meat followed an outbreak of African swine fever in Belgium which cost £70 million.

In 1987 the Commission coordinated checks on hard durum wheat subsidies in seven provinces of Italy and over several weeks made 'thousands of checks'. Italian authorities set up five teams with the Commission tagging along on each. It placed a heavy burden on the unit's manpower. The impact on cutting into this next Italian scam after olive oil and vegetables is not yet known. There will be those who suggest the Mafia has moved into wheat, especially since Sicily is one of the regions covered, but there are doubts on the extent of involvement by organised crime (see Chapter 11).

Swoops by Commission officials in countries have not been regular or successful. One of its more famous followed a tip-off from Piet Dankert, Dutch Socialist MEP. The Parliament is keen to see the Commission's anti-fraud unit endowed with powers to act as a flying squad. It sounds exciting and the Commission is not unenthusiastic. A 1985 raid applied the 1980 powers of 'surprise' in conjunction with customs authorities and national agricultural officials. A coordinated visit was made to several skimmed milk firms in six countries simultaneously at eleven o'clock in the morning.

The raid, designed to prove that skimmed milk was getting subsidies when it shouldn't, did not produce the evidence hoped for. Inquiries centring on The Netherlands are continuing into frauds costing up to £500,000. More widely used is the exchange of information between national authorities and coordinated by the Commission. The meat frauds in the mid-1980s were tackled in this way where there were countries outside the EC involved and complex questions of jurisdiction arose. Nabbing the villains in a different country from the evidence made prosecutions difficult to follow through.

Badly-planned raids based on insufficient information are a danger to efficient fraud eradication. The Commission can boast experienced customs investigators among its staff but without the full commitment of national resources, it is at a disadvantage. Well-planned raids often rely on informers and phone-taps. Unless these are fully at its disposal or other hard evidence is available, then it risks infringing public liberties. Only with sound coordination and hard evidence should it have the right to swoop on the private sector.

Other efforts at the pan-European level to improve the fight against fraud centre on expanding the anti-fraud manpower of the Commission. This involves the setting up of a ten-man central coordinating unit under the president of the Commission. This will study work methods, staff training, the use of legal provisions and new remedies. The unit will cover regional and employment training grants as well as agriculture. In the short term, staff may be pulled away from specifically tackling farm fraud and into the new coordinating unit.

In the long run, the anti-fraud staff should rise to fifty by 1990 though governments have still to back this move. Out of the ten additional posts created in 1988 only three will tackle agricultural fraud. Siegfried Reinke, head of the farm fraud unit, has been quoted as saying he needs a staff of sixty. He said he needed five for each country and to ensure closer cooperation with veterinary services and customs which is particularly important in the meat sector.

The farm unit is also proud of its IRENE computer database of the 3,000 fraud irregularities to date. It can classify them by type and product and teaches new recruits the problem they face. It also provides a permanent reminder of the EC's failure to clamp down as new incidents of typical frauds just keep on recurring.

When governments discussed farm fraud in March 1988, they asked the Commission to prepare a 'systematic analysis' of difficulties countries had in applying EC rules. Debate was on the Court of Auditors annual report and its chapter on fraud which 'pleased' governments. Finance and economic ministers also welcomed the setting-up of the anti-fraud coordination unit and any proposals for increasing cooperation between the Commission and national authorities. They said exchanges of Commission and national officials was one area it wanted to extend.

The introduction of semi-privatised national agencies to vet EC subsidies is one success story. These have focused on specific farm produce sectors and operate only within national borders. The trailblazer in this is Agecontrol in Italy, which has tackled the olive oil sector and may add wine to its brief. It has squeezed fraud from the industry until the pips have squeaked. From its hi-tech modern building in downtown Rome, it exudes more the feel of a private sector auditing firm than a stuffy government department. Its techniques go beyond straightforward auditing and break new ground with aerial photography and computers.

Its setting up as a private company, with the majority of shares owned by the ministry of agriculture, was not straightforward. There was a parliamentary row over granting Agecontrol inspectors the privileged powers of civil servants and the novel status of the agency prompted questions from the industry on whom it would report to. By the end of 1986 these issues were resolved and Agecontrol had gained widespread powers to collaborate with the Carabinieri, the Guardia di Finanza (financial police), the central fraud office of the agriculture ministry and Cadastral land registry offices.

In addition the ministry of finance authorised the release of data on the tax registration of oil producers and mill owners. The National Electricity Board issued instructions to its provincial departments to provide Agecontrol with electricity consumption data on mills. This will enable verification of mill activity and will justify the size of claims. The access to a variety of sources of information goes as far, if not further, than that normally available to tax authorities. Added to flexible management it makes a potent force.

Over the two annual campaigns of 1985/86 and 1986/87, Agecontrol has scrutinised the 1.1 million farmers, 8,200 approved mills and about 600 bottling industries. The majority of the 150 million olive trees are in the south of Italy and on small farms. Subsidies come in two forms: for the farmer according to a certificate of the volume of oil milled and to bottlers on a similar basis. Frauds in both sectors rely on over-declaration of volumes or quality to the authorities. Bottling, where those involved inflate the invoice value of sales, have been more difficult to thwart.

The first annual campaign in 1985/86 provided a warm-up and training for Agecontrol as it built up its staff to 58 inspectors out of a total of 138. In 1986/87, 675 mills were inspected and the main check involved predicting the production from the electricity consumption and type of machinery. This provided data for individual farmers' production at the mill to be compared to their subsidy

Table 5.5 Italian olive oil mills – withdrawal of recognitions proposed

Region	total mills	inspected mills	withdrawals number	%
Abruzzo	626	52	11	21
Basilicata	212	10	1	10
Calabria	1,322	80	11	14
Campania	242	61	8	13
Lazio	423	58	11	19
Liguria	282	57	4	7
Marche	185	48	–	–
Molise	121	19	2	11
Puglia	1,007	92	9	10
Sardegna	124	19	5	26
Sicilia	723	70	16	23
Toscana	477	83	5	6
Umbria	284	26	–	–
	6,028	675	83	12

(Source: Agecontrol, 1986/87 campaign)

claim and led to Agecontrol recommending that 83 mills, or 12.3 per cent, had their recognition withdrawn. Producer associations were another target and checks called for recognition to be withdrawn from 13 out of a total of 107.

The 1987/88 campaign has squeezed further the illegalities and by more selective sampling, made further inroads into mills, the worst area of abuse. Giovanni Guidice, Agecontrol's director of planning control procedures, says: 'This year we will propose twenty per cent of mills for revocation of recognition because we feel that fraud has been committed. This will be based on consumption of energy, or that the sums declared in oil compared to husk did not match, or there was a lack of agreement between documents for oil procedure and documents from fiscal law.

'Another way to get to mills is to go in through analysis of the area. There are communes where the number of trees is 10,000 and the number counted is 5,000. We can ask producers in that area how many trees they declare and how many were written in applications where they were milled. If he does not have the trees, he could not have the olives. That is a proof that the mill defrauded and this brings automatic revocation.'

Work has also progressed on a computer database of olive farmers and their cultivations built up by aerial photography. The aim is to check the cultivation register first proposed by the EC in 1976 as a means to control olive oil spending and on which tens of millions of pounds have been spent. It was half complete in May 1988 as returns from growers were married up with photographs by a powerful computer system. At that stage the data had only been used for regional yield checks and not on individual farms.

(Agecontrol staff dismiss a well-worn Brussels tale that the Mafia bribed the pilot of earlier aerial surveys to fly in gentle circles in order that the number of trees would be overstated. They say the computer will eliminate duplicate photos automatically and that checks against the land register would remove them. 'The only thing that could confuse the count is if the trees were cut down', says an official.)

Activities against bottlers are to begin in the 1987/88 campaign. The amount of EC subsidies is less but has grown during the 1980s to reach £152 million in 1986 out of a £423 million total in the three major producing countries. Frauds were mounting in bottling and packaging in Italy as quality checks were evaded, and fraudsters rebottled oil in a second country after claiming one lot of bottling subsidies in the first. A system where bottlers put up a financial guarantee during the period that authorities checked previous aid claims was not working well.

Agecontrol has proved a powerful weapon against fraud in the Italian olive oil sector with a welter of cases passed to prosecutors for further action. In direct savings, Agecontrol estimates its impact in recovered or not-granted aid at £3.5 million. Further indirect savings through deterrent effect is put at eight per cent of the 1987 spending or £19 million. It believes only a hard core of fraudsters may remain. Guidice says: 'Whoever is persisting after the second year should start to slow down. It is really hard to see what should be a physiological fraud level.

'We are trying to find what causes fraud. There was a lack of a presence. Payments are being made very late – one year after the end of a campaign at 80 per cent of average yields. Some are still there from 1978. This is an excellent reason for normal human beings to ask for higher amounts. Now the Community and the ministry have agreed on a procedure that payment is made all within six months of the closing of the campaign.'

Agecontrol in Italy has made strong progress in a short space of time and may be extended to the wine sector. There is some reluctance from Agecontrol itself, which wants to run in for a couple more years, and from the Commission in Brussels which talks of other measures. The idea has been copied in Greece, Spain and Portugal on olives and may be extended to other sectors in those states. The mix of disciplines of lawyers, economists and agricultural experts, many young graduates, has worked well. Accountants have been used in vetting union books and in the more paper-based bottling frauds.

Management emphasises the private sector skills. Guidice is an ex-materials manager from ITT, the US multinational. The personnel manager also comes from ITT. The Director General, Luciano Berni, is ex-Olivetti and ex-Ericsson. Prior to Agecontrol he spent two years building up management consulting at Arthur Young, the international accountants, in Italy from three people to forty. The chief of the inspectorate is a former Carabinieri. The part-time chairman Dino Cagetti, an appointee of Filippo Pandolfi the minister for agriculture, is an influential lawyer and entrepreneur.

Agecontrol has cost the EC Lira 15.6 billion (£7 million) for the campaigns up to 1986/87 – well under a Lira 20.6 billion budget. For the 1987/88 and 1988/89 campaigns, it is to be funded 50:50 with the ministry of agriculture. Against the fraud risk it is an economic solution and one that should have been tried years earlier. It was the EC's third attempt at hitting abuse after the 1976 cultivation register and the takeover of checking by producer associations in 1979. Agecontrol has since barred a number of associations from doing this work.

There is no shortage of descriptions of EC farm fraud in its various guises nor ideas for its remedy. On both national subsidies for intervention and on the international scene with export refunds, the analysis of how it takes place is sound. But the analysis of how often it takes place is less clear and requires research. On intervention subsidies, the evidence from studies, either in Germany, Italy or elsewhere, shows that amounts are overpaid by large percentages. On export refunds, the evidence is less clear despite the tighter customs scrutiny and the wide publicity usually given to these cases.

Remedies are many and include better implementation of national checking and the Commission's clearance system for paying out claims to government. A simple incentive would be to cut to 75 per cent the 100 per cent advances to national authorities. A restructuring of Commission departments would make efforts more cohesive. Efficient exploitation of agricultural products and markets should be linked to anti-fraud policy. The Commission is good at reacting to lobbying, preparing statistics and drafting new rules but seems short on sensible analysis and practical ideas.

Agecontrol has proved that bringing in private sector

skills works wonders. Its chairman Cagetti believes similar agencies ought to be set up in northern European countries. It could also be extended to a pan-European agency to hit the billions at stake on export refund fraud. This would require more anti-fraud rules common in all states and a commercial substance test to knock out those manipulating rules rather than breaking them. Many rules it would need are already in place but are not followed properly. Economic monitoring and a high-powered prosecuting team could finish the job.

6 WINE: COOKING UP A KILLER VINTAGE

With twenty-three people dead and hundreds of millions of pounds in subsidies defrauded, the European Community's wine sector is without doubt its largest scandal. Policy since the mid-1970s failed to curb excess production and led to a wine lake. Distilling excess wine created a sea of alcohol and just encouraged producers to claim billions more in subsidies. They made 'wine' with everything imaginable – including methanol which blinded and killed – and got paid for it. There is still no guarantee it won't happen again as the sea of alcohol grows and grows.

The European Commission, which proposes and manages the EC wine policy, faces huge damage claims from the victims' families who say it was negligent and could have prevented the deaths in March 1986. The families allege that the Commission 'failed seriously and in a repeated manner to meet its obligations, notably by the quite insufficient organisation of its services. Notwithstanding repeated warnings, the Commission didn't judge it good to modify its behaviour. It took no measure in order to prevent adulterated wines continuing to circulate in the EC'. The Commission is defending the case in the European Court of Justice.

Leading the campaign to bring the Commission, Italian and French authorities to book is Benito Francisconi. From his Italian National Wine Centre emporium in downtown Brussels, the wartime parachutist is fighting more battles. He declares his own interest as Belgium's leading importer of Italian wines and knows that each time a scandal breaks, his sales take a tumble. Dubbed Le Duce or Don Quixote of Chianti, Francisconi does not always have the smooth skills of the public relations expert or politician. But he can be charming and persuasive and there is no doubting his persistence.

Francisconi's campaign on behalf of the Italian wine cooperatives he represents first hit home in the 1970s. He gained a ruling in 1976 against a Belgian distributor of 'Valpolicella' and 'Chianti' who Francisconi said had no certificates of origin for his wine. On appeal the Belgian was fined on both counts. It had been a four-year fight to remove the Italian labels from a mixture of Greek and Algerian wines. It was not the first offence for the salesman. There were two earlier rulings against him in Luxembourg: one over a Luxembourg wine which proved to be no such thing, a second involving French wine mixed with glucose.

There were also claims of Mafia involvement in the mid-1970s. Vast 'chemical wine' factories had been discovered in Italy, which allowed the alcoholic strength and volume of poor wine to be boosted by mixing in water, sugar and other chemicals. In one example, concentrated raw wine and chemicals were shipped to Tunis, on the opposite side of the Mediterranean. On route, sea water was mixed in and on arrival contraband sugar. By the time the ship reached Marseilles, in the south of France, the wine was 14 degree *vin de coupage*, rated as not suitable for drinking but acceptable for improving the quality of poor French wine.

Since 1976 distillation aid has been the main way that the EC has subsidised the wine sector. At the beginning it must have looked like the ideal solution to over-production and the resulting surpluses. Distillation boils up wine so that the less dense alcohol content in the wine is evaporated off. It can be collected nearby through a network of pipes. It is a brutish process in comparison with the gentle six-week fermentation that produces wine from crushed fruit, juice and the sugar in the fruit. To the fraudsters, distillation offered a perfect means of destroying the evidence of their 'wine-making'.

The grower is relatively ignorant of this way of getting rid of surpluses. The more sensible curb on production – digging up vines – or a shift to better varieties was rarely tried. Instead the subsidies merely kept the price the

Table 6.1 **Trends in EC wine production and consumption** (millions of litres)

	European consumption	usable production
1973/74	14,900	17,500
1974/75	15,400	16,500
1975/76	15,200	15,000
1976/77	14,500	15,300
1977/78	14,100	13,400
1978/79	13,800	14,300
1979/80	14,400	18,200

(figures include quality and table wines)

(Long-term trends indicate that wine consumption per head is slowing down overall. The average Frenchman of 1955 drank 135 litres of wine each year but in the 1980s could only manage 82 litres. Each Italian, the second most energetic European drinker of wine, used to drink 99 litres a year but has cut down to about 80 litres. In the Northern states, wine drinking – mainly quality wines – is on the increase. The Luxembourg wine drinker consumes 64 litres a year instead of the 26 litres he did 30 years ago. The British have nearly doubled their capacity to 9 litres each a year, though the Irish remain at 3 litres.)

grower received at a stable level. In Southern Italy where the surpluses of cheap table wine from poor grapes were mounting, it kept the price from falling through the floor. It was the wine producer, mainly grower cooperatives, which received subsidies for storage or payments from distillers for surplus wine. The distillers received their cash from the authorities.

Francisconi claims the EC action only prompted the genuine good-strength wine to go for distillation at reputable Italian distilleries. This was encouraged by the better distillation subsidy for higher alcohol content wine. And once this first wine-making was complete, the wine industry's vats were free to make artificial wine from table grapes, sugar and concentrated must (raw grape juice) in varying proportions. Huge quantities of this 'wine' came onto the Italian market though the precise quantities will

Figure 4 **ANNUAL WINE TIMETABLE – STORAGE AND DISTILLATION**

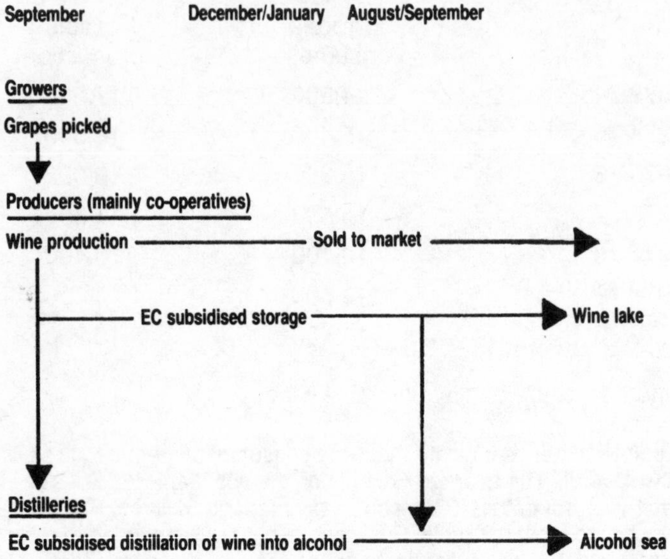

September   December/January August/September

Growers

Grapes picked

Producers (mainly co-operatives)

Wine production ——————— Sold to market ——————▶

├—— EC subsidised storage ————————————▶ Wine lake

▼

Distilleries

EC subsidised distillation of wine into alcohol ———————————▶ Alcohol sea

(The diagram indicates main scheme for wine under the EC regime. Once produced, wine either goes onto the open market, is stored or distilled into alcohol to remove it from the market.)

never be known. The distillation subsidies just encouraged these cheats to make more.

According to Francisconi, the major part of this second 'pressing' was sold to the French industry. He says hundreds of millions of litres of artificial wine were shipped from Italy to the port of Sète, in the south of France near Montpelier, to catch the 1 October to 15 January distilling season and EC subsidies. Until the 1981 season, much of the Italian wine entered France tax free and left the port gates as French origin wine. In August 1981, the wine growers of the Languedoc-Roussillon, angry at French official complicity in the trade, doused a load of wine aboard ship with fuel oil.

The new French government of President Francois Mitterand and Prime Minister Pierre Mauroy were finally forced to act. The temperature had risen dramatically with the added threat of Rioja wine from Spain and the arrest of the French agriculture minister, Edith Cresson, at Pisa as she sought a settlement with the Italians. Mauroy said taxes had to be levied on the Italian wine at Sète and it had to be registered as imported. The opportunity for sales of Italian wine at four to six times the value in Italy had to be cancelled out. Mauroy also put a cap on intensive growing by vineyards in the Languedoc.

By the autumn of 1981, there was a truce in one of France's largest wine-producing areas – Languedoc represents a third of French production. But the peace between France and Italy, and between wine-grower and the industrial combines was shattered in March 1982. The vats of Jean-Baptiste Doumeng, Communist senator and agri-industry millionaire, were blown up and seven million litres of Italian wine flowed across the quayside of Sète and into the sea. Doumeng, a key player in the East/West farm produce trade, defended his cheap purchases of Italian wine.

Table 6.2 Level of wine distillation – the early years

	production	distilled	%	wine sector
	(millions of litres)			cost (£m)
1976/77	15,014	539	4	63
1977/78	12,829	103	1	45
1978/79	13,834	167	1	43
1979/80	17,717	1,823	10	209
1980/81	16,387	2,293	14	321
1981/82	14,064	1,390	10	400

(Quality and table wine; includes Greek production of 539 and 547 million litres and its distillation of 18 million and 102 million litres in the latter two years.)

Even at this stage the fraud on subsidies was never properly exposed. Nor was the secondary trade in artificial wine from the South to the North of Italy, which later would allegedly prove fatal. But statistics show that distillation had risen dramatically since 1976, though both the poor 1977 and 1978 harvests prompted only marginal intervention. From 1979, good levels of production made distillation a permanent and increasingly expensive feature of the wine regime. Growers, wine producers and the authorities got a taste of what would later grow out of all proportion.

By the 1981/82 marketing year, it was clear that the 1976 distillation regime was doing little to tackle the average annual surplus in the 1970s of 500 million litres. At any level the policy had failed. Production showed no sign of falling back and distillation subsidies encouraged it instead of choking it off. The price of wine bought for distillation had been set too high. The policy was badly managed and prompted the fraudsters to step in and claim excessive subsidies.

The Commission's financial controllers began seeing irregularities in French claims for distillation aid as far back as 1975. Under the clearance system, governments receive 100 per cent of their share of farm subsidies, including those for wine, in advance. It reminds the Commission just who is in charge of the EC budget. Checks that the spending meets the regulations are often made by the Commission only years later. The Commission's controller may then refuse to confirm the spending and take it off their tab. The seventeen Commissioners can override this decision. Governments can appeal to the Court of Justice if they don't get their way.

The financial controller's doubts followed on-the-spot visits in France during November 1976 and June 1977. This led to him recommending disallowance of £76 million of distillation aid covering the years 1975 to 1979. From comparison with the spending for these years and comments by the European Court of Auditors, this may be as much as 100 per cent of the aid spent by the French intervention agency for wine distillation. The controller had found 'serious control weaknesses of long standing' in 1976 and 1977, which called for a more detailed investigation. It ought to have been carried out straight away – but wasn't.

In 1982 when the controller resumed his inquiry, he was unable to back his claim on all of the £76 million. The Court later said there were two 'perplexing' aspects to the Commission's conduct 'for which no satisfactory explanations can be found in the Commission's files. (These) are why the systems' weaknesses were not brought to light until 1977; why the Commission waited until 1982 to carry out a detailed investigation, the necessity for which must have been clear as early as 1977. Had the investigation taken place then, it would have been significantly simpler and the problem of missing documentation would have been less acute.

'Furthermore, three consecutive reservations in the clearance decisions relating to the accounts for 1975, 1976 and 1977, respectively, could have been avoided and the dimensions of the problem largely reduced.'

The investigation in 1982 conducted jointly with the French authorities was flawed, says the Court. It believes the control systems were designed to suit French fiscal arrangements and that they paid scant regard to ensuring that EC subsidies ended up in the right hands. For instance, there was no check that only table wine was distilled and that the wine was the subject of a minimum price contract between producer and distiller. The Court said that the Commission's conclusion that all materials entering the distillery were subsequently distilled was not enough. The checks had to be more thorough.

The Court complained that the French authorities were unable to say how many cases had been handled according to EC regulations. The joint investigation said that 87.3 per cent of cases were covered by valid distillation contracts and this percentage was used to approve £66 million worth of contracts. The Court disputes the way this percentage was arrived at from examining only a sample of contracts. It says that a sample ignored half of the 135 distilleries which had destroyed their documents; it also relied on 1975 spending and ignored the later four years and hence 33 per cent of spending.

The Court says: 'Even in the cases examined, the investigation was unsatisfactory in two important respects. First the status of the wine as "table wine" was insufficiently attested. In the complete absence of controls on the nature of these deliveries (particularly as regards the minimum acidity required), the favourable presumption made by the Commission in this regard, however justified it might be in normal circumstances, was not sufficient to allow the expenditure as a charge on the Community budget. Secondly there was insufficient evidence to show that the time limits for distillation had been respected.'

The Commission took its decision to overrule its financial controller in February 1984, approving £66 million out of the £76 million total for the five years. It said French controls had improved, the sample was unbiased and there was nothing to doubt the quality of the table wine. The Court said in December 1986 that the decision was 'unjustified'. It was a shabby affair. The Commission could have cleaned up a major abuse in the wine sector but missed its opportunity. In the end it was left covering up its own incompetence.

In the early 1980s the popular image of wine continued to be one where fraud was the order of the day. There were many bottles of Chianti, Valpolicella and Soave which had more to do with the chemistry set than the vineyard. Gianfranco Ferrari became a household name from flogging the stuff on television with the catchline 'Ferrari, the true wine'. He eventually got his comeuppance. Another organisation in Romagna earned a reputation for speed. Their coloured water and sugar mix turned into 'wine' in seventy-two hours, reports said.

The jokes would do the rounds again. The old Italian wine-maker on his deathbed still told his son the secret of the business: 'You can also make it with grapes.' But before long Italian table wine would be no laughing matter.

The nuts and bolts of the distillation mechanism were solidly in place in the early 1980s ready to be geared up for action. Let's concentrate on the harvests of 1983 and 1984 and the subsequent market conditions. It is the two years when hundreds of millions of pounds were paid out to subsidise the production of synthetic wine. The Commission was duped by governments into under-estimating the cost. But that was the least of it. Governments, Italy's in particular, had not kept their producers in check and they ran amok. Only later did auditors explain fully what took place.

Table 6.3 **EC table wine production and distillation in the 1980s**

| | production | distillation | percentage | distillation |
	millions of litres		distilled	subsidies (£m)
1981/82	10,400	1,318	12.7	273
1982/83	11,152	1,915	17.2	274
1983/84	11,560	3,399	29.4	597
1984/85	10,477	2,767	26.4	419
1985/86	9,276	2,008	21.6	284
1986/87	10,585	1,958	18.5	394

(excludes distillation of by-products)

They provided the hard systematic evidence that controls did not exist. It put the flesh on the anecdotal bones of all the stories of abuse. Armed with the reports from auditors it is clear how unscrupulous operators could make wine with all sorts of fruit, sugar to boost the strength, and a range of chemicals to clear and colour the wine. Even in 1983 and 1984, the signs became obvious enough even to the EC authorities.

Table 6.4 **Government distillation estimates – table wine 1983/4** (million litres)

	estimates in December '83	contracts April '84	final figures
Italy	1,010	2,050	2,199
France	570	760	821
West Germany	130	250	249
Greece	100	130	130
	1,810	3,190	3,399

By 12 December 1983, the Commission was able to make its estimate of table wine production at 11.1 billion

litres for the 1983/84 marketing year, pointing to 1.8 billion litres being distilled. But in the spring of 1984, an unexpected and massive rise in the quantity of wine under distillation contracts was revealed. The new figures showed that production had climbed to 11.8 billion litres and pointed to distillation of about 2.4 billion litres, or 20 per cent of production. The distillation estimates had been badly understated but these also soon proved to be inaccurate.

In April/May it emerged that 3.2 billion litres of distillation contracts had been concluded: the Commission's first estimate had been exceeded by 80 per cent. The Italian distillation had doubled, with the other countries showing smaller gains. The cost had risen from £412 million to £596 million and more attractive subsidies were available to producers than the basic preventive distillation at 65 per cent of the guide price. Either 82 or 91.5 per cent of the guide was handed out depending on whether producers chose market distillation covering only 500 million litres of *garantie de bonne fin* distillation linked to long term storage contracts.

Piet Dankert, the Dutch EuroMP who has campaigned against EC wine fraud, says: 'There would appear to be no rational arguments justifying this exceptional increase in expenditure. It is inconceivable that the member states most involved, such as Italy, France and the Federal Republic of Germany made such a monumental error that the Commission included completely inaccurate figures for the quantities of wine for distillation in its forecast supply balance. Theoretically, such an oversight is impossible.'

Dankert believes that governments were manipulating the data supplied to the Commission to improve the mix of subsidies that would be paid. He says that lowering the December estimate (see Table 6.4 above) stopped the Commission declaring compulsory distillation at only 60 per cent of the guide price and shifted payments to more lucrative forms of distillation. Producers could hang on to their wine in the hope – or expectation – of higher subsidies. Compulsory distillation began removing large quantities of quality wine from the market, mainly in France, from 1982/83 but was only extended to table wine in 1984/85.

And once one state had started this trend it was inevitable that all would do so. Hoodwinking the Commission and the non-wine-growing states who were footing the EC bill was fair game, they said. But in May 1984, the Commission forced agriculture ministers to order an inquiry and experts quickly proposed some reforms which gave the Commission powers to exploit new sources of information and not be obliged to follow the figures given by governments. It was the sort of power it needed as more data from the wine sector proved as worthless as the distillation estimates in December 1983.

Stocks of wine at the end of the 1983/84 marketing year on 31 August 1984 were adjusted down to 3.2 billion litres to take account of the extra distillation, putting the Italians' wine stock at 1.9 billion litres. But the Commission was in for a further surprise as it began planning the management of the 1984 crop of grapes, its production into wine and distillation to mop up surpluses. Italian projections, supplied in December 1984, indicated it was opening its account for 1984/85 not with the 1.9 billion litres stock with which it left the 1983/84 year but with twice as much – 4.0 billion litres.

It was an extraordinary accounting sleight of hand: overnight Italy's wine stocks had doubled and 20 per cent of the EC's annual production of table wine had appeared from nowhere. If a public limited company, such as UK chemical giant ICI, had accounted for its stocks in a similar manner its directors would be fired and its share quote immediately removed from the stock exchange. Nothing like that happened to the Italian government.

The doubling of Italian wine stocks is put down to a series of explanations including 'statistical and administrative deficiencies' in the way the Italian authorities prepare the figures. Commission officials believe that the previous statistics underestimated stocks of table wine. Producers feared that revealing their true figures would have drastically cut distillation which had become highly lucrative to them. The extent to which the extra stock included synthetic wine will probably never be known. Once wine is distilled, it becomes difficult to tell its origin.

The Commission's fullest official statement to date on the extra two billion litres found 'overnight' said: 'This phenomenon had of course alerted the services of the Commission, but the enquiries at the moment have not demonstrated that the emergence of this supplementary quantity was due, on the one hand from an underestimate of consumption or on the other, a change in the statistical methods. It is a tendentious argument to attribute this certainly important quantity one more time to a gigantic operation of fraud.'

This statement is arrogant tosh. It was filed in June 1987 by the Commission in early legal proceedings with Francisconi. Strictly speaking what it said may be correct – the inquiry was not complete and fraud has not been proved. But it was clear to the national authorities and Commission officials that Italy had been awash with synthetic wine.

Table 6.5 **Italian table wine – distillation**
(million litres)

	production total	compulsory distillation	voluntary distillation preventive	'g. de b. f'	support	distil total
1981/82	6,088	–	4	414	494	912
1982/83	6,148	–	438	356	212	1,006
1983/84	7,013	–	1,737	463	–	2,200
1984/85	5,939	345	389	700	121	1,555
1985/86	4,887		n/a			1,056

(During the 1980s four types of distillation have operated: compulsory distillation offers a subsidy of a minimum of 50 per cent of the guide price; preventive 65 per cent; *garantie de bonne fin*' (*g. de b. f.*) 90 per cent for white wine, 91.5 per cent for red; and support 82 per cent.)

The 1983 and 1984 harvests and the ensuing wine-making reveal unexpected quantities of Italian table wine. The figures show that from a steady 6 billion litres after the 1981 and 1982 harvests, production rose to 7 billion during the 1983/84 year. Distillation doubled, the majority via the preventive system with the producer having wide scope to choose how much he wanted bought up for alcohol. The *garantie de bonne fin* distillation also took off as producers realised it was an attractive way of ridding themselves of wine at the end of storage already subsidised under long-term contracts.

One persuasive explanation is that the southern Italian industry cranked up its synthetic wine production in 1983 and 1984 to create 3 billion litres extra production by boosting strength and quantity with the sugar/water mix and other ingredients. One billion litres mopped up distillation subsidies in 1983/84 with the 2 billion litres of new stocks at the beginning of the following season ready to pick up further subsidies. At a cost of 20 pence a litre in distillation aid, this handed EC taxpayers a bill of £600 million.

An investigation by the Commission into the stock discrepancies has made slow progress and was still underway during 1988. It was expected to lead to little more than reforms in the collection of statistics. It bore many similarities to earlier problems in the Italian olive oil sector where major statistical adjustments and widespread fraudulent claims for aid preceded reforms (see Chapter 5). The larger wine sector has proved more difficult to tame.

A special Court of Auditors report in 1987 into the distillation measures between 1981 and 1986 sheds a good deal of light on to the way the wine sector is run and whether EC rules are kept. It was the result of pressure from EuroMPs such as Dankert, and had good access to Commission and national officials spending twenty-three man weeks in the field. The report is one of the Court's better efforts. It reveals that basic record-keeping by Italian producers, distillers, intervention agencies and control authorities is appalling. France appears little better and Germany by no means perfect. Greece is not yet obliged to comply fully and make declarations.

Italian official controls on harvest, production and stock declarations ought to check that producers were accurately declaring the quantity of grapes grown and the wine pressed. According to the Court this control was 'inadequate' in the main wine-production regions such as Puglia and Sicily. Instead of weighing or measuring the quantities of wine, the Italian authorities relied on the producer's own paperwork. What the authorities needed was their own independent base of data to compare with declarations. It was scarcely surprising under this system that statistics were unreliable.

Accurate data on wine capacity and production in each country would fix effective short-term distillation targets and allow long-term planning such as digging up and destroying vines. But the information is just not available and the present statistics are a fiction. The Court concludes: 'The absence of a vineyard register twenty-four years after it was first envisaged, together with inadequate Community standards for establishing and verifying harvest, production and stock declarations, means that reliable statistics on production potential are not available in the main producing states with the exception of France.'

But it is the inadequacies in testing the wine quality and strength that garner the most savage criticism and where 'the greatest risk of irregularity or fraud arises', says the Court. Wine is examined on arrival at distilleries to see if it meets the quality set in the contract agreed by the intervention board between producer and distiller. The level of subsidy is proportional to the alcoholic strength and must be delivered within one per cent of the stated alcoholic strength. The higher the alcohol content, the greater the subsidy. Samples are taken for laboratory analysis by the distillery to check this.

The Court says the quality tests are inadequate. There are no tests to detect wine which has been strengthened by the addition of sugar, must or other substance. Nor is there a mandatory minimum level of sampling. Whereas quality wines must meet twenty-one different factors, table wine must only meet criteria of alcoholic strength, between 8.5 and 15 per cent by volume, and total acidity. The Court says: 'This lack of precision in the definition of table wine constitutes both a difficulty in ensuring adequate testing of wine at entry to the distillery, and a danger that adulterated wine presented for Community distillation measures may not be detected.'

The Court's special report confirms that all the ingredients for the easy production of synthetic wine were present in the early to mid-1980s: controls were loose enough to allow it to be produced and not be detected;

there were financial incentives to make it worthwhile. Having sold his first quality pressing, an Italian producer could use table grapes, sugar and water to turn out a second batch. Getting the distillery to accept this second batch appeared to be no problem. The Court identified the best locations – Sicily and Puglia – where it could be done. The Mafia was involved though it is unclear on what scale (see Chapter 11).

(It ought to be pointed out that there are many highly reputable vine growers and wine producers in Sicily. In May 1988, the author was provided by Francisconi with an introduction to Giuseppe Grasso who manages the Torrepalino cooperative in the east of the island. It lies behind the city of Catania on the side of the volcanic Mount Etna, 700 metres above sea level. Vines are grown on 350 hectares between olive trees which are used to break the wind. The volcanic ash gives the right balance of phosphorus, potassium chloride and silicates in the soil. It also aids drainage of precious water. It needs no fertilisers.

(Grasso produces one million litres of wine from the grapes grown by the cooperative. His plant is mechanised and computerised. Replacing the mashing, fermenting and bottling equipment today would cost £6 million. Refrigeration to stabilise wine is run from a computer console showing pressure, clarity and temperature. The successful range of white and red wines will soon expand with a champagne-style wine. In the laboratory there were samples ready for checking each week by customs. In the office export paperwork was well ordered with a statement from the producer and clearly stamped by 'repression of fraud' authorities, the town hall and customs.)

But not all synthetic wine, usually made with the addition of sugar and water, was distilled in Italy or, after export, in France. Large quantities found their way to bottlers in the north of the country and were distributed from there. Usually it needed its taste improved – it was not sweet enough and sometimes it needed its colour changed. Producers raided the cookbook of winemaking as surplus wine sought an outlet. This adulteration could be uncovered by rigorous testing, but hidden by certain additives such as glycol. In the summer of 1985 the evidence emerged of the chemical glycol, or antifreeze, in wine.

Austria, not a member of the EC club, took the brunt of this scandal. Five hundred wine growers were under suspicion and fifty held in jail as millions of litres of wine proved to be adulterated by glycol. It made it smooth and sweet and it is not certain that all the glycol was designed to hide a synthetic origin. The reputation of Austrian wine was destroyed overnight. Exports of table wine to West Germany no longer earned three times the domestic price as the sweet taste popular with German wine drinkers turned sour. But a far more lethal scandal was just around the corner.

In August 1985 the glycol scandal was in full flow and the European Commission network of health experts worked efficiently in circulating health ministries in the EC states with details. To the list of Austrian wines was added German wines and some from the Piedmont region of Italy. Nine wines were involved from three companies in this north-west region of Italy. When the news reached the ever alert Francisconi, his reactions were swift. The Belgian newspapers, relying on Commission data, had not detailed the names of the wines and Francisconi was alarmed. He wanted to know if he was carrying any glycol wine in his stock.

Francisconi, whose sales dropped by 50 per cent at one point, says: 'I announced first, proceedings against the national organisations for Italian wine for being lax, for passive complicity and for non-assistance for the endangered wine. Secondly proceedings against the companies (who had sold the contaminated wine) for disloyal competition and for tainting the reputation of Italian wine, because of the sale of Italian table wine in unspeakable two-litre bottles which need pure disinfectant to clean away the traces fallen on the table (according to consumers).'

This legal action had scarcely begun when on 18 March 1986, the first of twenty-three Italians from the north of the country began dying after drinking wine contaminated with deadly methanol. Whereas glycol was relatively harmless if off-putting, methanol or meths, is lethal in large doses, causing blindness and death. It used to be the cheap killer of alcoholic vagrants. Another thirty Italians were in a serious condition and fought for their lives. About a hundred were blinded. Their ages ranged from 20 to 79. The majority were middle-aged and came from Milan, Turin or Genoa. It is one of the worst consumer tragedies of recent times.

Francisconi believes that this wine originated in the south of Italy from a second 'pressing' in the vats after the first had gone for EC-subsidised distillation. He says this artificial wine contained little more than water, one-tenth noceanine colouring and at least one-tenth methanol. Use of methanol instead of sugar was prompted by the abolition of duty on it by the Italian government in 1984. Shipments towards France had followed. One load of methanol wine was stopped on the south coast of France in March 1985 by the authorities. Francisconi claims that more wine from the south of Italy entered France at Sète in December 1985 and that the authorities knew of this.

'The EEC, the Italian state, the French state, the wine authorities already knew of it before the end of 1985. The EEC in particular could have intervened immediately to prevent the deaths. The proof that the EEC can intervene is the ban of May 9, 1986 on the import of meat and fresh products of the seven countries of the East after the Chernobyl nuclear catastrophe. Why didn't it intervene in the Italian methanol affair?' asks Francisconi.

He makes two complaints against the Commission and other authorities. He says that the EC wine and distillation regime promoted fraud and synthetic wine. Everything since the 1970s had predicted it, but it had not been countered. The trade in synthetic wine from the south of Italy was another product of the policy: 70 per cent went to France for strengthening weak wines and 30 per cent to the north of Italy for bottling. Secondly he says the Commission's action over the Italian glycol wine in August 1985 was inadequate. It should have named the Piedmont firms and brought it out into the open. This would have prevented other Piedmont firms selling wine contaminated by methanol.

The Commission says the first it heard of methanol

wine was on 19 March when it was notified by the Italian health minister. The next day it told other capitals. At the same time it telephoned the Italian authorities and ordered them to keep the Commission informed of developments. The French authorities had also told the Commission they had discovered lethal doses of methanol in Italian wine. From 22 March, an Italian decree made it obligatory for all wine exports to carry a certificate of analysis.

Reaction to the scandal in Italy was wide-ranging. The health minister declared that it was widely known that each year, one billion litres of 'artificial wine' either went to France to defraud EC distillations or was bottled in the north. The agriculture minister confirmed that this view was widely held at the highest level. The Vatican newspaper said it cried 'not so much for the innocent victims who have drunk, as for the image of wine'.

Ripa di Meana, one of two European Commissioners from Italy, wrote to his socialist colleague, the Italian Prime Minister Bettino Craxi, suggesting that there was EC fraud involving 500 million litres of wine. It had been a spontaneous move and was another urgent appeal for reform. The only negative comment was unproven claims that some of those who had died were already ill.

Francisconi has campaigned hard since the spring of 1986. He regularly fires off dossiers of his claims and press cuttings to back them to European government leaders and other politicians. His legal claims, brought with other Belgian and Dutch importers and Northern Italian wine growers, are being pursued in the European Court of Justice in Luxembourg. Each claims a provisional £70,000 in damages. He hopes to cite both Jacques Delors, the president of the European Commission, and Filippo Pandolfi, the Italian agriculture minister on 'involuntary homicide' charges.

In early 1988 Francisconi extended the case by bringing the families of five of the victims into the action. The families are each claiming one billion lira (£430,000). The legal hearings will begin in late 1988 and no decisions are expected before 1989. Witnesses may include European commissioners, EuroMPs and Italian ministers. The complaint drew heavily on the findings of the special report from the Court of Auditors. It added: 'They (the families) consider that the Commission is directly responsible for the death of their close relation and beg for compensation for damage caused to them.'

As the Francisconi side batted claim and counterclaim back and forth, the Commission began to take the case more seriously. It tried to separate the claims of fraudulent distillation from adulteration by methanol. It said there was no evidence that wine containing glycol or methanol had been intended for distillation. Investigations in Italy had not shown this, said the Commission. The five million litres of methanol wine intercepted and destroyed in France was destined for human consumption and not distillation. The Commission also disputed the link between glycol wine in August 1985 and methanol wine in March 1986.

Italian authorities are also unsure that methanol was introduced at the production stage in their interpretation of findings from criminal and Ministry of Agriculture investigations. They put the blame for methanol in wine on two 'fairly big' traders – Odore and Ciravegna – from the Piedmont towns of Asti and Cuneo. (Francisconi wants these firms to appear in his Luxembourg court case.) They also blame a third trader, not producer, from Puglia and say that all three added methanol after production but before bottling. But they admit they can't be certain methanol was not used more widely.

The prospects of a Francisconi victory in court are not strong, according to legal observers. The Commission's responsibility for the deaths may be too remote with most of the EC regulation relying on controls in Italy. Tying the fraud on EC distillation subsidies to the twenty-three deaths may prove difficult. The European Court's poor reputation for gathering evidence and examining witnesses does not bode well. It is better at interpreting dry legal texts and handling lengthy written pleadings. But there are cases where it has ordered the Commission to pay damages and this may prove another.

Since the methanol scandal the wine sector has come under increasing close examination. The Commission has two inquiries underway in Italy, one into synthetic and methanol wine, the other covering the appearance of 2.1 billion litres at the beginning of September 1984. Much of the spadework is being conducted by Italian officials.

Checks on fraudulent claims and adulteration of wine have been stepped up in the wake of the methanol affair. A big package of anti-fraud measures has been brought in by the Italian government and others are proposed EC-wide by the Commission. Italian authorities have speeded up introduction of the wine register to give a computerised record of each producer's output and introduced better coordination of fraud authorities such as the agriculture ministry and *guardia di finanzia*. The Commission plans to extend this coordination to France, Germany and Greece and introduce a central twelve-man flying squad of Commission officials.

This latter proposal is making slow progress with governments. Officials with powers to swoop in nation states are never popular with governments, though they have been used in the fishing sector and for fruit and vegetables. But their numbers have been kept small. German regional authorities, which would need to be involved, have not been constructive and the French and Italians can't decide which anti-fraud services will lead the wine attack and liaise with the Commission.

Given the success of the semi-privatised olive oil agency in Italy (see Chapter 5), it is surprising this means of attacking fraud has not been proposed for wine. Officials quote the success of the fish inspectors to justify their choice and are nervous about putting the role out to the private sector. Officials drafting the wine rules have not studied the olive agency 'in detail'. They should have. Leaving future controls in the hands of Commission and national officials, who have made such a mess of things in the past, seems an unsatisfactory solution.

Checks on the quality of table wine entering distilleries are even further down the line. In 1988, Commission officials were planning the structural and price reforms before dealing with the latest control plans and quality checking. 'The discussion on fraud is a little quiet', was how one official put it. Plans for highly-sophisticated chemical testing techniques, with EC subsidies, have still to be proposed. The technology for the 'Martin method' has been around for a number of years and works well. It can tell if wine is made with added sugar. Nuclear magnetic resonance checks that the wine is made from sugar in grapes and not out of a sack.

With each machine costing £350,000, there is a reluctance to install the number needed. The aim is for three in France, one in Germany and three or four in Italy. Europe's largest wine producer, Italy, has yet to install a machine. Samples would be taken to the centre for checking but until they are in place there is no still no bar to synthetic wine. Barring the use of sugar in EC wine is often proposed, but is politically unacceptable to northern states with poorer climates. In any case it would not stop the fraudsters continuing the practice. Only a method like Martin will deter adulteration.

Wider criticism of the wine sector and the distillation measures came with the Court of Auditors' special report completed in the autumn of 1987. It lambasts the distillation measures, which it says 'lack coherence', removing wine to create 'unwanted' stocks of alcohol. It says the structural surplus is 'perpetuated' by offering distillation to mediocre table wine. The reforms in 1985 introducing compulsory distillation are 'unlikely' to reduce producer yields. It wasn't just the distillation measures which were at fault, the economics of the whole wine sector were wrong.

It specifically attacks *garantie de bonne fin* distillation where the minimum buying-in price at 90 per cent of the guide 'guarantees the producer a price significantly in excess of market prices'. Under the wine regime, market prices ought to be at 82 per cent of the guide price but have been consistently in the 70 per cent region. The Court questions EC funding for the nine-month subsidised storage prior to the linked *de bonne fin* distillation where a 'large percentage' of producers only sign storage contracts 'to take advantage of these distillation measures to the maximum extent possible'.

The only *bonne fin*, or satisfactory outcome, is the one for the producer. First he gets paid for storing his wine, then after nine months, the wine gets distilled. It would have been cheaper to distil it in the first place. Offering the best price of all EC distillation, it was no wonder it became so popular, covering 1.1 billion litres by 1984/85 and costing about £200 million a year in distillation subsidies alone. It certainly was not a satisfactory outcome for European taxpayers.

The Court considers the consequences of distillation: masses of alcohol. (The EC's mythical wine lake is really of alcohol. Excess stocks of wine belong to producers. Only their short-term storage is EC-subsidised.) Turning wine into alcohol looked a sound option for many years and up until 1985, the EC itself carried no stocks on its own books. As the butter and grain mountains grew from EC purchases, wine and alcohol remained the responsibility of either producers, distillers or national governments. But the increasing quantities of alcohol eventually swamped the market and outlets for distillers, forcing national authorities to intervene to buy up excess stocks.

Under the longer-running voluntary distillation measures, it is left to national authorities to buy up excess alcohol stocks. Only with the introduction of compulsory distillation for table wine in 1984/85, did the EC begin saddling itself with its own alcohol stocks, though here too, the storage and disposal costs were often paid by governments. For instance at the end of August 1986, of the total alcohol stocks from wine distillation of 1.4 billion litres, one billion was at the full cost of governments. Of the 400 million litres from compulsory distillation, only about 67 million litres was fully on the EC's books.

The immediate cost to the EC of supporting its wine alcohol market is low. The cost of alcohol buying-in by the EC was only £1 million in 1985 and £2.5 million in 1986. (Some have questioned whether this subsidy is legally within the terms of an EC agricultural policy, because alcohol is also an industrial product. But perhaps because of the relatively small sums, this has not been pursued.)

The cost quickly rises in a saturated market. If sales of compulsory distilled alcohol are made below 70p a litre, taken to be the normal market price, then the EC pays the difference. The cost of ridding the EC of the 400 million litres of this alcohol at the end of November 1986 was put at £270 million by the Court of Auditors. This disposal cost of 67p a litre was based on a Commission estimate for sales at 1p a litre. The market was so over-supplied that there were no longer any outlets. The alcohol was literally worthless.

In practice, sales as fuel oil have fetched up to 7p a litre. The Italian authorities sold 520 million litres for delivery over a two-year period. But according to the Court of Auditors in July 1987: 'This sale has effectively saturated traditional market outlets for the foreseeable future. In addition, the presence of the remaining significant stocks of 450 million litres overhanging the market inevitably depresses market prices.' With distillation continuing at the 2 billion litres/year plus figure in 1986/87 and consumption of table wine dropping further, there were more supplies of alcohol coming onto the market with nowhere to go.

This has alarmed producers of synthetic alcohol, such as BP Chemicals, the largest in the EC. The synthetic and agricultural products are chemically indistinguishable. BP produces about 375 million litres a year, equivalent to just over half of the EC's synthetic production, though some is exported. In the mid-1980s it successfully stopped subsidised French alcohol from sugar beet coming onto its industrial market of solvents. Alcohol is a good medium for printers' inks, quickly evaporating to leave the ink on the page. A BP manager says: 'We face this endless battle trying to maintain our market in the face of state subsidy.'

Table 6.6 **Cost comparisons of alcohol production**
(pence/litre)

Synthetic alcohol	25 – 29
Wheat alcohol	39 – 44
Wine alcohol	about 272

(Court of Auditors 1987 calculations. Large subsidies make wine alcohol ten times more expensive to produce than alcohol extracted from petroleum or from distilling the fermented products of other agricultural commodities.)

BP has tried hard to keep agricultural alcohol separate from its own industrial product. Likewise, BP has not gone into the drinks business. It is unfair competition when BP, which must cover all its costs, has to compete with subsidised alcohol coming onto the market at as little as 5p a litre (even though it has cost more than £2.70 a litre to produce it). It may be a good deal for the buyer but it turns economics on their head. Much of the EC or national sales of wine alcohol have been to fuel oil markets or outside the EC. But there are also suspicions that exports of wine alcohol come back to the EC after picking up further subsidies in the US, via the Caribbean, or from Scandinavian countries.

There have been moves to use the alcohol distilled from agricultural surpluses as a petrol substitute or additive for cars. It runs quite well, says BP. The EC considered it as a way of removing the grain mountain but said it was too expensive. BP was strongly against the move. It would have been another step against its valuable alcohol market and its opposition was less to do with the effect on its petrol sales. The petrol user would not get the best price, paying through taxes to keep alcohol competitive with petrol.

Distillation is a crazy part of the EC wine policy. The audit court estimated the cost of producing the 1.3 billion litre surplus of alcohol in August 1986 at £2.4 billion. It said these were the EC subsidies paid between 1980 to 1986 in distillation aid on stocks accumulated over the same period. Now they were nearly worthless to the owner and would incur a further £270 million in EC subsidies, and probably a further sum in national aid before they were disposed of. It was a dismal investment of taxpayers' money, and one which is still continuing. The major gainers were an expanding distillation industry in Italy and to a lesser extent, France.

The overall economics of the wine sector are wayward. The imbalance between supply and demand remain, despite more than ten years of distillation. The surplus remains as large as ever. The trends had been clear enough: falling table-wine consumption and greater yields from vines. But effective measures to counter them were few and far between. The audit court said the quality of table wine could be improved and alternative uses for grapes or wine, such as blush wines or wine coolers, should be found. More importantly, it called for a 'significant reduction' of the area under vines. It also said alternatives to distillation ought to be sought.

Some steps towards reform were taken in 1984 and 1986. Most are too little and too late. Limits were introduced in 1984/85 to restrict preventive distillation to 13 per cent of production. But compulsory distillation for table wine was introduced the same year. The more expensive *garantie de bonne fin* distillation was similarly restricted to 13 per cent of production for 1986/87. The trade, centring on Sicily, of transfers of wine for compulsory distillation has also been stamped on.

The toughest cutbacks came after the 1988 Brussels summit, when farm ministers limited compulsory distillation subsidies at 50 per cent of the guide price to about the first one billion litres, instead of 1.25 billion litres by 1991. After this threshold is breached, only 7.5 per cent of the guide price is available in subsidy instead of 40 per cent. There is greater encouragement to dig up vines though premiums are restricted on low yielding land, with up to 10 per cent of a country's vineyards exempted. The impact on the industry has to be planned far more carefully and there are fears of desertification, particularly in Spain.

It is still a half-hearted attack. The main measure to reduce production – digging up vines – lacks any clear targets. There will be a review of progress before April 1990, but it is unclear at this stage how attractive the digging-up premiums will be, though at least they offer more money to higher yielding growers. Distillation is to continue and more than a billion litres of alcohol is likely to come onto the market each year. The cost is not being cut. The 1986 wine measures cost £760 million, in 1987 they rose to £890 million and were expected to reach over £1 billion in 1988.

The record on wine over fifteen years is a sorry one. Most European taxpayers have just paid, but some have paid with their lives. The Commission and EC governments continue to take the policy cul-de-sac of distillation. They have done so since 1976 and show no sign of turning back. Matching production with consumption plus exports is not an equation that is seriously considered yet it ought to be the long term goal. But it can only be attained by less quantity and more quality. The Italians have been shocked into tough anti-fraud measures but the definitive test of alcohol content is not in place. It's food for thought the next time you open a bottle of table wine.

TOBACCO:
SUBSIDY MILLIONS
GO UP IN SMOKE

European Community governments have declared 1989 as European Year of Information on Cancer. They have been asked to put aside £7 million to warn the public of the dangers of the killer disease. It follows the widely-publicised European Cancer Week in May 1988 with a smaller budget. In addition, £13 million is to be spent up to 1991 to coordinate medical research across the twelve countries to track down the causes of the disease and come up with cures. Yet over the same four-year period up to 1991, the EC's common agriculture policy will spend 150 times more – about £2 billion – on subsidies to tobacco growers.

There are stark financial contradictions of EC policy towards a major cause of many diseases. On the one hand, tobacco is top of health officials' list of targets in their Europe against Cancer programme. On the other hand, the European Commission and governments have no plans to phase out subsidies on growing tobacco. On the contrary: they will undertake research to improve the varieties grown. Instead of outlawing this unhealthy and unpleasant weed, EC anti-cancer efforts will concentrate on tax policy, greater publicity of the dangers and cuts in tar levels in cigarettes.

Another contradiction is that the tobacco crop offers poor peasant farmers in the Mediterranean a better income than most farming alternatives. And in northern Europe, it is giving a strong boost to farmers' profits, contributing up to 60 per cent farmer's gross margin from only 10 per cent of his land.

Tobacco growing is the most highly subsidised crop in

the EC's farm policy at £3,000 a hectare (£1,200 an acre). Wine subsidies cost only £290, olive oil £180 and cereals £60 for each hectare in 1985. Europe is also growing what auditors called 'rubbish' varieties. It would have been cheaper for the EC to destroy this crop before processing and would certainly have left the farmer no worse off. Bizarre discrepancies have been uncovered in the setting of 'norm' prices and premiums (subsidies), which have cost the EC up to £100 million. On one occasion, Commission officials ignored experts' advice, a decision which was to cost them £7 million a year.

The European Court of Auditors said: 'Unless varieties which are really in demand can be produced at reasonably competitive prices, Community preference involving a high level of support is difficult to justify. The tobacco regime is now costing 800 million ecus (£560 million) for the Community of ten alone (excluding Spain and Portugal). In so far as a significant portion of this expenditure continues to benefit varieties for which there is little or no demand, the Court believes that the time is overdue for a close examination of policy in the tobacco sector.'

It continues: 'As a result of sixteen years of Community support, only 29 per cent of the crop is in real demand. In addition, the high ratio of aid to the final value of the crop reflects the low average quality of the tobacco produced and, in terms of support per hectare, the budgetary cost of the problem varieties in particular, appears to be untenable. The cost of paying premiums alone for the problem varieties is of the order of 130 million ecus (£90 million).'

Europe has about 220,000 tobacco growers, mostly concentrated in Greece and Italy. These two countries grow 150,000 tonnes each a year whereas France, West Germany and Belgium grow less than 50,000 tonnes together. Many of the growers cultivate no more than one hectare and it is their chief or only source of income. The land is usually of reasonable quality and not the stony ground of olive groves. Tobacco is an annual crop, with EC support coming in the form of a premium paid to those who buy from the grower and bale the leaf. The intention is to keep the price paid to growers at the EC norm.

The Commission claims its subsidies are not excessive and prices are half those guaranteed to US growers and one-fifth those to Japanese growers. It says: 'A certain balance has to be maintained between Community production and imports, so that the Community manufacturing industry is supplied with raw tobacco without excessive dependence on suppliers in non-Community countries. At present, nearly twice as much raw tobacco is used by the Community manufacturing industry as is produced by Community growers.' But if the growers produced the tobacco which the industry wants, the EC would have little need to depend on imports.

Management of the system operates as in many other agricultural sectors, and governments have to supervise examination of the crop at the first processing stage and check the weight, quality, moisture and impurities level. This allows a premium certificate to be issued by the intervention agency for subsequent claims by the processor. In Greece, the checking is handled by the National

Table 7.1 **European tobacco production – groups of varieties**

Group of varieties	1981	1982	1983	1984	1985	1986
1. Greatest demand	22%	24%	22%	24%	27%	29%
2. Moderate demand	35%	34%	39%	41%	40%	33%
3. Low demand	29%	28%	23%	20%	19%	21%
4. Problem varieties	14%	14%	16%	15%	14%	17%
	100%	100%	100%	100%	100%	100%
Total production ('000 tonnes)	309	332	313	348	344	353

(Groups changed after 1986: excludes Spain and Portugal)

(The table indicates that varieties in greatest demand slowly increased their share of overall production. Those in moderate demand were on the decline after peaking in 1984. But efforts to contain low demand and problem varieties showed more patchy results with the shares of both on the rise again.)

Tobacco Board at the growers' premises, and further spot checks are made at each processing plant. Italian officials say they weigh all tobacco, though auditors found no evidence of this in 1987.

Production peaked at 400,000 tonnes in 1986 after Spain and Portugal joined the EC. The underlying problem is not over-supply but growing the wrong sort of tobacco. The Court of Auditors in 1987 could not understand why the EC persisted with poor varieties. The Court said: 'Action should have been taken several years ago to discourage production of the problem varieties and steer production towards those varieties in real demand. It is regrettable that, since the scheme began in 1970, the Commission has not proposed premiums that reflected market requirements.'

The EC's annual price fixing sets norm prices for more than thirty varieties of tobacco. At the same time, farm ministers set the premium to be paid to producers to subsidise their buying-in cost, and so that they can buy tobacco at the norm price from growers. This premium is supposed to be fixed on the basis of two 'standard components'. The first is forecasts for sales in Europe and the impact that overseas tobacco will have on European prices. The second component is aimed at securing 'in the best possible manner' the guaranteed price and income.

The Commission says it has tried to use this complex formula to correct the mix of varieties as consumers have moved towards 'American-blended' varieties and demand for the EC's traditional sun-cured tobacco has fallen. Sales of the traditional dark Gauloise or Gitane cigarette have been replaced by the Marlboro or Rothmans type of cigarette. The EC has failed to follow this trend quickly and successfully. Instead, growers carry on with unwanted varieties and European cigarette makers import the tobacco they need.

Premium fixing has involved a ragbag of methods since the Europe-wide tobacco regime began in 1970. At first, world and domestic price levels were compared arithmetically to arrive at producer premiums. The difference was made up by an EC subsidy. Since 1975, most methods have involved a comparison between the European variety and a competing basket of overseas varieties.

Thus between 1977 and 1983, premiums rose at the same annual percentage rate as norm prices. Since 1984, prices have been reduced and premiums have moved either in line or more sharply downwards.

Fixing premiums proved a wayward affair. The two 'standard components' in the premium calculation were lost as ministers focused on the key difference between the EC variety price and the prices of the basket of competing varieties. They neglected to look at the sales outlets for the problem varieties, say auditors. The Commission, which proposes the rules, says there are 'serious difficulties' in applying the two components in a 'consistent and transparent manner'. And it believes that a more rigid method of calculation would only distort competition.

Much effort has been spent in drawing up the competing varieties of non-EC tobacco varieties to compare with European prices. The Commission has drawn on advice from government experts in setting up the rival varieties, though the results have been less than ideal. Auditors complained that instead of choosing varieties which competed with EC strains, the Commission established that a variety 'could theoretically compete' and used its price data. The Commission had only limited information on the quantity of EC imports of these varieties and this could 'unduly influence' premium setting, the auditors suggested.

Specifically they criticised the choice of two baskets of overseas varieties which competed with the EC varieties Perustitza and Erzegovinia. They said the Commission did not follow experts' advice on competing varieties. Doing so would have led to premiums being set 30 and 27 per cent lower than those subsequently set. The Court of Auditors said: 'A lack of supporting documentation has hampered the evaluation of whether the Commission's amendments were justified. The potential financial cost of the Commission's decision is 10m ecu (£7 million) a year.'

The Commission replied that it consulted experts in 1984 before choosing the competing substitute varieties and that it was given, in succession, two different opinions. 'Thanks to the information provided by the member state directly concerned (Italy), a consensus of expert opinion was subsequently arrived at with regard to the composition of the relevant baskets of competing varieties, and the Commission's decision was based on this consensus.' But the auditors have stuck to their complaint despite the Commission's explanation.

The Commission also dismisses the potential cost of £7 million. It says: 'It would be easier to argue that the decision has helped to cut costs. When allowance is made for the level of the fixed premium, production of those varieties is marking time and there is no record that any quantities have been bought in over the last few years.'

The Commission's argument is less than convincing. It claims that because it did not have to pay out to buy up surplus stocks, costs were saved. On the surface this makes some sense: the buying-in price is set at 85 per cent of the norm price and higher than the premiums which overall were 44 to 79 per cent of the norm. But there is no firm evidence that buying-in would have taken place if the alternative choice of substitute varieties had been made. And with the buying-in price – unlike the premium – dependent on quality, the cost could have been pushed well below the level of the premium.

Some auditors have suggested the incident indicates corruption but there is no evidence of this. On the surface, it appears to be a decision, bucking the experts' advice, which could benefit those growing the two varieties concerned. There have always been claims that Commission agricultural officials have directed policies towards their own friends or countrymen through leaking inside information or by manipulation policy making. Some say there are too many checks on an individual official to allow this to happen and that rival lobbies or government officials will quickly expose this fiddling.

Other more seasoned Commission officials know this takes place in certain sectors of the EC, but there is no firm evidence that it has happened with tobacco although one former senior official says it could have happened in 1984. He says: 'It is quite possible. I was very often confronted with that situation. I did not agree with the market directorate. They made black arrangements with a member state, and tried to convince the Agricultural Commissioner and then the whole Commission with the wrong figures.

'I remember an example in the milk sector where

internally they were falsifying the price elasticity, so as to give better consumption and convince the agricultural Commissioner. When I came to verify the figures they were wrong. There was no additional demand (for milk). They were using figures. They even asked experts externally to give them elasticity figures so they could sell this type of measure. He was doing it for money or his country.'

According to this official the rigging of figures went all the way to the top. The 'worst manipulator of figures' was Finn Gunderlach, the farm commissioner between 1977 and 1981 when he died in a Strasburg hotel during a European Parliament session. The motive in this case was personal ambition. On one occasion Gunderlach just changed the figures given to him for a speech at the parliament. The official says: 'He had to defend a prudent price policy, and the income figure I gave him showed a deterioration. He changed the figures so they weren't so detrimental. He wanted me to produce the figures. I refused. He just did it himself.'

In the 1984 tobacco case the lack of documents, the number of years since the decisions were taken and Court of Auditors' 'political' reluctance to single out culprits leaves the charge unproven. Commission officials who investigated the rates of subsidy also found no evidence to justify action against any official: the chief of the tobacco division in the agricultural directorate was still in the same post in 1988. He had been there since 1980. Belatedly, measures have been taken to scrutinise more closely the way Commission agricultural officials propose subsidies.

In 1988 Henning Christophersen, the Commissioner for budget and financial controls, brought in tougher internal checks on the agricultural directorate. It requires periodic reports 'on both the internal market and the world market (supply, demand, prices) for the main market organisations, so that all the appropriate conclusions can be drawn as regards likely trade flows (imports and exports) and storage'. The reports will be sent by the agriculture directorate to the financial directorate within the Commission. The two were also to cooperate on three-year forecasts of farm spending.

The financial directorate, which operates more like an

internal audit than a cashier's office, was clearly taking a firmer line over free-spending agricultural officials. But there are still major gaps. Setting of export refund subsidy rates lacks the same stringent scrutiny and there is no limit on the amounts that agricultural officials can set by themselves. A small change in the rate per kilo of produce can cost millions. Given the scope for fraud on these subsidies (see Chapter 5), all those above certain levels, such as £500,000, ought to get approval from finance officials.

Rotation of staff is another issue not properly tackled in the agricultural sector and there is nothing to prevent unhealthy relationships developing between officials and the industry they pay subsidies to. Italians and Greeks very often deal with wine and tobacco in the same way that Dutch and British deal with milk and grain. The counter-argument says it allows them to get to know the intricacies of their market. This latter argument is over-played and if an official is up to scratch he can easily cope with regular and mandatory three-year rotation of his sector.

The Commission denies a failure of judgement in 1984 and that the tobacco decision cost money. And the audit court didn't have the evidence to be more specific. But the suspicions over many policy decisions remain. The scope for financial killings in the agricultural commodity markets is plain to see. By gearing up with options, the rewards can be maximised. The main restrictions on access to inside information focus on industry lobbyists or journalists, who could abuse the information by cashing in directly or indirectly. With a toothless watchdog in the Court of Auditors, the villains inside the Commission are likely to escape their just deserts.

Further discrepancies in tobacco subsidies emerged when premium rates were compared, one country to another, for the same variety. When the Burley tobacco was grown in Italy, it received a 63 per cent premium of the norm price, but in Greece the premium was only 43 per cent. This was surprising to say the least, because the same basket of varieties had been used for price fixing. The Greek Burley was also generally of higher quality, while Italian Burley proved difficult to sell. Auditors said the extra cost of the Italian premium in 1986 alone was £27 million. Between 1981 and 1985, the extra bill was £122 million.

The Commission defended its policy, saying that the two Burley tobaccos were no longer the same variety because of the different soil, climatic condition and growing methods. 'Each of these different varieties of Burley has its particular characteristics, production costs and marketing conditions, and this justifies different prices and premiums. All the governments and tobacco experts who have been consulted agree with the Commission on this point, and unanimously recognise the individual identity of the different varieties of Burley grown in the Community.'

The premiums revealed further disincentives and crazy economics when compared to average prices actually paid to growers. The Court of Auditors discovered that these were well below the norm prices fixed only annually by farm ministers. The premiums were between 39 and 115 per cent of growers' prices depending on the variety. For three problem varieties grown in Italy, the premiums of £45 million exceeded the price paid to the growers. Tobacco processors, who bale raw leaves, were getting an extra EC bonus just for being there. The farmers were being paid 100 per cent out of EC funds in what amounted to pure income support.

The Commission claimed that the cost of sorting these three Italian varieties was expensive. The Court of Auditors retorted that it was relatively simple. Its comparisons with two of the varieties grown in France and Germany found their premiums were between only 64 and 87 per cent of the average producer prices. The Commission examined the matter 'in depth', deciding that 'this apparent discrepancy between the premiums and the prices paid to growers for certain varieties is accounted for by differences in quality, the different grading and packaging processes and certain peculiar market conditions.'

The Court said that with export refunds – further subsidies for sales onto world markets – the total subsidy for the three varieties rose to 125 per cent of the actual prices paid to the grower. The Court said: 'Destruction of the tobacco with compensation, at an earlier stage, would have produced a budgetary saving without financial loss to the producer.' The Commission replied that the cost of destruction at about 15p a kilo and the 'practical and environmental problems would outweigh the budgetary savings hoped for'.

Once again the Commission's mathematics were at fault. The premiums for these three Italian varieties were about £1.50 a kilo and thus indicate a saving of 34p a kilo, including export refunds, if the crop had been destroyed before processing. This figure is larger than the 15p kilo cost for destruction. Unless the 'practical and environmental problems' are greater than 19p a kilo, putting a match to the three problem varieties in Italy would have clearly saved EC cash.

Table 7.2 **Tobacco – EC funding**
(£ millions)

	1982	1983	1984	1985	1986	1987	1988
Export refunds	12	20	26	22	22	27	27
Premiums	403	430	498	573	514	553*	631*
Storage	21	20	20	8	11		
Total	436	470	544	603	547	580	658

(*= premiums and storage subsidies. 1987 and 1988 based on budgetary information)

(The table shows a steady upward trend overall, though 1985 was particularly expensive. Premiums to support price levels are the dominant form of subsidy and subsidies for exports or buying-in for storage are small by comparison)

One success the EC can claim for its tobacco policy is negligible surplus stocks. Purchases were up in 1986 to £28 million but the previous year's purchases had all been disposed of. One reason is the over-generous premium payments paid, whatever the quality of the crop. The price of bought-in tobacco varies with quality and the purchase price can drop below premium. The Commission is reluctant to introduce quality-related premiums because it may encourage fraudulent over-declarations, which has happened in other sectors such as wine, with an inflated alcohol strength.

Reforms at the Brussels summit meeting in February 1988 on farm policy preserved the status quo on production levels and made steps in the direction of improved price and premium incentives for varieties in demand. Overall EC production, including Spain and Portugal, was levelling off at the 385,000 tonne level with a one per cent decline in the area under cultivation. The five groups of varieties were retained for 1988 and put the Greek Burley into a group of varieties facing temporary difficulties. Norm prices of these were kept the same as 1987, and premiums were raised one per cent.

Table 7.3 Tobacco production – groups of varieties

Groups of varieties	1985	1986	1987	1988
1. Commercially sought after	25%	28%	28%	30%
2. Facing temporary difficulties	24%	21%	20%	25%
3. Well-suited to EC demand	18%	16%	17%	14%
4. Partly for buying-in	19%	18%	18%	17%
5. Grown in less-favoured regions	14%	17%	17%	14%
	100%	100%	100%	100%
Total production ('000 tonnes)	406	383	387	385

(Figures for 1985 and 1986 indicative only; 1987 provisional; 1988 are the amounts guaranteed for subsidy)
(Table shows the latest groupings of varieties introduced for 1987 and the trends in their share of production. There was marginal improvement in sought after varieties but a decline in well-suited varieties for Europe. Those grown for buying-in and in less-favoured regions, the latter including at least two problem varieties from the old groupings, show some decline. Those facing temporary difficulties, all different Burley varieties, are on the up)

Of the three varieties which the Court had said would be better-off destroyed with compensation because premiums were so high, two were now 'well suited to demand' from EC manufacturers, said the Commission. The rise in output of one of these two varieties, Badischer Geudertheimer in Italy, showed that 'price and premiums for that variety can be fairly attractive to growers'. There appeared to be a sharp turn-around though no new figures matching premiums to actual prices to growers were available.

The third troublesome variety from Italy, Forchheimer Havanna, remained in the problem category and both premiums and norm prices were being cut by eight per cent in 1988. The Commission believed that production is 'now being adjusted'. But two other varieties in this fifth group were showing 30 and 25 per cent growth in production and more land under their cultivation. Overall trends for the two latest problem groups of varieties are showing steady upward growth. New 'rubbish' varieties are replacing old 'rubbish' varieties.

The Commission's latest 1988 price proposals and review of the tobacco sector pointed to growing stocks being bought-in, though this was partly prompted by an 'overreaction' in Greece to the Chernobyl nuclear accident and its fall-out. But support is not even proving an effective social security payment for many tobacco growers. A separate survey of production costs spelt out their pitiful situation. Norm prices were just covering production costs and premiums were between 35 and 75 per cent of production costs. Hourly wages for growers were 'invariably lower' than local wage levels and between 50 per cent of the labour came from the family of the grower.

North European governments, which pay for these subsidies, have put a cap on cost. The 'stabiliser' mechanism introduced by the Brussels summit penalises production over the guaranteed maximum and has already proved effective in other farm sectors. But the measures to improve the varieties grown lack targets and there is not enough encouragement to grow the varieties in demand. With an annual crop it should be easier to change varieties than in other sectors such as olive oil, citrus or wine where trees or vines need to be dug up. The obvious alternative – cotton – is another expensive crop. And long-term phasing out, which on health grounds should surely have been a key issue, has never been suggested.

Table 7.4 European cigarette consumption and trends

	cigarettes smoked (billion/year)	per head consumption (cigs/head)	trend in consumption
Greece	28.9	2,921	+1.5%
Spain	76.8	2,001	−1.3%
West Germany	121.7	1,989	−1.2%
Italy	105.2	1,845	−6.8%
Ireland	6.3	1,782	−2.0%
France	94.6	1,722	−1.7%
United Kingdom	96.0	1,700	−0.9%
Denmark	8.5	1,663	−2.7%
Belgium/ Luxembourg	14.2	1,389	−13.9%
Portugal	13.7	1,358	−2.1%
Netherlands	15.9	1,102	+2.3%
Europe total	581.8	1,808	−2.6%

(1986 consumption figures)

(This table is based on statistics from production, imports and exports and puts Greece clearly at the top of the European smokers league. Other tobacco-growing countries smoke more than the average. The UK is below the average and getting lower. Most dramatic decline is in Belgium and Luxemburg. Smoking in The Netherlands the bottom-placed in the league is on the increase.)

(Anti-cancer studies suggest the levels may be higher, closer to a 2,000 cigarette a year average, and put the number of smokers at 37 per cent of the population. These opinion polls indicate that the Dutch and Danes are more likely to smoke than the average European, but the individual consumption is lower – one to nine cigarettes a day.)

There are no plans by the European Commission to phase out tobacco subsidies even in the long term, despite a growing tide of criticism and the clash with the latest anti-cancer campaign. Its two reactions to such a call are the claim that wine, which it also subsidises, is another health hazard and secondly that it is researching tobacco varieties with less tar. A spokesman said in 1988: 'We do not deny tobacco has negative effects. But saying there can't be any kind of support for tobacco growing is going too far. We are aware of the problem and that is why there is the shift (to different varieties).

'As far as I am aware there are no Commissioners who believe we should stop completely any kind of aid. It is not a reasonable option.'

The barrier to such a radical move is the opposition it would attract from major producer-countries Italy and Greece. Already Commission anti-cancer plans to introduce a directive cutting the maximum level of tar in cigarettes to 15 milligrams by the end of 1992 and 12 milligrams by the end of 1995 have hit Greek opposition. Health ministers in June 1988 told the Commission to consider if flanking measures could be worked out: the Greeks were to be bought off with development aid for new crops. Even the UK only wanted voluntary measures along the lines of its own advertising code.

In all, there are fourteen measures proposed by the Commission to tackle tobacco smoking. They include awareness campaigns and studies on smoking in public places where non-smokers are believed to face a lung cancer risk. A number of measures to end tax-free sales and to uprate tobacco taxes will receive a non-committal response from governments: setting fiscal policy from Brussels is not popular. The principle is all very fine but the EC cannot hide the fact that it is continuing to subsidise tobacco growing, and ultimately helping people to smoke.

8

MILK
THE TAX HAVEN
THAT TURNED SOUR

The European Community's agriculture policy contains more detailed regulations, generous financial resources and scope to intervene than any of its other policies. Yet its ability to regulate Europe's farming scene on the ground is often woefully inadequate. Luxembourg's milk sector may be only the worst example. In 1984, after years of suspicion, police and judicial officials raided the Grand Duchy's main government-approved farm organisation and began uncovering massive financial manipulation and tax fiddling. It revealed an undisclosed 'economy' going back many years and was still being pieced together in 1988.

Investigators found a network of bank accounts and companies, some in neighbouring Belgium, which milked the profits from dairy farmers and creamed off subsidies from the EC. Two chiefs from the Centrale Paysanne farming cooperative-cum-trade union face charges of preparing false financial accounts. The scandal and the failure to tackle it sooner raises serious questions for a country which prides itself on its financial sector and is attracting banks such as Lloyds, the TSB and others from the City of London. The authorities eventually employed seasoned Banco Ambrosiano investigators to crack it open.

The milk sector in Luxemburg is typical of many EC countries. Farmers sell their cows' milk to the dairy cooperatives to which they belong. Day-to-day running of these 'dairies' is handled by a full-time staff who fix the price for buying the milk, handle storage, processing and sales. In the UK, the Milk Marketing Board buys from

172

farmers and sells to retailers. In Luxembourg, the job is split so that Centrale Paysanne handles the retail side after buying milk from the Luxlait cooperative of dairy farmers. And by a series of takeovers, Luxlait has become the dominant dairy, notching up sales of LFr3 billion (£50 million) a year.

But in the late 1970s, Luxlait's farmer-members began questioning the price they received for their milk. They found that by selling to West German dairies, over the adjacent border, they could get two francs (about 3p) more per litre of milk. On the LFr12 price that milk was fetching at the time, it was an important discrepancy. It proved to be the first backing to claims that Luxembourg's dairy sector was financing a complete agricultural empire. These claims have still not been answered satisfactorily.

It is a messy story that reveals that other side to the 'better-than-most' image Luxembourg has as a tax haven. (Strictly it is not a tax haven, because its tax rates are not negligible and capital requirements to set up a bank are quite substantial. But its many tax treaties make it a handy financial centre.) The Centrale Paysanne/Luxlait scandal lends credence to a view of the Grand Duchy bordering on the Ruritanian.

Jean Hamilius is a former Luxembourg minister for agriculture and leading figure in the financial scene. He says: 'There is no doubt that Luxembourg's agriculture – Centrale Paysanne – empire has been set up from the beginning by people who wanted it to be shielded from interference from government and from the basics. Like monasteries or churches, the ownership is organised in such a way that no one knows who owns it, and there is no real democratic control. People do not steal money there, but may make wrong investments and errors of judgement, and juggle figures around if it does not come out.'

Hamilius is a straightforward man, a 61-year-old accountant and management consultant who has sat on the boards of several banks and was a senior member of the 1974-9 Democratic (Liberal)/Socialist government. It is the only government to break the Christian Democrat party's stranglehold on the post-Second World War levers of Luxembourg power. As its minister for agriculture, he began bringing that sector to book. But he never had the access to Centrale Paysanne's books gained by investigators after raids on its offices and the home of Mathias Berns, Centrale Paysanne's autocratic Secretary General.

Hamilius's financial background and no-nonsense style allowed him to make a start on attacking the network of farmers' cooperatives. During his five-year ministerial term he stood down from his partnership with accountants Compagnie Fiduciaire, part of the Arthur Young international network, to avoid conflicts of interest. And he wanted to gain a cross-party consensus for his reforms. 'I did not want to start a war between Liberal and other farmers to give Mr Berns an excuse to say: "Hamilius is a member of the financial establishment and wants to destroy farmers" – so that Mr Berns had a Jew to point a finger at.'

Hamilius at times considered sending in his officials to analyse the farming associations and their payments to farmers, but was reluctant without the backing from the Socialist minister of finance. He says: 'All the agricultural associations should be audited by the ministry of agriculture. And all these organisations should come under the control of the tax department. Once or twice they moved in and were booted out. There was never a finance minister who encouraged the tax people to do their job. Why should I send in my people from the agricultural service to be beaten up?'

In 1979 Hamilius's tenure at the ministry of agriculture gave way once again to a Christian Democrat agriculture minister and Berns breathed again – or at least briefly. By then many farmers were querying the price they were getting for their milk, notably from sales to the US Army in West Germany. They began to challenge the grip of Berns head-on. Their leader was Robert Mehlen, who farms 210 cows for milk and 130 for beef in Montenach, 35 kilometres from Luxembourg Ville and close to the border with Germany. His Fraie Letzeburger Bauvreverband (Free Luxembourg Farmers Federation) has become the main opposition and claims 570 farmers.

The youthful Mehlen says: 'Many farmers don't have time to campaign. In 1978 there were elections for the committee of the Luxlait cooperative. Berns lost his

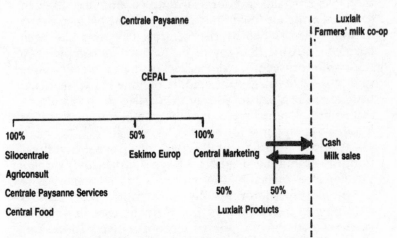

Figure 5 **ORGANISATION OF THE LUXEMBOURG MILK SECTOR**

Main players only. Solid lines indicate shareholding links. Broken lines indicate that Centrale Paysanne and Luxlait are separate legal entities, economically linked via milk sales.

majority in the southern region. I became the spokesman for the opposition. It took a year to understand the committee, but little by little it was coming and I told the general assembly of Luxlait that officially we are not happy with Central Marketing and Luxlait Products (two companies under Centrale Paysanne control which bought farmers' milk). I asked for explanations and he refused to give answers and then I knew something was wrong.'

Luxlait and Centrale Paysanne are supposed to be separate organisations but Berns had a foot in both camps – he was Centrale Paysanne's secretary general and also sat on Luxlait's supervisory committee. And he was able to retain control over the Luxlait cooperative after a consolidation of its three regions. Mehlen had hoped to split off the southern region where his followers had gained a hold. He had around him nearly eighty of the larger producers some of whom were already offering their milk to German dairies for better rates. In 1979 there was growing opposition in the more widely drawn Centrale Paysanne membership. But the campaign from the inside was not working.

Mehlen resigned from the Luxlait committee in January 1981 and the FLB was set up soon after. Through the close-knit Luxembourg farming community, Mehlen gathered evidence to support claims that the balance sheets of companies owned by the Centrale Paysanne had been falsified. In April 1984 the FLB presented its complaint to the public prosecutor who called in the Surete Publique (police detectives). By the middle of June it had reported back to the prosecutor who in turn called in an examining magistrate. Events were rapidly coming to a head as Mehlen's complaints hit home.

Under the continental system of criminal investigation, the examining magistrate (*juge d'instruction*) gathers the evidence, questions the witnesses and recommends to the public prosecutor whether to mount a trial. He has wide powers to tap phones (not normally used in financial cases such as this one), detain uncooperative witnesses or the accused, to enter premises and seize documents. Despite his title of judge, he does not give final judgement or sentence on the accused. His role has been compared to that of a coroner in the UK – deciding how a person died but not who did it.

Andre Lutgen, a young and eager magistrate, was given the task of getting to the bottom of Centrale Paysanne and Luxlait. He expects to handle up to 300 cases a year from robberies to murder. His experience includes supervising the liquidation of Banco Ambrosiano Holdings in Luxembourg. This company was a linch-pin in Roberto – 'God's Banker' – Calvi's failed empire through which more than US$1 billion in dubious loans were channelled. At first the Lutgen-led investigation was shunned by the Italians but in 1988 they pleaded for access to his Swiss findings.

Through Ambrosiano, Lutgen has become Luxembourg's expert in unravelling complex financial scandals and tracking down the culprits, though he left it to the Italians to bring Licio Gelli, the freemason chief, to book. While Luxlait and Centrale Paysanne don't involve as large sums as Banco Ambrosiano, in terms of the Grand Duchy's economy they are large. And in the same way, Luxlait struck deep into the roots of the country's political establishment. Luxembourg's external image as a strong and safe financial centre was secure so long as the scandal stayed in the farming sector.

Lutgen moved quickly after his late June 1984 appointment but the counter-attack was equally rapid. On 9 July a team of fifteen police officers and detectives from the Surete Publique descended on the Centrale Paysanne premises in the centre of Luxembourg Ville and at Berns's own home. Many documents were taken away for examination. Then Lutgen made what was probably a mistake – it being August, he took a holiday. By the time he returned, the course of the inquiry had been dramatically upset.

Lawyers in Luxembourg had probably never had a busier August. First the raids at the Centrale Paysanne were annulled after a plea by its main holding company whose books had been seized. Then Lutgen's staff appealed and won. But that was not the end of it, as dozens of magistrates became involved in more appeals. In all, there were four decisions by the supreme court of which two were in Lutgen's favour. Each time the warrants were withdrawn, the papers had to go back and the investigators fumed. The chances of finding hard evidence dwindled daily.

Between 7 and 8 August, when documents were successfully re-seized, details on one Centrale Paysanne bank account disappeared, according to Lutgen. This covered an account entitled 'milk products'. The investigation was also hampered by the lack of cooperation from Centrale Paysanne staff who at first had made statements to Lutgen. After the series of court cases over the seizures, this assistance dried up and employees at all levels remained mum, allegedly under instructions not to talk.

But the seized documents were dynamite. These were 200 files of financial records and bank accounts found during the raids which disclosed money from Centrale Paysanne activities not included in its annual accounts or balance sheet – or at least not in the one-page affair circulated to ordinary members. LFr820 million (£13 million) had passed through three bank accounts held at the Caisse Centrale des Associations Agricoles, a Luxem-

Figure 6 CENTRALE PAYSANNE'S HIDDEN OPERATIONS

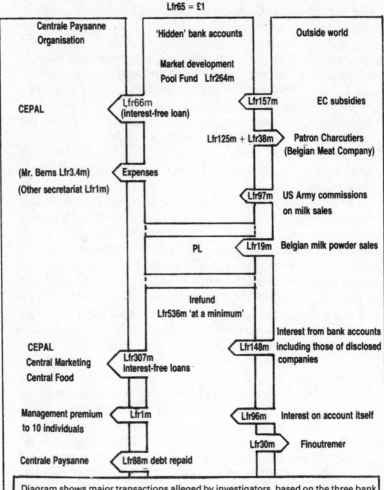

Lfr65 = £1

| Centrale Paysanne Organisation | 'Hidden' bank accounts | Outside world |

Market development
Pool Fund Lfr264m

CEPAL — Lfr66m (interest-free loan) — Lfr157m — EC subsidies

Lfr125m + Lfr38m — Patron Charcutiers (Belgian Meat Company)

(Mr. Berns Lfr3.4m) — Expenses
(Other secretariat Lfr1m)

Lfr97m — US Army commissions on milk sales

PL — Lfr19m — Belgian milk powder sales

Irefund Lfr536m 'at a minimum'

Interest from bank accounts including those of disclosed companies — Lfr148m

CEPAL Central Marketing Central Food — Lfr307m Interest-free loans

Management premium to 10 individuals — Lfr1m — Lfr96m — Interest on account itself

Lfr30m — Finoutremer

Centrale Paysanne — Lfr88m debt repaid

Diagram shows major transactions alleged by investigators, based on the three bank accounts discovered in July 1984 raids; arrows indicate direction of cash movements from outside sources, through the 'hidden' bank accounts to other parts of the Centrale Paysanne empire. Patron Charcutiers is believed to be owned by Centrale Paysanne interests. Statements on the first two accounts had been discovered at Berns' home in Keispelt, ten kilometres from Luxembourg Ville.

Four individuals were named as receiving sums. These included LFr770,000 (£12,000) and LFr640,000 paid to two senior employees at Centrale Paysanne and LFr80,000 to Henri Medernach and Jules Meyers who were the *commissaires aux comptes*, or accounting commissioners, to CEPAL and one of its subsidiaries. An accounting commissioner is a very limited equivalent to an auditor. Medernach is a former director at Caisse Centrale bank, Meyers a former Centrale Paysanne president.

Lutgen and his team believed a further LFr118 million in an allied longer-term Irefund account was transferred to another separate account on 7 August 1984, at the time of the raids.

bourg bank primarily used by the farming community. It was not one of the banks named on the December 1983 balance sheet of Centrale Paysanne.

Examining magistrate Lutgen concluded that the three accounts, all under the sole signature of Berns, had been hidden from the general assembly of Centrale Paysanne, its administrative council, its accounting commissioners (a limited equivalent to an auditor) and others. Considerable sums had failed to appear in the account of any company or the Centrale Paysanne itself. 'Very important profits, without being justified by expenditure, had been realised on the back of the Luxlait cooperative and have led to manipulations on black accounts.'

The management and finances department of Centrale Paysanne, which Lutgen said was directed by Jos Ewert, also came in for flak. Ewert, Berns' nephew, disputes the title finance director and claims he is the 'internal auditor' who checks the accounts. It was not the independent check for general assemblies that it was made out to be. Documents showed that Ewert changed figures in provisional balance sheets and Lutgen accused him of false accounting. Lutgen said: 'There exists a parallel economy hidden from the group controlled by Mathias Berns and some members of the secretariat general.

'The members of a producer cooperative such as Luxlait are deliberately kept in ignorance of the profits made with the help of their produce.'

It was a stirring conclusion but do the facts bear it out? Does it stand up to the claims of Mehlen and the FLB that the price of milk bought from the Luxlait farmers was unfairly low and the financial accounts were being rigged? Certainly there was a lot of cash sloshing through bank accounts which Lutgen called 'hidden' or 'black' when he first accused Berns and Ewert, but the latter says this is no longer the charge. A final verdict on these three bank accounts awaits a criminal trial – unlikely before 1989 and by no means a certain outcome.

There is no dispute that the bank accounts exist. But there is a wider argument over what interpretation to put on them and the rest of Centrale Paysanne and Luxlait's finances. They hint at a diversion of funds from a profitable milk sector to an investment fund used for loans to

Centrale Paysanne companies for capital investment often in the less profitable meat sector. They don't suggest gross personal enrichment. There are no payments for yachts, fast cars or villas in the south of France.

But who owns the three bank accounts; in which organisation's books do they appear? At first sight they don't appear to be in the books of the Centrale Paysanne cooperative-cum-trade union. The December 1983 balance sheet, the last before the raids, consisted of bank accounts (with the Banque Generale and Postbank), inventory and debtors amounting to LFr17 million (£260,000). Other assets were *'pour memoire'*. At the bottom of the balance sheet it was noted that building and portfolio were 'pm', or 'for memory'. It was a highly unconventional form of accounting.

Much of the Centrale Paysanne's activities appeared to have been forgotten when accounts were drawn up. It wasn't just the three bank accounts that were missing. The network of subsidiaries which ran the show – buying and selling produce – weren't included either. These substantial companies were included neither as investments nor consolidated into Centrale Paysanne as a group of companies. (Shares in CEPAL, the holding company, were issued in 1955 to twelve leading farmers. Further shares were issued in 1976 though it is unclear who took these up. Control rested with leading Centrale Paysanne figures.)

Ewert, the finance chief, says that there are no laws covering trade union accounts in Luxembourg. 'Trade unions have the right to dispose money as they like,' he says. It is up to each union to make its own rules. Accounts are well separated inside the Centrale Paysanne set-up. The trade union, youth service and women's section each have their own accounts. The members in each of these sections can see their accounts. The brief accounts for December 1983 are those for the trade union. Ewert, interviewed in 1988, told the author: 'All the members of Centrale Paysanne are informed who ought to be. Centrale Paysanne is not responsible to you.'

The pyramid-like structure of the organisation gives those at the top extra powers or responsibilities, says Ewert. The committee decides 'in the best interests of Centrale Paysanne it is better to individualise and separate the departments'. The inevitable conclusion is that a high-level group ran the three bank accounts, uncovered in the raids, and were the only people to receive financial reports on the transactions. 'We organised the accounting. We respect the Luxembourg legislation.'

Ewert, a graduate from the Fontainebleau-based INSEAD business school, at one time suggested that most trade unions and political parties in Luxembourg keep 'black' bank accounts. He has since denied this. But the omission of industrial investments from the accounts of non-profit making organisations puts their non-taxable status in doubt. Hamilius, the top accountant, says: 'It is true that unions and parties are not from that point of view properly organised, and have not been investigated by the tax authorities up to now. But they (the trade unions) do not run businesses.'

Something was clearly wrong with this set-up. Subscription-paying members of trade unions or political parties deserved a democratic accounting of what is done in their organisation. The full disclosure rules were not in place and the tax authorities were not doing their job. Further discoveries were later to bring reforms – at least to the agricultural sector. But there was still some way to go in uncovering the nature of the Centrale Paysanne's hidden economy. The questions were only just beginning.

With the evidence from the raids and based on his conclusions, magistrate Lutgen ordered Berns and Ewert to appear in his Palais de Justice office in January 1985. With the lessons learned from Italian lawyers in the Ambrosiano inquiry he drafted a detailed questionnaire. He wanted to know the economic reason for 13 per cent deducted on milk sales to US troops, who had decided on it, and if the Luxlait cooperative had been told. There were questions about the payments to the Belgian companies and to Centrale Paysanne officials. Lutgen also asked for the bank statements missing when the second raid was undertaken.

Berns refused to make a statement and the meeting ended with his lawyer asking to know the charges and being handed the questionnaire. He claimed that until the Supreme Court ruled he would not answer the questions. More court cases followed in which Berns attempted to impeach Lutgen, and Ewert accused Lutgen of defamation. Luxembourg lawyers were split over the investigation, though eventually they made a 'cool-it' plea to both sides.

In February 1985 two public demonstrations supported Centrale Paysanne and claimed the legal investigations were a threat to employment. The second involved 3,000 demonstrators and 350 tractors in the centre of Luxembourg Ville. Centrale Paysanne and Luxlait had retained their support despite the breakaway FLB led by Mehlen. The close-knit Luxembourg farming community was heavily tied in economically with Centrale Paysanne, not just from the payments for produce but more directly through wages as workers. If one member of a family worked there, it often carried the votes of many other farming folk.

Lutgen was not to be cowed by this attempt at intimidation and used his own version of softening up the opposition. One morning in April, he called in Berns and Ewert and slapped them in jail. In the afternoon he called them to his office and they told him that everything they had done was correct. Ewert succeeded in getting some minor corrections made to the complaints against him. Apart from that there was little progress on either side: both sides stuck to their versions of the story.

Lutgen had a specific reason for calling the meeting. He wanted to prevent Centrale Paysanne presenting more false balance sheets to its members for the December 1984 year-end, due in May. The two Centrale Paysanne chiefs were released at 8 p.m. They said they would not be issuing the latest accounts because Lutgen had the documentation they needed. It was a game of snub and counter-snub.

The next step by the examining magistrate was another trick learned from Ambrosiano. He called in a top team of accountants from Touche Ross, the international firm, and asked them to make a detailed report. The choice of this firm was dictated by a need to avoid conflicts of interest with local experts, most of whom had relatives who were farmers. Touche's London partner Brian Smouha had also become a favourite from his successful, if expensive, recovery of 70 per cent of Ambrosiano monies.

By choosing Smouha and three other Touche experts

from Germany and Switzerland, Lutgen hoped he would get a clearer account of what had gone on. A jury, if a trial was called, would find the complex financial network easier to understand. The danger was that the time it would take would diminish the enthusiasm for a trial.

Progress had been slow and Lutgen was forced to put a March-1988 deadline on replies from Berns, Ewert and their lawyers and experts to a second questionnaire. The questions remained the same: What was the legal status of Centrale Paysanne and who owns the meat company in Belgium; where do the hidden bank accounts fit in and how was the US Army contract handled? A letter from a Berns lawyer in February 1988 was still disputing the years to be covered by the questions. He wanted it restricted to 1978 to 1983.

After two and half years, answers from Centrale Paysanne were still thin on the ground. It stuck to its claim that it had done nothing wrong. In May 1988, Touche Ross delivered its long-awaited report confirming the facts but leaving the interpretation unclear in many places. The Berns line said that funds for long-term agricultural development had to be handled separately. After further interviews of Berns and Ewert, Lutgen will send his file to the public prosecutor. He will decide whether to lay formal charges and ask the Chambre de Conseil either to withdraw or bring the case to trial.

The criminal investigation was only one line of inquiry as farmers continued to graze their cattle and seek the most profitable outlet for their milk. The Government also began taking steps to clean up the sector as even the Christian Democrat party tired of the Centrale Paysanne antics. The organisation carried on business as normal after the raids. Its Central Marketing company still bought milk from Luxlait. But the Luxlait membership was wiser and more began to quit. Many followed Mehlen and took their milk to Ekabe, the last independent dairy in Luxembourg, or to outlets in Germany.

And when the farmers left, they expected to be paid back not just the nominal value of their share but the full asset-backed stake. The cooperative faced mounting pressure with the resignations, which it resisted. Court cases followed, which the farmers won all the way up to the supreme court. The danger of Luxlait collapsing became acute by 1986 and it called on the government to act. Rene Steichen, secretary of state for agriculture, says: 'They (the leaving members) wanted to get their shares back on the basis of the balance sheet of Luxlait.

'There were a lot of public aids that Luxlait said were not to be shared between the living members. There was a sentence in the court judgement that went another way and partly as a result of this text, it was not very clear and we introduced a law that was confirming the old practice. The second part was that from this date (July 1986), agricultural associations had to have an auditor, as other companies of major importance have had for seven or eight years in Luxemburg.'

The right of departing Luxlait members to get a fair share of the cooperative's assets was retrospectively taken away, a move approved by the Parliament in August 1986. It seemed to be another slap in the face for those seeking to clean up the sector. The appointment of a qualified auditor was some compensation and proved a valuable check on abuse. Steichen says: 'His report raised big problems in the agricultural profession. In fact he said things that we knew. In the government we decided to suspend all aids until conditions were resolved in Luxlait.'

Why, if Steichen knew what his auditor would report, had he and his senior colleague, the minister of agriculture Marc Fischbach, done nothing to clean up the situation before? Steichen answers obliquely that the FLB, the free farmers federation, made their decision to quit when the failed to get 'transparency'. There would be more transparency in the future. It was a belated step by a Christian Democrat government after years spent ignoring the wayward practices of Luxlait and Centrale Paysanne.

Steichen appointed Jean Reuter as the Luxlait auditor. Reuter is a member of a famous Luxembourg family and runs his own accounting practice in the Grand Duchy. It is an independent outfit not connected to any of the international practices that are increasingly trying to improve their presence in this growing financial centre. He began his assignment to audit the 1986 accounts of the Luxlait cooperative in February 1987.

The latest 1985 accounts showed total assets on Luxlait's balance sheet of LFr1.2 billion (£20 million) and a profit and loss account showing sales of LFr2.9 billion (£48 million). Profits, as they should be in a cooperative, are negligible as they are paid back to the farmer-members.

He summarised the results of the four financial years from 1982 to 1985 as reviewed by the supervisory committee and after checking by the management and finance service of Centrale Paysanne. Its Central Marketing arm is the sole buyer of Luxlait's milk and it wanted to check its purchases to ensure that Luxlait's production tallied with the output of its farmer-members. With Berns on Luxlait's supervisory committee and Ewert checking the accounts, it was clear that Centrale Paysanne and its two chiefs wielded considerable influence with the supposedly independent Luxlait. It extended their grip on Luxembourg farming.

Milk sales were Reuter's next target and the crucial issue. He quickly tackled the dual interest of Berns and his cronies. He said that Central Marketing is 'in the happy situation of fixing its purchase price from Luxlait'. Berns was speaking for both buyer and seller: as Director General of Central Marketing and member of Luxlait's supervisory committee. Reuter says Luxlait ought to be able to review Central Marketing's books and at the end of April 1987 asked for his own access. Berns refused and Reuter was forced to make his own deductions.

From analysing Central Marketing's invoices to Luxlait, Reuter reckoned that it earned an inflated margin of 10.4 per cent. He said the milk was delivered and invoiced by Luxlait itself. All that Central Marketing did for its LFr200 million (£3 million) a year profit was supply a list of prices and take on the risk of selling the milk. Reuter said he couldn't be sure that the price Luxlait farmers were paid for their milk was the correct one. 'I cannot advise the committee to submit this balance sheet to the general assembly without making some restrictions as for the position taken by Berns.'

In a final bid to get to the bottom of the pricing, Reuter asked examining magistrate Lutgen for access to the 200 files of seized records. The request was granted – the two had worked together before. It allowed Reuter to uncover the way that LFr58 million (£900,000) of government subsidies were switched around between Luxlait and Centrale Paysanne. The cash was first received by Luxlait in the early 1960s and spent on two installations, one for milk powder. Then in 1970, Berns called for the money to be paid back into one of the hidden bank accounts under a 'revolving fund' arrangement.

The suggestion was that subsidies, whether to Luxlait or part of Centrale Paysanne, went into a single pot run by Berns which he then loaned out. It was another indication that Luxlait was not its own master and that state subsidies were not ending up in the right place. It was only a small slice of much larger sums which disappeared into hidden accounts in the way of subsidies and included EC funds.

Reuter turned to the US Army contract. Since after the Second World War, Luxlait and its predecessor organisations had sold high-quality milk to servicemen in the Rhine Army over the border in West Germany. Because the sales to the US Army are considered to be made outside the EC, they have the same status as exports onto the world market and hence attract EC export refund subsidies. Thus the business was much more lucrative than an ordinary sale to a German consumer. Together with other commissions, Reuter estimated the sales should have boosted Luxlait's price by 13 per cent.

But none of this extra 13 per cent ever reached Luxlait. According to Reuter, the export refunds and commissions for the costs of handling orders were cashed on the Centrale Paysanne market development pool fund. This was one of the hidden bank accounts and passed LFr264 million (£4 million) between the early 1970s and mid-1984 when it was seized at Berns' home. Centrale Paysanne was doing rather nicely out of the deal but Luxlait farmers, who produced the milk, never got the benefit.

Legally the Luxlait members may have no claim on these funds. Under an agreement, all their milk is sold by Central Marketing and any export subsidies would be correctly paid to Central Marketing. (This is a view unofficially confirmed by the European Commission.) What it did with the money within the Centrale Paysanne empire would be its own business. Economically the

Luxlait members have been defrauded. They were denied a fair price for export sales and denied the information to make their own judgement on whether they were being paid a fair price. It was a shabby and well-concealed scandal which went on for years.

Reuter also queried the transfer of EC subsidies for the private storage of butter to a Centrale Paysanne Produit Laitiers account. This would appear to be the bank account which, according to Lutgen, disappeared when his raids were overturned by the courts. The bank statements were no longer available when his troops returned.

Reuter concluded with a rousing appeal to the Luxlait general assembly where his report was to be discussed on 15 May 1987. Some of the language was a little out of place for an auditor's report. He said: 'I hope that my advice will find an open ear on the part of milk producers in promoting some initiatives and clarity; from the committee in preparing a reorganisation of statutes and markets without the intervention of Central Marketing; from Centrale Paysanne in rendering to Caesar what is Caesar's; from the government substantial reorganisation aid. . . '

The reaction of the Luxlait committee was not as Reuter expected, though it correctly informed the membership of his rejection of the accounts. The committee called for a counter-appraisal – a second audit. It was a move which smacked of Berns and Ewert's move over the examining magistrate's allegation in 1985. Then they had engaged their own set of experts to counter the Touche Ross report ordered by Lutgen. The Luxlait committee called in Coopers and Lybrand, an international firm of accountants, to review Reuter's report and carry out an audit of the 1987 accounts.

So Luxlait had two firms of auditors: Reuter for the agriculture minister and Coopers for the Luxlait committee. It was an unusual situation and an indication that government reforms of the milk sector still had some way to go. Would the auditors, both supposedly offering an independent professional viewpoint, come to the same conclusions on Luxlait? It was not to be the case. Coopers says it was 'not always in accord' with Reuter's report. This covered a 'number of points'. For Coopers it was a question of how 'material' the points were. Many of Reuter's 'small anomalies were not material' to the accounts.

Marie-Jeanne Chevremont, Coopers' Luxembourg partner, questions Reuter's objectivity and some of his comments on Berns. 'Reuter has accused certain managers of Centrale Paysanne to the detriment of Luxlait. He has no elements of objectivity. It is subjective on the part of Reuter.' But on two crucial elements, Coopers agreed with Reuter. These were Berns's conflict of interest from sitting on Luxlait's supervisory committee and secondly the restrictive milk purchase agreement with Central Marketing. After Coopers' audit, the Luxlait general assembly accepted the 1986 accounts.

Ewert from Centrale Paysanne is vitriolic in his comments on Reuter's report. He calls it *une betise*, a silliness or a nonsense, and goes on to call it a fabrication. For good measure he calls the original FLB complaint a calculated contrivance. Ewert has the benefit of checking Luxlait's accounts over a number of years on behalf of Central Marketing. Specifically he criticises Reuter's unconvincing comments on packaging and computer costs. Ewert saves his wrath for Reuter's alleged leaking of his report. 'This disqualifies an auditor', Ewert says.

The dispute between the auditors was an embarassment to the government's efforts to clean up the milk sector. As the 1987 audit continued, further obstacles blocked Reuter, the government's auditor. He wanted to attend Luxlait's annual stocktaking to check that the figures were backed by actual produce in the warehouse. It is a standard audit practice. He was refused access. Coopers, on a LFr2 million (£30,000) fee, were not present at the annual stocktaking either. Chevremont says: 'We have adopted alternative methods to our satisfaction.'

Steichen, the secretary for agriculture, said in mid-1988: 'We are talking about making these two reports concur. For the essence it (Coopers report) was the same.' Bringing widely-used auditing practices to Luxembourg's agricultural sector was proving a hard task. This was surprising given the Grand Duchy's desire to keep up with the financial services revolution.

The different views of the two audit firms were soon put to the test on a major issue. Reuter had been insistent that a provision should be set aside for a contested tax demand covering many years. Luxlait's tax-exempt status was at stake and it would lose, he said. On the other hand Coopers told the cooperative that the taxation of Luxlait was 'very improbable' and that not to provide the tax 'is acceptable and in accordance with US (accounting standards)'. The reference to US standards was because there were no accounting standards in Luxembourg covering the point – another omission for this European financial centre.

In February 1988 the Luxemburg taxman finally won his LFr127 million (£2 million) claim when the Conseil d'Etat, the top civil court, ruled that Luxlait's 50 per cent ownership of Luxlait Products during the 1960s deprived it of the tax exemption normally held by an agricultural association. It would have to pay the tax on business revenues like other enterprises. It was a costly bill and is likely to be only the first of many to clobber those who run the agricultural sector. Once again the taxman was proving effective in bringing empires down to size.

Chevremont explains Coopers' error as 'a question of judgement'. But it was a judgement contrary to the basic accounting guideline: be prudent. It was not advice that an international firm expanding along with the Luxembourg financial service industry could afford to make too often. Only two years before, it had comprised ten staff and was run by a partner in Brussels, 200 kilometres away. In spring 1988 it was telling unit trust managers how to set up in the Grand Duchy and expanding its staff to thirty by September. The many new trust managers expected to get reliable tax advice.

The financial position of Luxlait has become difficult as members resign and it pays off its tax bill. It has sought government subsidies to put it on a sensible footing. These would come from national coffers but still require European Commission approval to ensure they are not excessive and do not give Luxembourg milk an unfair lead over the neighbouring and competing countries. The Commission took its time to consider the initial LFr140 million (£2.1 million) subsidy.

In mid-1988 the Commission was still investigating the Luxembourg plan. It was not clear if it quizzed the

Luxembourg authorities about why EC export refund subsidies had not remained with Luxlait and about the other Centrale Paysanne arrangements to bleed the cash out of the milk farmers' cooperative. These arrangements ought to make it think twice about approving the latest subsidy injections. Instead the Commission ought to urge reparation payments back from Central Paysanne to Luxlait in order to save taxpayers' cash.

More reforms to Luxembourg's agricultural sector were approved by the Parliament in July 1987. They set up a democratically-elected chamber to represent the views of farmers. The FLB expected to gain nearly 40 per cent of the votes in elections in April 1988 and was campaigning vigorously for the nineteen-seat Chambre d'Agriculture. When the results were announced, Central Paysanne led with 54 per cent of farmers' votes, the FLB with 28 per cent and a third list of farmers opposing the Centrale Paysanne with nearly 18 per cent. Berns had fought the reforms, which cut the influence of his own organisation, and lost. Clearly inside Centrale Paysanne he still held sway.

The opposition had divided between those farmers who had left Luxlait and those opposing its policies from within. Mehlen, the FLB leader, had won a seat but complained that 50 per cent of Centrale Paysanne's vote came from farmers who were retired or who had sold up. He was concerned that Centrale Paysanne would take over the running of the Chambre and that the 75-year-old Berns would be installed as its director. The fear was the old discredited guard would carry on where they had left off. Until any criminal trials that will very much remain the case.

There is no sign that Berns and Ewert, who both still faced charges of false accounting, would step down from the management of Centrale Paysanne. The only move Berns had taken was to quit Luxlait's supervisory committee in 1987. It brought one long-standing conflict of interest to an end. Agriculture secretary Steichen rejects calls for the two to be removed from Centrale Paysanne's management. He says: 'In the government we don't bother what goes on in the courts.' He rejects allegations that Berns is protected by family ties to a former Christian Democrat prime minister.

Judicial officials mounted searches in 1986 as part of a separate investigation involving Central Marketing and allegedly fraudulent slaughter tickets for beef bought from farmers. The sums were not large but the inqury was complex and incomplete in 1988. No formal charges had been laid. There were sales to Belgium but EC monetary compensation subsidies were not said to be at stake.

The lucky years of Centrale Paysanne were ending. Centrale Marketing, its main sales arm, was caught out when an Italian outfit descended on Luxembourg. The two signed a contract for deliveries of 60 tonnes of meat a week. But the buyers never paid, claiming the meat was not up to scratch. The court cases continued in Rome in 1988 over this. The Italians were linked to the 'World Financial Establishment' which also set up shop selling share certificates and which had bases in tax havens. The finance house and the meat buyers were quickly drummed out of town. The unsavoury side of international investment and farm deals had come together.

Most Luxembourg observers believe that the Luxlait/ Centrale Paysanne scandal does not cross over into the international finance sector. They say that the poor standards of accounting disclosure and fiscal reporting are unique to the farming sector. The banking sector is well controlled by the Institut Monetaire Luxembourgeois. It scans the local scene and international publications to check that those claiming to be Luxembourg licensed banks have IML licences. There are high minimum capital requirements. The insurance sector has yet to go beyond the captive-type operation.

The major recent casualty, Banco Ambrosiano Holdings, was not a bank. It was only an unregulated investment holding company. It owned banks and was owned by a bank. It also borrowed large sums from banks. With the title 'banco' many, including those unfortunate lenders, believed it was a bank but it fell outside IML regulation.

IML dismissed claims that it ought to have queried the way Centrale Paysanne used the Caisse Centrale des Associations Agricoles, now renamed Caisse Centrale Raiffeisen, for the three hidden bank accounts kept there. Banking practice continues to protect account holders from reporting to tax or other regulatory services of unusual transactions. This is only beginning to change in the US and UK, with disclosure of the rewards of drugs and other crime. Nor can the aggregating of interest on the Centrale Paysanne bank accounts be seriously questioned.

But there have been reforms to the way CCAA is run. It carries a unique status in the Luxembourg banking world as a cooperative society and central bank for a fifty-branch network of Caisse Rurale Raiffeisen. Others with a say in its running include Centrale Paysanne and its group of companies, Luxlait and Berns. CCAA and the rural branches held LFr24 billion (£370 million) in customer deposits at the end of 1986. Traditionally the branches operated with part-time staff and undertook activities which were not strictly banking, such as buying equipment and services for local farmers.

In 1984, the finance ministry forced some changes to the banks' statutes to restrict their activities to pure financial business. In some branches there was discussion about the part-time staff and in larger branches the managing director or secretary general had to be full-time. At the CCAA Rene Wolter became the president in 1986. He had just retired as head of the ministry of finance's bank surveillance department. The appointment was more of a personal one than under ministry pressure but it still gave greater confidence.

Surveillance by the IML is independent from political influence and covers the CCAA in the same way as other banks. Observers believe the finance industry is free from the day-to-day political interference that allowed Centrale Paysanne and Luxlait to remain free from accounting or fiscal controls. One seasoned investigator says: 'The IML is strong enough to get rid of problems of that kind. They would not let some weak politician interfere in their affairs. And neither (Jacques) Santer (premier and finance minister) nor (Jacques) Poos (the economic and treasury minister) would interfere in the IML.'

How did the manipulation of accounts go on for so long undetected? Mehlen, the FLB leader, believes that for many years, Berns' own success masked what was going on. Early efforts paid off in a long period of improving prosperity. After the Luxembourg government returned from exile in London in 1944, Berns with Christian Democrat party support was able to set up the farmers' cooperatives and trade unions. Milk quality was radically improved in the 1950s through a tough policy of slaughter. Former farm minister Hamilius remembers returning from a year at University in the US in 1951 to find a major improvement.

It enabled Berns to sell to the US troops over the border in Germany who demanded milk as they knew it back home. This lucrative contract kept dairy farmers better-off than rivals in neighbouring countries. The profits were invested in buying up rival dairies. There also followed a series of grandiose projects including grain silos, a milk powder factory and an artificial insemination laboratory which were impressive and provided up to date services for farmers. But some, such as the abattoir at Mersch, were out of proportion and the European Commission baulked at funding this project.

The poor Luxlait price to farmers for their milk eventually persuaded the more intelligent ones to sell elsewhere, mainly in Germany. In 1987 it was estimated that one-sixth of milk production headed east over the border to dairies where the breath of competition kept costs down. Meanwhile Luxembourg was becoming saddled with under-used milk treatment and processing equipment as EC quotas reduced capacity further.

What lessons can be learned from Luxembourg and can they be applied to the farming economies of other EC countries? To make direct comparisons without the hard evidence that is available from Luxembourg would be dangerous. But there are suspicions in other northern countries that cooperatives have shifted profits from milk to beef and that government or EC subsidies for milk farmers have gone to support their beef counterparts. In some cooperatives, this may be approved but in the long run it distorts prices and stores up trouble.

The sheer power which these cooperatives wield is not healthy for farmers or consumers. The UK's Milk Marketing Board, a similar organisation to Luxlait, has been taken through the civil courts more than once for trying to keep rivals out of its market. Via the UK Government, it has also faced a series of infringement proceedings from the

European Commission for its spending of subsidies. In 1988 the UK Government began considering some changes to this monopolistic organisation.

And Centrale Paysanne/Luxlait shows that despite a welter of regulations, directives and edicts, the EC has only limited influence over Europe's agriculture. It can't make sure that its subsidies end up in the hands of those that have earned them; it can't prevent one sector cross-subsidising another; and it can't do a great deal to protect working farmers. The more recent quotas on each country's milk production will prove a blunt but more effective weapon on farmers' incomes. While for Luxemburg's financial centre, the saga may just prove a come-on to less than wholesome operators.

Section 3
POLLUTION, THE THIRD WORLD, MAFIA AND THE 1990s

9 WATER: THE DIRTY OLD MAN OF EUROPE

Pollution is the scourge of the modern world. The waste from factories pours into rivers and seas; the emissions from smokestacks dirty the air and kill trees; more sophisticated chemicals wreak their own particular vengeance on human, animal and plant life. European Community measures ought to counter these pollutions. But despite being agreed in Brussels, governments have not put them on their national statute books, or if they have, they forget to report progress or just don't bother to apply them. The EC's environment law is honoured in its breach. And the UK is one of the worst culprits.

Take water. It is a beautiful natural element perfect for washing, bathing and swimming. Polluted, it becomes an unpleasant and unhealthy commodity. Out of the tap, British water often contains more hazardous chemicals than are permitted under an EC drinking water directive. Nitrates, for example, are the result of prolonged over-use of agricultural fertilisers and can harm young babies. The sea around Britain is another cesspit – literally in some places. Official tests show that thirty per cent of beaches break EC health levels on sewage and germs in bathing water. This allegedly causes stomach upsets and headaches.

And getting the UK to change its ways is like asking a young child not play in the mud. It just doesn't hear. Both drinking and bathing water directives prompted legal threats from the European Commission before the UK even contemplated taking any action. It took eight years for the government to raise the number of nominated beaches from a ridiculous 27 to a more reasonable 389. Cleaning bathing water is now underway. On drinking

196

water it was the same story – first there was a climbdown over what the law meant, then came the measures to clear up. It will be years before the UK toes the line.

The UK government claims to have thought hard about the implications of the directives – harder, it says, than other governments which don't police the rules. But the UK didn't even comply with its own, misinterpreted, versions of the two directives. Andrew Lees, a leading campaigner with Friends of the Earth, says: 'In our view the government wilfully misinterpreted the (drinking water) directive. It beggars belief that it had to take legal advice. The wording of the directive is clear. The government record is one of delay, delay and delay and prevaricate as long as possible.'

And the changes, when they have come, appear aimed at smoothing the path for the privatisation of the UK water industry – removing financial uncertainties over the £7 billion share sale due in 1990. But major doubts persist over the scale of spending needed before UK water meets the EC directives. Some say the clean-up bill may rise to £6 billion. The government thinks it's much smaller. It makes privatisation a risky investment for prospective shareholders.

It is still not clear, thirteen years after the bathing water directive was agreed, whether Belgium, Italy and the UK have put the legislation on their own statute books. Belgium, Italy and The Netherlands had to be taken before the European Court of Justice before this point got home to them. In 1988, Belgium had yet to adopt all the 1975 directive's provisions at regional level and Italy had introduced a number of exceptions to the mandatory and recommended levels of pollutants. The UK has never introduced specific legislation and relies on an administrative circular issued by the Department of the Environment.

But it was not this aspect of the UK's approach which prompted the first threat of court action by the Commission. In 1979 the UK had nominated only 27 beaches as bathing areas under the directive, a list which had excluded Brighton and Blackpool, the most popular UK resort in 1987 with more than six million visitors. The UK thought it had spotted a loophole and by keeping its list short, it would not be liable to maintain standards for all the other beaches. Even landlocked Luxembourg had told the Commission it had 39 'beaches' on its lakeside and river resorts and West Berlin counts 16 bathing waters. In February 1987 the UK, after Commission pressure, reluctantly named a further 362.

As Stanley Clinton Davis, European Commissioner for the environment and former Labour minister, said: 'It was clearly unacceptable for a country with a coastline as long as Britain's to name only 27 beaches where the Community rules of cleanness and hygiene would be applied.'

It was one of the first rebuffs to the UK's arrogant attitude to EC environment legislation. It was a sign that the European Commission could humble Whitehall, its ministers and officials. It is the start to many cases brought after complaints from the environmental lobby. But the February 1987 decision making the number of beaches covered by the directive up to 389 was just the first step. Bringing those up to the standards required by the directive should be the second step. But the government has admitted there is still a long way to go and 'inevitably this will take a number of years'.

In any case the UK government believes the dangers from bathing in dirty water are limited. It says bathing in sewage-polluted sea water 'carries only a negligible risk to health, even on beaches that are aesthetically very unsatisfactory'. This has been the view since 1959, when its concern was the transmission of serious diseases such as polio though this is not thought to be carried by seawater. In 1987, the British Medical Association said it was reviewing its position that there was no quantifiable health risk. In time the government may change its view which is looking increasingly out of line.

In the US and Canada, governments would probably say EC standards were not strict enough. Latest rules in these two countries insist on more frequent testing, daily in the case of Toronto, and with tougher mandatory levels. Both suggest a maximum bacteria level which is a fifth of the EC mandatory level but which is still four times higher than the EC guideline. In practice viruses are a major cause of swimmers' stomach complaints. But tests for their presence are rarely made because no easy and quick scientific tests are currently available. Instead, most results rely on tests of bacteria levels.

A study by the University of Surrey's Robens Institute of Industrial and Environmental Health and Safety for Greenpeace, the environment group, produced disturbing results of bathers' reactions to dirty bathing water. Holiday-makers on two unnamed South Coast beaches – one 40 times more polluted than the other – were quizzed. The 'dirty' resort had four times more than the recommended EC level of bacteria. The detailed poll asked 1,900 people their reactions to physical rubbish in the sea, whether they thought the water was polluted, if it had put them off swimming and whether any had felt ill after immersion.

The poll found that dirty resort swimmers were more likely to report having felt generally ill and to complain of stomach upsets, nausea, diarrhoea and headaches. It said that 4.4 per cent of the dirty beach swimmers who put their heads under the water either sought a doctor or took medication for a stomach upset. 12.4 per cent of this same group of bathers complained of 'generally feeling ill' after their swim, compared to 6.7 per cent of swimmers at the dirty beach who kept their heads above water. Only 1.1 per cent of all other swimmers from both resorts complained of stomach upsets.

The study says it cannot establish a direct connection between dirty water and illness. But the results were enough for Greenpeace in November 1987 to call for a full epidemiological survey to test further for a causal link. It noted the finding that more than 80 per cent of the public are worried about bathing in polluted water. Drawing on separate tests of water quality at 30 beaches, it called for more rigorous testing by the Department of the Environment. It said the government ought to make sufficient funds available to water authorities to ensure an immediate clean-up programme.

Widespread tests of water quality at the UK's beaches were first revealed in April 1987. It followed a survey ordered in December 1985 by Environment Minister William Waldegrave and covers the 1986 bathing season. Waldegrave, a competent minister with a genuine concern for the environment, was 'encouraged' by the results. He said: 'They show that 228 out of 368 bathing waters in England, Northern Ireland and Wales – 62 per cent – meet the directive's standards, although I am advised that the conclusions, drawn only from the first year's monitoring results, should be regarded as provisional.'

A close reading of the DoE survey disclosed that at least two out of the first tranche of 27 nominated beaches – Scarborough's South Bay and Southend's Thorpe Bay – had failed to meet EC standards. Ryde on the Isle of Wight also failed, though only the East Sands were originally nominated. Thus the government had not even met the lower standards of bathing water quality which it originally decided for itself to take on. But at least on the basis that three out of the 27 failed, then 89 per cent passed the standard – a significantly higher proportion than overall including the more recent beaches.

Results for testing during 1987, released by the DoE in May 1988, claimed 'continuing improvement'. Out of the 374 bathing waters then nominated under the directive, 262 or 70 per cent met the mandatory EC bacteria levels. This was up on the overall 62 per cent in 1986. But the detailed figures revealed some setbacks. Two more out of the original 27 beaches no longer met the EC standard. These were Southend's Westcliff Bay and the Goodrington beach at Paignton. Since the three others from 1986 remained dirty, it meant the pass rate of this 27 was down to 81 per cent. It was still above the overall figure but some bathing water was obviously getting dirtier.

The Commission has pursued action against the quality of water at Blackpool, Southport and Formby after complaints from residents and environmental groups. It was only a step away from taking the UK to the European Court of Justice in January 1987, but has since been negotiating a settlement with the UK government. The stumbling block was the timetable. The Commission said the directive applied today, the UK said it wanted to comply 'as soon as possible' and said that plans were being drawn up for the works. Government limits on water authority spending were one reason for the slow moves.

In the four years to 1985, the nine English and Welsh water authorities with nominated beaches spent an average of £37 million, and the rate has doubled since then to about

Table 9.1 Bathing water quality at selected UK beaches

(p=pass EC mandatory bacteria standards; f=fail)

	1987 Greenpeace	1987 DoE	1986 DoE
Yorkshire			
Whitby	p	p	p
Scarborough North Bay	f	p	p
Scarborough South Bay	f	f	f
Filey	f	p	p
Bridlington North Beach	p	p	p
Bridlington South Beach	p	p	p
Hornsea	f	p	p
Kent			
Deal Castle	f	f	f (i/r)
Margate	p	p/p	p/f (i/r)
Ramsgate	f	f	p (i/r)
Herne Bay	f	f	p (i/r)
Whitstable	p	(not EC	beach)
Southend Westcliff	f	f	p
Southend Thorpe Bay	f	f	f
Fylde			
Fleetwood Pier	f	f	f
Cleveleys	f	f	f
Anchsholm	f	f	f
Blackpool North Pier	f	f	f
Blackpool Man Squ	f	f	f
Blackpool Squires Gate	f	f	f
St Annes Pier	f	f	f
Grans Bay	f	(not EC	beach)

Cornwall

Wherry Town	f	(not EC beach)	
Marazion and Mounts Bay	f	f	f
St Ives Porthminster	p	p	p
St Ives Porthmeor	p	p	p
Porth Towan	p	p	p
Trevaunance Cove	p	p	f
Newquay Fistral	p	p	p
Newquay Towan	p	p	p
Pass rate	37%	50%	54%

(Table compares 30 beaches tested by the University of Surrey's Robens Institute, on behalf of Greenpeace, as closely as possible with official DoE bathing waters. The only significant differences on sampling sites involve the Fylde coast which fails on either basis. The DoE beaches also include incomplete returns (i/r) by some water authorities but this has been ignored on pass rate calculation. DoE returns include two Margate beaches.

(Overall the Greenpeace results were worse than the 1987 and 1986 ones from the DoE with only 37 per cent meeting the standards. And Greenpeace expressed surprise that its figures were so high. It claimed that in less favourable conditions, the failure rate would have been even greater.)

£70 million a year with many major projects under way. It involves the building of 'long sea outfalls' – piping sewage well beyond the shoreline to ensure rapid dilution. It is a method recommended by the 1984 Royal Commission on Environmental Pollution. In May 1988, the Water Authorities Association detailed the efforts being made by their members in studies and spending on improvements.

The Fylde coast of Lancashire, which includes Blackpool, is expected to meet EC standards by the early 1990s. A £1 million coastal survey is underway. £10 million has already been spent on construction and a further '£40 million would see work completed by 1993'. In the South West, where 100 beaches are located, £200 million is being set aside. Nine beaches that failed the standard in 1987 are being worked on, including £40 million at Penzance, £4 million for Bude and £4 million for Lyme Regis.

Further ahead, Southern Water is spending £125 million to bring the whole of the south coast up to EC standards by the middle of the 1990s. It said 20 long sea outfalls and the shore-based installations had been built over the last seven years. Wales is spending £90 million over the next decade. Llandudno and Barry were two particular targets for remedial work.

The Water Authorities Association accepted that the monitoring figures indicated a major effort was required. It said: 'There is some variability year upon year, dependent upon the weather conditions during each summer and whether there is sufficient sunlight to cause the rapid death of bacteria. However, the overall results do give a clear indication of where priority has to be given to schemes for improvement with long sea outfalls, and the water authorities are proceeding as rapidly as possible with the major expenditure that is required.'

Exact levels of bathing pollution are impossible to determine. Not because the scientists are working for different interests but because the levels themselves are never the same. Time and tide is continually on the move. What is not in doubt is that many UK beaches are not meeting the EC standards. Despite the ten-year phasing in of the 1975 directive, the UK is still going to be another ten years in meeting its full requirements. It was a pretty off-hand attitude by a government to its international obligations and one which left bathers risking stomach complaints.

Studies released in 1988 showed that bathing water in many resorts around Europe failed to meet EC standards. So think again if you are planning a holiday on the west sands of St Andrews, Fife, Scotland, at Peniscola, south of Barcelona, Spain, Puerto Alcudia on Minorca, Strande-Kiel and Norderney, West Germany or Corfu in Greece. Bacteriological studies of germ and pollution levels at these beaches made their bathing water the most unhealthy during July 1987. They were 'very polluted' and broke mandatory rules, according to an extensive study organised by the Bureau for European Consumer Unions (BEUC).

In Spain, Marbella and Benidorm in the south and Lloret de Mar on the Costa Brava failed to meet less strict EC guideline levels. Albufeira on Portugal's Algarve and many more bathing areas in Ireland, France, Belgium, Denmark, The Netherlands, Italy and Greece had more than the recommended level of bacteria. Out of 312 visited by investigators ony 206 beaches, or 66 per cent, met the recommended EC standard with 100, or 32 per cent, suffering some pollution.

Visual inspection by BEUC rated beaches on a scale of one to five depending on the number of types of pollution such as oils, detergents or tar that were present. No beach scores worse than three. Those with three black marks are Lyngvig in Denmark and Salou and Montgat, both near Barcelona in Spain. The study says: 'For 36 per cent of the beaches tested visual examination has noted the presence of one or several types of pollution, various discharges, residues of mineral oil, detergents, tar. . . '

Bathing water, under the directive, must be clear enough to allow a swimmer to see one metre under the water and preferably two. BEUC tested for better than one-metre vision and at various shorter distances. All nineteen Belgian beaches and all nineteen, bar one, of the Dutch beaches fail to meet the directive. A number are close to the one-metre threshold. Most other countries show a patchy picture. Greek and Canary Island sea water is very clear.

Chemical testing of heavy metals like zinc, lead, cadmium, copper and mercury is the final area of the BEUC study and one of the more alarming. The directive sets no levels but governments are supposed to report values to the Commission so that levels can be firmed up. BEUC adopted a five-level scale of pollution for these metals, from no pollution to very heavy pollution on the advice of 'world experts'. On this scale more than half of the 312 beaches that BEUC tested are at least lightly polluted by all five heavy metals. Many suffer average or heavy pollution. Eleven per cent suffer very heavy zinc pollution.

A low level of these metals is normal in water but it is increased by industrial discharges. Dangers to bathers may be limited but fish and seafood accumulate these metals in significant quantities. The results show that some North Sea countries are badly contaminated, with UK and The Netherlands worst hit, but Denmark is the least contaminated. France has localised troublespots. According to BEUC, 'some countries are distinguished by their high rates of individual metals: Belgium and Great Britain for cadmium, France and Spain for copper, Spain again for lead and Greece for mercury.'

Overall, the results show a distinct reduction in bacterial pollution and an increase in chemical pollution over recent years. The results at the bacteriological level are not appalling, but just bad and unsavoury.

BEUC suggests that the directive has produced some 'positive effects. On one side, concerning the bacterial pollution, one can consider, subject to certain reserves, that the results are rather encouraging, while those on chemical pollution are frankly disturbing.' The obvious dangers from holiday resorts tipping their sewage into the nearest part of the sea are being tackled, though there is still a long way to go. Many resorts around Europe were no better than the UK on this count. The dangers from industrial plants further down the coast is an unchecked problem. EC limits on metals would be a start.

Implementation of this directive, which has a direct impact on the man or woman in the street, has not surprisingly been poor. Within the directive's rules, countries have taken advantage of options on what is a nominated 'bathing area' under the directive. Some states prohibit bathing in other areas, some publish data on their water quality. There have been calls for more uniform testing rules and the Commission may be considering halving the mandatory level of bacteria. This would still leave it two and half times the US limit. There may also be a binding limit on the streptococci bacteria which clearly cause infection.

The water around the coastline may be less than satisfactory, but the water that comes out of the British tap often fails to conform to EC standards too.

After its climbdown over bathing water, the Department of the Environment has been forced to retreat on drinking water because its lawyers had misinterpreted a 1980 directive on the quality of water for human consumption. This means that a range of pollutants, some cancer-linked are exceeding the limits set in the directive. In the face of farmers' opposition and the government's own

desire to privatise the water industry, the DoE's performance has been found wanting. Once again it has been left to
the environmental lobby and the European Commission to
force compliance.

Friends of the Earth, the UK environmental group,
has filed a lengthening list of complaints to the Commission in Brussels over the UK failure to meet drinking water
standards. The list covers nitrate pollution, mainly caused
by agricultural fertilisers; lead, particularly in Scotland;
pesticides of various types and a series of solvents.
According to Andrew Lees, FOE's countryside and
pesticides campaigner: 'The Commission puts teeth into
our argument. The government might not do everything it
asks but it does not like going before the court.'

FOE complaints have come thick and fast. In November 1986 it tackled nitrate levels and the failure of the UK
to implement the EC legislation. The UK was relying on
existing law, in this case the Water Act of 1973. In various
sections, this requires water to be 'wholesome' before it is
consumed by the public. Local authorities have to regularly check 'the sufficiency and wholesomeness' of water
supplies in their area. They have to notify water undertak-
ings and authorities, if there is 'any insufficiency or
unwholesomeness'. In their turn, water authorities have to
provide 'a supply of wholesome water'.

But when is water 'wholesome'? The DoE issued a
circular in 1982 which told authorities that it would 'regard
compliance with the terms of the directive as a necessary
characteristic but not a complete definition of any water
that is to be considered wholesome'. The FOE complained: 'The UK has not integrated the Community
measure into national law by the most appropriate forms
and measures to ensure that the directive is effective. There
is no statutory definition of "wholesome" drinking water
in UK law and there is no statutory reference to the
parameters in the directive.'

It is a formal infringement of the Community measure, said FOE. Some would say it was a legal technicality
of no consequence. But it may offer an astute lawyer
defending a dirty water claim just the get-out he needed.
The UK consumer could lose the protection of the EC

directive which lays down maximum admissible concentrations (MACs) on a large number of water constitutents. Officials say EC environment legislation has 'very commonly' been implemented via circulars, and dismiss complaints as a 'sterile' legal argument. The approach is to use a circular until the Commission spots it.

The 'actual infringement' of the directive concerned the high levels of nitrates in various areas of England and Wales and how the DoE has coped with them. FOE questioned the classification of nitrates as 'undesirable' and not toxic; the way that the DoE calculated the figures for MACs by a rolling three-month average instead of one-off tests; and 52 'derogations' allowing nitrate levels to exceed the 50 mg/litre level because of 'situations arising from the nature and structure of the ground' where the water was drawn. FOE believed that widespread pollution was being covered up.

The dangers of nitrates are disputed but sufficient to grant babies protection. The government's chief medical officer has called on water authorities to inform doctors and hospitals when levels exceed 50 mg/litre so that they can monitor for infantile methaemoglobinaemia, or 'blue-baby' syndrome. This is potentially fatal to infants and where levels exceed 100 mg/litre, at any time, then low nitrate water is recommended for infant feeding. The last confirmed UK case was in 1972. The French government ruled in April 1985 that water with more than 50 mg/litre should not be supplied to pregnant women or babies.

The actual level where danger increases is difficult to pin down. World Health Organisation says that symptoms of blue-baby syndrome may not be evident at up to 89 mg/litre but warns that 'undesirable increases in methaemoglobin in blood do occur'. WHO set a guideline in 1984 of 44.5 mg/litre for drinking water. There are also animal experiments suggesting that nitrates may be carcinogenic. A Chinese study hinted that high levels of nitrates caused gastric cancer in a particular region. The official UK line is that research 'gives no support to the suggestion that nitrate is a cause of cancer'.

FOE stands little chance on this part of its complaint to the Commission. The directive itself classifies nitrates as only 'undesirable'. FOE said: 'It is certainly arguable that excessive amounts of nitrate in water are toxic and thus ineligible for derogation.'

The FOE next accused the DoE of 'massaging the data'. Day-to-day tests could regularly breach the 50 mg/litre limit. This is not acceptable, said FOE. It quoted studies of the River Dart, using hourly concentrations for 1975–83. These showed that 90 per cent of the nitrate load was transported in 37 per cent of the period. Rolling averages smooth out peak concentrations where nitrate levels rise rapidly in autumn/winter periods. Over any three-month period the average nitrate level was under 50 mg/litre. But taken in shorter 'bites', perhaps even on a monthly average, the level recorded was closer to the limit.

'In other words, the Government's concept of "compliance" with the directive is to allow drinking water to contain more than 50 mg of nitrate per litre, as long as that level is not exceeded when the sampling results are averaged over three months. This approach ridicules the concept of a maximum admissible concentration,' said FOE.

The FOE complaint to the Commission was by no means the first over nitrates or other aspects of the drinking water directive. By November 1986 the Commission had challenged the UK government over the lack of legislation for private water supplies which were not covered by the DoE circulars, and its method of measuring MACs. A separate complaint over nitrite levels in water in the Borough of Tower Hamlets, East London was also being pursued. (Nitrites have been linked to stomach cancer.) Talks began with the UK government after it offered to change its approach on nitrates but with 'prolonged delays'.

1987 was a bad year for the UK. In the European Year of the Environment, it gained a reputation as 'the dirty old man of Europe'. It did not meet its obligations on bathing and drinking water, air pollution or disposal of chemicals. In June, Commissioner Clinton Davis had a list of twenty-two infringements against the UK on environmental issues at various stages in the legal process, though some other states face actions as serious as the UK's. The UK was also criticised for holding up EC proposals on scrubbers, which filter emissions from the smoke stacks of coal-fired power stations, to cut future sulphur and nitrous emissions – the cause of acid rain.

The UK eventually held its corner and committed heavy spending on the scrubbers. It was part of its policy to fit environment laws to what it could afford to clean up. Progress on drinking water came in December 1987 when Nicholas Ridley, the Secretary of State for the Environment, had 'a technical point' to announce to the House of Commons. Ridley's acid tongue may hide a cultured and nature-loving intellectual but his record and presentation have not endeared him to the environment lobby. Other responsibilities and lobbying from other ministries, such as agriculture and industry, have not made his department appear pro-environment.

Ridley said he was considering a number of intitiatives for strengthening and extending water pollution controls. He said: 'As to drinking water quality, I have decided, after taking legal advice that the term "maximum admissible concentration" in the European Community drinking water directive should relate to individual samples and not averages over a period. This is a technical point. It concerns the appearance of water supplied and does not have health implications.'

But despite the 'technical' tag, Ridley had made a major climbdown and accepted the FOE and Commission's complaints. The lack of reported damage to human health and the claim that nitrate pollution levels have flattened off gives the impression that there are no dangers. Yet removing the rolling average method of calculating the 50 mg/litre nitrate content of water meant many supplies broke the law. The announcement displayed a cavalier attitude to public health.

Friends of the Earth responded quickly to winning on one of their complaints and said that Commission legal action in August had 'forced the government to stop bending the rules'. They claimed that £6 billion would have to be spent on additional investment before the water authorities could be privatised as the government hoped. There would also be 'powerful new controls' over agricultural and industrial pollution. FOE rounded off its blast against the government with a new complaint to the

Figure 7 **NITRATE POLLUTION**

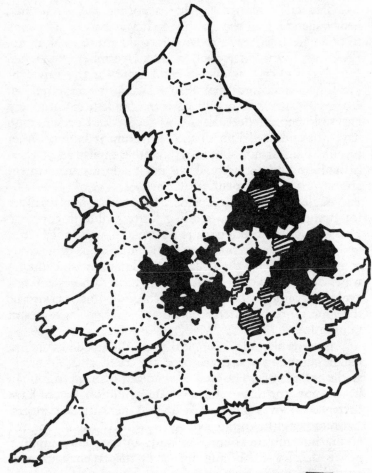

 Areas with no derogation where nitrates occasionally exceed 50mg/ litre.

 Areas which are 'derogated' and where water contained more than 50mg/litre of nitrates on a 3 months rolling average.

European Commission over nitrate pollution of drinking water.

Lees, the environment group's campaigner, said: 'FOE have won this round. The next battle is to force the government to accept that it is illegal for them to allow any drinking water supplies to contain nitrate levels above the EEC limit, and to get them to bring in new controls over agricultural pollution.'

Ridley's decision that MACs had to be measured on single samples and not on rolling three-monthly average levels had a major impact. The government had admitted earlier that 920,000 people were receiving water with nitrates over the 50 mg/litre level but this number had been measured on the three-monthly average. FOE claimed that without massaging the figures, five million people were receiving water breaking the EC standard. Thus it extended its complaint to 49 more sources of water where any sample had breached the 50 mg/litre level since the directive came into force in August 1985.

Because of its slipshod implementation of the EC directive, the government was now caught between the devil and the deep blue sea. It could either apply for more derogations to cover water where nitrate levels were over 50 mg/litre or it could give up the fight and clean up the pollution. Both courses had a number of drawbacks. More derogations would cause further public outcry and had to be cleared with the Commission in Brussels. A clean-up programme was financially costly and involved an embarrassing admission of failure. Further legal challenges against the derogations narrowed the UK's options.

The derogations – departures from the directive – are designed for 'situations arising from the nature and structure of the ground in the area from which the supply in question is drawn'. If water sources contain an impurity it is difficult to remove it from a kilometre underground. But the derogations are not to be used where water is polluted. Because of the 'structure of the ground', the DoE had granted extensive derogations to three water authorities, the Anglian, Severn-Trent and Yorkshire. They covered the water supply of an estimated 920,000 people.

It was the FOE and the Commission's next task to show that agricultural pollution, mainly from nitrogenous fertilisers, was the main cause of excessive nitrates in the water supply. Neither organisation believed that nitrates were due to 'the structure of the ground'. They certainly flowed into the ground but they were not part of the geology itself. The DoE said it was unconvinced and scientific evidence had to be used to spell it out.

Much of the pollution stems from the heavy use of fertilisers in the grain belt of East Anglia and Lincolnshire. From here water supplies are drawn into neighbouring areas, which also show the high nitrate levels in drinking water. Intensive farming – to a large extent due to the EC's own policies – has dramatically built up the level of this pollution. Some basics explain how this underlying change has taken place. Nitrates, the oxidised compounds of nitrogen, are contained in artificial fertilisers, farmyard manure, and other slurry. They are strongly soluble and quickly slip into rivers or underground sources from where drinking water is drawn.

Publicly, the UK government claims nitrate levels are no longer rising. DoE long-term data up to the early 1980s showed some signs of flattening towards the end of the period after a steady rise in most areas. Commission studies put this down to the nature of the sites tested. Its studies showed continuing increases in fertilisers in rural areas against declining industrial activity and better sewage treatment. More specific testing of the ground beneath different types of farming may suggest a rise in agricultural nitrate pollution.

The UK's interdepartmental Nitrate Coordination Group (NCG) in 1986 quoted research revealing high concentrations of nitrates in the UK. It says: 'Research undertaken during 1975–82 in the outcrop areas of major aquifers showed high concentrations of nitrate, generally in excess of 100mg/litre, invariably present in the unsaturated zone pore-water beneath long-standing arable land, suggesting leaching losses in excess of 50 kilogram nitrogen per hectare. By comparison, the concentrations beneath unfertilised and lightly fertilised permanent grassland were much lower (normally less than 10mg nitrate/litre).

'A relationship between intensive arable cropping sustained by increasingly large nitrogen fertiliser applications and high rates of nitrate leaching to groundwater was inferred. High nitrate concentrations were accompanied by elevated levels of other solutes, notably sulphate, chloride and some trace elements, derived either directly from fertilisers or mobilised from soils by farming practices.'

The FOE used NCG statements to back its claim that arable farming in East Anglia is the cause of higher nitrate concentrations. FOE argued: 'There is thus strong evidence showing that nitrate in both ground and surface water sources is largely derived from agricultural inputs. The maximum admissible concentration (MAC) is not exceeded because of "situations arising from the nature and structure of the ground in the area from which the supply in question emanates". The government used article 9.1 (in the directive) as a device to evade compliance with the MAC for nitrate.'

Eventually the government was forced to give up derogations covering large expanses of Lincolnshire, Nottinghamshire, Cambridgeshire, Norfolk and Staffordshire. It was the second climbdown in the space of two months. In January 1988, Colin Moynihan, Parliamentary Under Secretary at the DoE, announced: 'There are currently 48 supplies with nitrate derogations, serving some 900,000 people. These derogations were granted because the concentrations in the supplies are not a health risk. However, in the light of recent legal advice, I have decided that these derogations should be withdrawn.

'The government will in due course publish its proposals for limiting nitrate concentrations in water. In the meantime studies are proceeding into solutions to the problem, including water de-nitrification processes and the feasibility of protection zones.'

With that statement, FOE had won the second and perhaps most important line of its complaint: that water quality suffered because of agricultural pollution, not because of some special geological factor as the government tried to suggest. Confidently the FOE stated that nitrate pollution of tap water extended beyond the three water authority areas of Anglian, Severn–Trent, Yorkshire, and into Thames, Southern and Wessex. It called for a fertiliser tax to pay for the clean-up operation so that water authorities did not just pass on the bill to those who paid their water rates in those areas.

Other complaints on the UK's drinking water cover the high levels of lead coming out of Scottish taps. In 1985, when the directive came into force, the government applied for derogations to cover this excessive level. In December 1987 the government told the House of Commons that 85 water supplies in Scotland exceeded the EC threshold and that 38 would be unable to meet a target, set in 1985, that lead in Scottish drinking water would be cut by the end of 1989. FOE filed a formal complaint to the Commission in December 1987 over this excessive lead, which dissolves off old water pipes.

Lead is a well-recognised danger to young children causing brain damage. But as with nitrates there is no clear level which is proven to be dangerous. The EC drinking water directive sets a 50 parts/billion maximum but this is beginning to look out of line with practice around the world, though it remains the World Health Organisation's guideline value. The US is considering cutting its permissible level in tap water to only 20 parts/billion as concern grows that relatively low concentrations in blood impair a child's learning ability.

In February 1988 FOE complained to the Commission about the pesticide lindane in two Yorkshire rivers under an EC directive covering dangerous substances. This pesticide has already been barred from some uses. Other pollution of water under the drinking water directive has prompted concern about 'phenolic taste problems' in Yorkshire and solvents in Coventry, Cambridge, Norwich and at military airfields. The idea that you can turn the tap on and feel confident about the quality of the water that comes out is rapidly disappearing. The government's performance on EC water directives does little to dispel the concern.

The cost of cleaning up water is also rising. The FOE's £6 billion is plucked from the air and at different times, it has suggested only £4 billion. But water authorities accept it could be that much. Anglian Water alone is spending £70 million on measures to remove nitrates from farm pollution. About half of the fifty, now cancelled, derogations covered Anglian. Some estimates suggest 70 per cent of its water supplies will exceed 50mg/litre of nitrate unless corrective action is taken. Five other less affected authorities will have to spend on denitrification. The Water Authorities Association estimates £200 million spending over the next ten years.

That is only the part of the bill arising from the removal of the derogations covering the setting-up of nitrate protection zones, the closing down of sources and the mixing of supplies to get below the 50mg/litre threshold. Another bill comes from the change to the sampling methods and the removal of three-monthly rolling averages of concentrations. This covers the whole range of pollutants laid down in the directive. A spokesman for the Water Authorities Association said in April 1988: 'I can't say how much it will be. It could be several millions or it could be several billions. We are trying desperately hard to get that figure correct.

'It varies from authority to authority and from area to area. It can't be solved in a week or two. It could be due to nitrates or coloration because of a peat bog. I am not happy with the use of £6 billion, but it could be several billion,' he admitted.

The other complaints that the EC drinking water directive is being breached have a financial cost. On lead pollution, FOE suggests a £750 million budget just for stripping old piping in Scotland, while the government figure is 'tens of millions'. Pesticides require expensive activated carbon filters at treatment works. The other individual breaches require costly counter-measures to preserve the purity of drinking water. Breaches of the bathing water directive are another ingredient. Improvement schemes are costing currently £70 million a year and expected to last ten years: a £1 billion bill would be a fair overall estimate.

These costs are a crucial element in the future privatisation of UK water authorities, and will have to be disclosed in the prospectus sent to potential investors. Privatisation is unlikely to take place before the end of 1989 after government legislation is put in place. Merchant bankers Schroeders, the government's advisers on water privatisation, were unclear of its impact in Spring 1988 and whether it would be a contingent liability or a direct

Table 9.2 **Cleaning up UK water – the cost over the next 10 years**
(£ millions)

	minimum estimate	maximum estimate
Bathing water	700	1,000
Drinking water		
– nitrate measures	200	2,500
– lead	50*	2,000
– other pollutants	40*	500
	290	5,000
total	990	6,000

(*=estimates. This table compares official figures from water authorities, and others bandied about by the environment lobby.)

liability to revenue or capital. It was merely one of a number of unresolved issues at that stage. Non-compliance with the directive was common in Europe, the DoE had told Schroeders.

The government was well aware of the looming threat to its privatisation programme and moved to soothe the concerns. The statements by Ridley and his DoE colleagues in late 1987 and early 1988 were followed by another in April. Joyce Quin, Labour MP and former EuroMP, had been told in a House of Commons answer by Ridley that he expected 'most public water supplies to comply by 1990'. FOE believes these statements are designed to smooth privatisation's path. FOE's Lees says: 'In a large part, it is not a change of heart by the government but more to reassure a jittery City. They don't want large uncertainties.'

But the government does not intend to foot the bill. It has made clear to water and local authorities that they will have to find the cash, though the door has been left open to a tax on fertilisers. The aim will be to go some way to applying the polluter-pays principle, enshrined in the latest

1987 EC treaty. On bathing water, where replumbing of the foreshore will be a costly exercise, consumers will pay. It is their dirty water and detritus being flushed down the pan into the sea. Water authorities accept they will pass the cost on and are only limited in making the renovations by government restrictions on their spending and borrowing.

With drinking water, the polluter will be charged differently. Existing law allows water authorities to fine farmers who tip silage into rivers: it is a criminal offence. The causal link between fertiliser spread on the soil by the farmer and the subsequent pollution of water from the tap is less obvious, though accepted. Getting the farmer to pay will not be easy: the National Farmers Union and the Ministry of Agriculture are resisting a levy on fertiliser sales. The FOE backs a levy 'not as a consumption limiter; it should be an important redistributive mechanism'. It also wants it non-deductible by farmers against other taxes.

FOE claimed in April 1988 that the Cabinet Office had set up a working group of DoE and MAFF officials to find a compromise. It said MAFF was insisting that farmers with land in the planned water protection zones should be compensated for any lost profits. It was not the first time MAFF had tried this ruse. In late 1986 William Waldegrave, the Environment Minister, had resisted the move because it breached the polluter-pays principle. He likened it to compensating polluters. Splitting the cost between farmers and water authorities is the likely outcome.

The authorities are against paying for the farmers' pollution and will put the ball back in the farmers' court with a study of farm waste in mid-1988. A government decision to get water authorities to pay, and hence put up their charges, could be contrary to the polluter-pays principle: nitrate pollution is clearly caused by intensive farming. Environment groups may complain to the European Commission again. UK government believes it would be too much of 'a general point on which to base a European court case'.

The UK government has been criticised for not complying with existing directives and for blocking future ones. Partly this is the fault of the directives themselves, which were agreed ambitiously in the 1970s or early 1980s without much analysis of how they would work in practice or their cost. The UK also says it has never been taken to court over an environment directive, a fate which has befallen a number of other governments. Between 1983 and 1986 the only court judgement in the environment field was one against Belgium in 1986 over non-compliance with a toxic waste directive. In 1987 there were at least four judgements involving directives on pollution.

Table 9.5 **Breaking of environment laws – the dirty men of Europe**

	water	air	waste	chemicals	nature	noise	total
Belgium	9	–	10	7	3	1	30
Italy	7	2	5	8	4	–	26
Greece	5	3	5	2	1	1	17
Denmark	5	2	5	2	2	1	17
UK	6	2	2	1	4	1	16
Netherlands	2	2	1	3	7	1	16
Germany	4	2	5	2	1	1	15
Luxembourg	1	2	6	4	1	1	15
Ireland	1	2	3	1	1	1	9
France	1	2	1	–	3	–	7
	41	19	43	30	27	8	168

(Snapshot of complaints being dealt with by Commission against governments at the beginning of the Year of the Environment in March 1987. Some are more advanced than others and include one court judgement not complied with. Some were close to settlement with governments introducing laws to implement the various directives. Other complaints were on the way: the UK's tally reached 22 by June 1987. Spain and Portugal were not tackled because they are new EC entrants.)

At the start of 1987 Clinton Davis, the European Commissioner for Environment Policy, warned governments over growing disregard of the directives. Each country was supplied with a long list of alleged breaches.

Belgium, Greece and The Netherlands had problems putting the laws on their national statute books and the port of Antwerp was polluted by carcinogenic substances; Denmark, Germany, Ireland and Luxembourg had failed to report progress to the Commission; France had too much lead in some of its air; Italy had a mix of problems with a row over a directive to prevent major industrial accidents.

Apart from the water directives, the UK had not completely implemented directives on cadmium and hexachlorocyclohexane, had no mandatory legislation on sulphur dioxide and lead in the air nor pollution by dangerous substances. It had failed to inform the Commission over alleged breaches of a directive on PCB waste from transformers which, when incinerated, had caused deformities in cattle in Wales. It had not told the Commission it had implemented the trans-frontier shipment of wastes directive of 1984. A year later, many of these infringements remained, the Commission said.

Tougher policing of the environment directives by the Commission is limited by its staffing. Governments are reluctant to increase numbers and sanction a plan for EC inspectors to supplement national environmental health officers. UK officials say the government was 'inexperienced in negotiating' the earlier directives and 'not so much attention was given to the minute detail that should have been. We all know better and realise something that looks minor, such as maximum admissible concentrations (in drinking water) can have major policy implications. We now write these directives much better.'

By mid-1988 the challenges to the UK on water were moving towards a resolution. The government had accepted the argument, and it merely remained a question of setting the timetable for cleaning up effluent sent into the sea and organising measures to reduce nitrates in the grainbelt. The government was unlikely to risk a lengthy court case in the run-up to privatisation. Further complaints were filed with the Commission, some with a wider geographical coverage than others. Aluminium levels appeared to be one problem. It increased doubts over the values on the water authorities' balance sheets for privatisation.

The cost of meeting EC environmental laws is becoming an important input in the UK's privatisation plans. Plans for the electricity industry will have to take account of the £1 billion bill for a directive agreed in 1988 to cut sulphur dioxide and nitrogen oxide emissions from coal-fired power stations. Future shareholders will pay the price of meeting target emissions fixed up to the year 2003.

Industry, quite rightly, ought to bear the cost of its pollution. Pressure from environment groups via the Commission is starting to make that happen. It explains why new directives are taking longer to agree. In 1988, these proposals included cleaning up the North Sea and shipboard waste burning; cutting down on the chloro-fluorocarbons in aerosols and refrigerators which destroy the ozone layer; and exhaust fumes from small cars. Policing the measures was rarely considered by governments. It was to be left to the environmental lobby and the European Commission: EuroMPs began handing out do-it-yourself complaint forms.

10 DEVELOPMENT AID: POOR RETURNS ON A MASSIVE INVESTMENT

Help for the struggling African, Caribbean and Pacific countries is a worthy endeavour, and doing it efficiently is even better. But the European Community's efforts on this front have duplicated all the wastefulness and inefficiencies that it exhibits on its home ground. Contracts for development projects are handed out in a suspect way and go wrong in startling proportions. Up to ten per cent of emergency food aid arrives short on quality and quantity. When EuroMPs go off to an exotic hotspot to consider development policy, they do so with umpteen unnecessary hangers-on.

Millions of pounds are spent each year on highly-paid consultants to research the feasibility of capital projects and to monitor their progress. But despite a complex set of rules and tendering and vetting of firms, the choice of consultants is often no more than the first out of the hat: shortlists of suitable candidates regularly contain just one name. And when the European Commission backtracked on its removal of national quotas in choosing consultants, it was challenged by the UK government. The evidence of its move was plain to see, but the Commission claimed it had never taken such a decision.

As governments get down to considering the five-year allocation of aid from 1990 onwards, the debris from previous rounds of spending lies around their feet. Tea grown in a Madagascar plantation project was left to rot in the warehouse. In Mali, a drinking water project could not sell supplies because they were too expensive for locals to buy. A sewage plant in Senegal was out of order for over a year. The wrong equipment had been selected for a

Table 10.1 **European Development Fund – five-year tranches**

	£million
1971–76	620
1977–80	2,237
1981–86	3,440
1986–90	5,250

(Spending does not strictly adhere to the five-year EDF timespan)

Table 10.2 **EDF funding – 1986–90**

	£million	%
Germany	1,366	26.1
France	1,239	23.6
UK	871	16.6
Italy	661	12.6
Spain	350	6.7
Netherlands	296	5.6
Belgium	208	3.9
Denmark	109	2.1
Greece	65	1.2
Portugal	46	0.9
Ireland	29	0.5
Luxembourg	10	0.2
total	5,250	100.0

(Table indicates the contributions put into the EDF by governments for spending on aid projects)

hospital in Benin. Each time auditors visited new countries, they uncovered new abuses. Nothing seems to have been learnt from previous mistakes.

Peter Price, MEP for London South East, has led a campaign to boost the number of Commission staff monitoring aid for capital projects. He says: 'In international aid agencies you find that normally one-third of all projects are a complete failure and that one-third have to be put back on the rails. One-third of schemes are a success straightaway, with no problems. If you could improve the quality of aid, you could contribute more than ten per cent of the funds available. To improve the quality is better than an increase in quantity. Leading from that, if you have proper evaluation you can learn from past projects.'

The aid contracts from the £5 billion five-year European Development Fund up to 1990 follow similar lines to previous tranches of the cash, but there is more of it. Often the sums are added to loans from the European Investment Bank, owned by EC governments, or 'soft' loans from other development organisations, such as the World Bank. There are sixty-six countries in the African, Caribbean and Pacific (ACP) which are part of the scheme, with the first area getting the most money. The funds, while managed by a European Commission directorate, are not part of the EC budget but in a separate pot put up by the twelve governments.

Three main areas benefit: agriculture, transport infrastructure and the energy and mining industries. The cash is spent on anything from farm vehicles, fertilisers and pesticides to roads, ports, railways and schools. Just under twenty per cent of all contracts awarded are for feasibility studies, training programmes or works supervision. European contractors from the largest construction groups to the smaller specialist consultancy vie for contracts. The latest trend in spending is away from one-off projects, towards programmes to improve an industrial sector and including training.

Each year about 200 tender invitations are issued by the Commission, asking interested companies to bid for contracts. This figure excludes those contracts for less than £2.8 million which are only advertised in the ACP country involved. Contracts fall into three different types: works, supplies and consulting. A larger works contract to build a dam or a dock could rise to £30 million and involve a number of individual contractors. Supplies for fitting out buildings or for vehicles tend to be of a lower value.

The aim is for European or developing countries to get

the contracts. They have a built-in 'preference' or right to a certain proportion of contracts. Results show that ACP firms gain more than 40 per cent of works contracts, 16 per cent of supplies contracts but only 6 per cent of the consulting work. The expertise and more advanced skills remain the province of the developed world. Companies from outside Europe or the ACP have only ever won 3 per cent of EDF financed contracts.

Bidding for contracts is intended to be transparent and free from bias. Tenders are advertised openly and often ahead of their formal invitation. But lobbyists and those who follow the aid scene tend to know of projects before this. Details are prepared by ACP country officials or a consultancy they employ. Once published, contractors have four months for works and two months for supplies contracts in which to send in a bid. At the end of the invitation period, the bids are opened publicly by a tender board of ACP government ministers or officials and in the presence of the locally-based Commission delegate.

It is similar to the way you might choose a builder to add an extension to your house. Builder A will offer a cheap price but without the clever design and extra finish that more expensive Builder B offers. Meanwhile Builder C says he can offer a long-term financing route. Then Builder D comes along with a difficult-to-resist offer to build a garage at the same time. It is a tough choice. The only difference with EDF projects is a set of clear rules and their use of public money.

A first assessment will weed out bids not meeting the technical terms of the contract; the second will rank the bids on price. The assessment is handled in the ACP state by government officials, the Commission delegate and any consultancy involved in assessing the bids. Legally only the Commission may award the contract, and the delegate on the ground can only do this if he chooses the bid which is the cheapest, 'economically the most advantageous' and which is within the EDF funding earmarked for the project. Otherwise the decision must be referred to Brussels.

This is the admirable theory of the awarding of contracts funded by EDF money. The practice has not always lived up to these high levels. One early 1980s row involved Rush & Tompkins, the UK-quoted construction company, and a multi-million pound plan to divert the Amarti river in Northern Ethiopia with a massive dam. As with many large contracts, only three reached the final selection for contractor. Alongside R&T was an Italian consortium of three cooperatives, CMC from Ravenna, CRC from Reggio Emilia and CMB from Carpi, Modena. The third bidder was Boskalis Westminster-Baresel, an international construction group based in the UK.

The final selection of the winning bidder was the task of Kampsax, a Danish firm of consulting engineers. It had been chosen by the Ethiopian authorities but was paid for by the EDF. The Commission later said it was there to advise the Ethiopian government but that its assessment of the tenders was not binding on the Commission, which had the final say. When the three tenders had been opened in November 1982, R&T were cheapest at £17 million with the other two bidders £2 million and £3 million more expensive respectively. This was a major project with large sums at stake.

The crucial meeting to decide who won the contract took place in February 1983. The tender committee, with the Commission delegate present, examined draft and final reports from Kampsax which showed late changes because of the arrival of additional R&T documents, relating to financial guarantees. Evidently these amendments were not helpful to the UK group because its offer was rejected unanimously by the committee on its 'lack of technical and financial capability'. Clearly price was not the deciding factor. The Italians were asked to open negotiations on a contract. The other group was waiting in the wings to see if the Italians fell out.

The Ethiopian authorities were keen to do business with the Italians and a meeting was set for March in Addis Ababa. But both were in for a shock. The Commission, instead of agreeing with the Ethiopians' choice, ordered them to start negotiations with R&T. It had not been happy with the dismissal of R&T on financial grounds. It was a well-known group with a strong financial reputation. The rejection did not make sense. The R&T offer had been dismissed because the bid was made via its less-substantial Dutch subsidiary. (The reasons for this were never very clear.)

During the spring of 1983, a series of meetings took place between the Commission, Kampsax and the tender committee to resolve the dispute. Eventually the consultants were pursuaded that R&T was a financially sound operation though the UK group had to supply financial guarantees for its Dutch subsidiary. Initially the Ethiopians were reluctant and told the Italian consortium that the Commission was twisting their arm.

In June, Kampsax filed a report recommending that R&T get the contract, to which the Ethiopians duly added their name. The formal contract was signed in July and endorsed by the Commission delegate on the authority of the Brussels-based chief authorising officer. It was a sorry saga but European taxpayers were saved a £2 million bill.

The Italians, who were furious, later brought a legal action against the Commission for depriving them of the contract. During a hearing in the European Court of Justice, two experts in international contracting said that the guarantees from R&T amounted to a new bid because they were filed after the final date for bids. The Commission refused to release various documents and the crucial February 1983 meeting was never fully analysed. The court threw the case out for legal reasons: disputes of this kind are supposed to be settled through arbitration and not in the Luxembourg court.

The case of the Amarti Dam contract is the best documented of recent projects where international contractors have ended up attacking their competitors after a contract dispute. The legal precedent it set meant that it was unlikely that other such disputes would end up going to court and receiving the same unfavourable glare of publicity. It was a glimpse into the hard commercial world that accompanies contract negotiations. But it left many unanswered questions: had there been corruption? Had the Commission or R&T played the lead role in correcting the bidding? How effective had the consultants been?

A dispute in 1987 suggested that Amarti was not an isolated case. This time UK construction company Mowlem and a West German contractor, Frank und Held, were arguing over a contract in Malawi. Three or four more similar lucrative contracts in East Africa were said to be due and observers feared there would be tactical bidding. A Commission official in the EDF area had also gone to work for the German company and this raised anxieties of using his influence and knowledge to give an unfair advantage. Officials sought assurances that he was not involved in lobbying.

The Commission was concerned that the contract was 'pre-arranged' and that the Malawi government favoured Mowlem. The consultant's report also leaked out, leading to suggestions that Mowlem's bid was not 'compliant' and that the German firm was £700,000 cheaper. In fact there was little to choose between the two firms which were both ahead of the rest of the field. The Malawi government put Mowlem at the top of its list but the Commission wanted a second round run-off between the two to make sure the choice was 'absolutely impeccable'. It is an unusual practice but gets the contract awarded to the right company.

The second round put the German firm clearly ahead. It was 'substantially low enough to award to Frank und Held', according to officials. One comments: 'What the government wants is not absolutely relevant, what is relevant is what were the ground rules and were they being adhered to.' In this case, as in the case of Amarti in 1983, the Commission was forced to overrule the ACP government's preference and rule in favour of value for money. In this type of large construction contracts the Commission has to be alert to what it going on in the ACP country itself. It is a continual battle.

Lobbying is often intense and the system allows non-financial factors to play a role. 'Wild allegations' regularly flow when these large works contracts are up for grabs. Some come from the losing company, which is naturally feeling aggrieved. The system is not as smooth as it might be. Business practice in Third World countries is not as scrupulous as in Europe. The Commission has one safety check, through its delegate having to refer all decisions to Brussels, when the lowest bidder is not recommended by the government authorities in the ACP state.

One continual suspicion is that ex-colonial ties play a hand: France and Belgium to francophone Africa, the UK to its old Commonwealth countries and Italy to Ethiopia and Somalia. The British Overseas Trade Board carried out a study of francophone Africa and decided that there was no inside track for its old colonial masters – they were just bidding better. The British have been slow to move more strongly into Africa after their success in the Middle East. The Italians are better at employing local staff and have fewer expatriate supervisors. Margins in Italy are also more competitive because of lower wages.

(If there is corruption in overseas aid spending, then the finger usually points to Thailand or Indonesia, where civil servants are very poorly-paid and are on the lookout for a little extra. But those two countries are not in the ACP club and receive funds direct from EC coffers. A European Court of Auditors report made a stinging attack on spending on the two countries in December 1985 and over 'inadequate' files in the Commission in Brussels.)

Reports on how contracts have worked out on the ground are not impressive. Visits by auditors to scrutinise progress and to evaluate completed projects have covered considerable ground during recent years. Too often their reports show a dismal performance. The three most recent bear this out. In 1984 they visited eight ACP countries and found that feasibility studies had commonly underestimated actual costs. The civil engineering works for a power station in Samoa cost double the £2 million estimate. A road in New Guinea cost 68 per cent more than expected. These failings put the financing of the whole project in jeopardy, said auditors.

In 1985 the Court of Auditors returned to Madagascar, Kenya and Somalia to see if earlier complaints had been followed up. In 1980 it had found substantial underestimates in the cost of an irrigation project in Bura, Kenya. Remedial action had taken three years to implement and by then the problems had been aggravated. In Madagascar a project to develop the Andapa Basin was still being delayed by a shortage of spare parts and no action had been taken over the poor maintenance of a pumping station. The Commission answered it was not all its fault.

The auditors' report on 1986 looked at training and

trade promotion. The latest EDF spending was to be directed less at grandiose construction schemes and more at programmes, mainly in the farming field. At the end of the year about £300 million had been earmarked for training over ten years. Many of the awards sent students from the Third World to European colleges. This led to spending on expensive overseas training and underspending on training at home.

In Somalia, £1 million was spent on European training but a £32 million allocation for training coupled to development projects was left unspent. In Ethiopia, this trend led to an increase in spending abroad and a cutback at home on training for staff to manage the distribution of aid to famine victims. In Swaziland three students were sent on £7,000 a year courses in the UK and Italy, which were available at half the cost in the country itself. Another £700,000 was spent on training officials from customs, the national bank and broadcasting who were not a priority target.

European taxpayers who stumped up the cash had expected these emerging countries to develop new industries and their own prosperity. But each time, all the auditors could report was money wasted and excuses. Even the new types of spending plans – designed to be more cost-effective – ran into trouble. Training had been one area, trade promotion was to prove another.

The trade promotion spending that auditors examined in 1986 lacked coordination. More than £15 million was set aside but promotional events were not linked to those organised by other aid organisations to make the most of the spending. Nor did the Commission consider if trade fairs were the best way of sales promotion. The auditors said that specialist exhibitions in Europe were a better bet and would prevent products from ACP countries being submerged by Western products. A strategy was needed to tackle pricing in the marketplace and to ensure that quantities were available for export.

The sales representatives sent by ACP countries to trade fairs were criticised. These were supposed to be experienced but often weren't and did not even know the prices of the products. They spent their time collecting business cards to send back home to exporting firms. When

Uganda exhibited coffee at a fair in Trieste, it was not able to make any sales because its agent already held the monopoly over sales in Italy. Leather sellers from Mali and Niger did not have enough space in Paris to display their goods. There were last-minute withdrawals at shows where the Commission had not bothered to recover the stand booking fees.

As Tory MEP Price had predicted, a large proportion, as much as two-thirds of projects, went wrong or had to be put back on the rails. The audit visits certainly confirmed that a large proportion were not well conceived or managed. But was the Commission in Brussels prepared to play its part in improving its role? Price had persuaded the Commission to amend its 1986 budget and create seven new posts, including four A grade officials, to evaluate development projects. In March 1988 he complained that only two of the new staff were tackling this and five others were doing other work.

To force the Commission to play ball, he put down a new amendment calling for twenty-five new staff. It was a tactical move which paid off. Price said in May 1988: 'It had the desired effect and the Commission entered into negotiations. I had discussions at all levels in directorate general 8 (which handles development aid) and with Henning Christophersen (the budget commissioner). They will fill three of the posts this year and the other two next year so that within ten months all will be filled. It is a real success for the European Parliament and I withdrew my amendment for twenty-five posts.

'They confirmed in writing that this would not in any way be taken into account from other DG8 staff. They would not lose other posts in DG8.'

Making sure the Commission, the manager of aid projects, learnt the lessons of the past is hard going. The spending had been going on for twenty years and only now is systematic evaluation taking place. The unit will build up a computer database of past projects which will be available to those planning new ones. It won't mean similar projects are not carried out, but it will make sure the pitfalls on the way to successful completion are avoided. It was a start. Price said: 'Nine people in the unit is minuscule but it will improve the quality greater than the cost of it.'

Price believes that the Commission is no worse or better than other aid agencies in managing projects. 'It is roughly average – you get more publicity for failures from the Court of Auditors.' He believes that the Commission copes with fewer staff per pound spent than other aid agencies such as the World Bank or national aid agencies. But unlike the World Bank the Commission has been slow to appreciate the benefits of ex-post evaluation of projects.

The Commission, with the backing of EC governments, ought to review staffing levels against the expanding demands of projects and the latest techniques to manage them. Instead of taking on new posts willy nilly, staffing should be re-assessed from the ground up. The likely expansion of funds and more permanent footing of the EDF after 1990 offers an opportune time for this to be carried out.

The award of consultancy contracts has become an equally controversial area. Consulting contracts are a major attraction with UK firms, who make up nearly a quarter of the 4,000 European consultants who pitch for this work.

Putting all these contracts out to full tender would delay the award of a chosen contractor and cost the time of officials. This cost has to be traded off with the need to get value for money, through low-priced and competitive bids. It is difficult to get a balance and puts heavy reliance on Commission and ACP officials awarding contracts in a fair and efficient way.

Finding a consultant is like a house owner finding a surveyor or architect to design the extension to a home. If all you want is a basic service with no frills, you might take the word of your builder and hire the first surveyor he recommends. More in-depth inquiries would extend to friends in the local bar or pub. A better selection would come from searching out people who had had extensions built previously. As the cost goes up, you would want to be even more sure of making the right decision.

The Commission vets consultants by competitive open tendering or a restricted tender where it asks only a selection – a shortlist – of companies to bid. But in practice neither method is used as much as it should be. The first hard evidence that all was not well emerged in the form of a special report from the EC's own financial watchdog, the Court of Auditors, in 1985. At this time the Commission was recommending that only two or exceptionally four to six firms be put on a shortlist for consulting contracts. This cut down its own workload in vetting firms. But it soon became clear that even this level was not being met.

The Court examined 230 shortlists for consulting contracts worth more than £35,000 and awarded in 1983. It found that over 40 per cent of these lists contained just one name and only 10 per cent two names. 6 per cent of the shortlists included five names or more. It left less than 44 per cent of contracts with shortlists of three or four names on them. The Commission's recommendation to its staff was being widely ignored. In nearly half of the contracts, it was unrealistic to call the system 'shortlisting'.

The Court said that the Commission ought to monitor progress and completion of contracts more closely. It received voluminous details on some aspects but little on project progress. The *curriculum vitae* of staff used by consultants were not systematically provided and junior staff were sometimes used instead of the highly-qualified consultants proposed in the contracts. The final evaluation only consisted of a one to five mark from 'very good' to 'bad' with just a few lines of comments from the delegate on the spot. There was no blacklist of consultants to prevent their re-employment.

It was a pretty sorry picture. The Court of Auditors called for a computerised register to be introduced and more standardised procedures such as a scale of fees and thorough progress reporting. The Commission claimed its procedures were within the agreement with the ACP countries, and used this to duck a number of criticisms. It said computerisation had been under consideration since 1979.

Later figures suggest that large volumes of consulting contracts are still being awarded without full competitive tendering. In the fourteen months to the middle of November 1985, £79 million of funding was approved via the restricted – shortlist – tendering system. It represents a significant proportion, probably a majority, of all consult-ing contracts in the period. It included over £1 million on extensions to fifteen contracts agreed without any other firm being considered. The largest was an extension of £206,000 on a £130,000 contract for analysing ACP country debt exposure granted to a British bank.

Over one hundred contracts were awarded under the shortlist system during this period in 1985, though it is unclear how many names were put on the lists. But it is understood that only one company was suitable for the largest £322,000 contract and that the same applied to many more. In some cases shortlists of one firm were permissible under the Commission's guidelines because the contract value was less than £105,000. More recent figures covering 1987 show that at least 30 per cent out of £120 million of consulting contracts was awarded on shortlists of one. It was a level which 'stunned' even the officials in charge when they made the analysis.

Reforms have made slow progress. The computerised register began running during 1987 and all contract files must now include a computer printout confirming that a search has been made for suitable candidate firms. The 4,000 registered on the ACP/World Bank DACON system can be narrowed down to a manageable shortlist as the criteria are made more precise. But while the computer includes details on the firm's experience, further data on assessment of its past performance will not be installed until 1989.

And the system remains loose enough for specialised contracts over £105,000, such as for training, to be agreed without any shortlist. In this case the 'intellectual content' rather than price determines who gets the contract. Officials also claim that certain specialised contracts can be agreed in the ACP country up to £350,000 which also breaks the limit. It is high time that auditors gave the latest system the once-over. It is five years after their damning report and there is no guarantee that the latest system is running smoothly. Some consultants claim quite the contrary.

One lobbyist said in 1988: 'If there is only one firm on the shortlist I would ask why. But I don't always know. Sometimes people say, "Don't pursue that" and I say, "What is going on?" With a shortlist of say three or five firms, who are doing a good job, why (should the Commission) take a chance with someone they don't know? But I get annoyed with the Commission when consultants have done a poor job, particularly in West Africa. There is not a lot of scope for this unless the Commission gives contracts to firms without a competitive tender. You don't like to see one firm rising ahead of all the others.

'Sometimes a firm wants to be on a shortlist and Commission officials say it's difficult. The Commission will not publish any information on shortlists. If the Commission was forced by the Court of Auditors to give shortlists, I bet you would see peaks. You are going to see some people who are partial to particular firms: not one person getting contracts across the board, but each year you would see several contracts whereas most firms get one or nothing.'

But the UK claims the Commission has been involved in more systematic breaking of tendering procedures. It believes that UK firms could be frozen out of consultancy contracts through a quota system to share out contracts between the EC states. In the long term, it wants consultancy contracts to be awarded in the same way as the larger works and supplies contracts – under a full open tender system. In the short term, it is fighting the withdrawal of a semi-quota system. (Quotas are based on each country's share of EDF funding – see Table 10.1 at the start of this chapter.)

Until June 1983, consultancy contracts were on a full quota system and awarded according to the level of contributions by the EC countries to the EDF. Then the system was changed so that 18.25 per cent of consultancy contracts were put out to open tender with the remainder still subject to national quotas. It does not sound a large proportion, but in practice it allowed the UK to take up much more of its natural share in a market it dominates.

But in March 1986 the Commission re-imposed full quotas, arguing that the previous system 'could not be regarded as satisfactory'. Of the five-year tranche of ACP cash to the end of 1985, £200 million went on consulting. At that stage the league table showed Germany with 23 per cent, the UK with 18 per cent and France with 17 per cent. The fourth large EC state, Italy, had 10 per cent with The

Netherlands on 9 per cent. (The two other types of contracts, works and supplies, where tendering was fully open, showed ACP countries getting 42 per cent of works, followed by France with 23 per cent, Italy 10 per cent and UK 9 per cent. On supplies UK, France and Germany were in the 20 per cent region.)

The UK was quick to complain. Lynda Chalker, junior Foreign Office minister, told other governments in April 1986 that the experimental tender scheme had been a step towards full liberalisation. The latest move was 'a step backwards', she said. The UK's EC ambassador sought clarification from Commission officials but was rebuffed. It was unclear exactly how the latest system was operating, though there was to be no discrimination on shortlists. The Commission said: 'It is only in the second stage that the Commission introduces the consideration of the distribution of contracts between candidates from different member states.'

When countries had reached their quota of contracts, then their firms stood no chance of being selected. It meant that it was pretty pointless trying to get shortlisted in the first place. And by the middle of 1988 there were some indications that the UK was being ruled out of contracts with spending on the latest five-year plan scarcely underway. But the UK levels gave an indication as to why the Commission had reacted. By the beginning of 1988, more than 30 per cent of contracts were going to the numerous UK consultancies. Under a quota system, in line with its contribution to funds, the UK share would be around 17 per cent.

The Commission refuses to explain its decision in response to legal proceedings taken by the UK government before the European Court of Justice. It says that legally speaking there is 'no such decision' because it has not been taken by the full college of seventeen European Commissioners. The UK says all governments were told of the move at a meeting of officials on 6 March 1986. The Commission says the new rules are 'only part of a number of elements' in a series of 'flexible' criteria. There are no quotas, only 'nationality targets or guidelines'. The UK accused the Commission of 'holding up' a settlement.

The Commission has adopted a legal-style reminiscent of *Alice in Wonderland* to rebuff the UK complaint. Decisions weren't decisions and criteria had become 'flexible'. It was the sort of argument beloved of civil servants and public sector lawyers. It left the consultants, who were eager for work, fuming on the sidelines. The Dutch government backed the UK's case and the Italians opposed it alongside the Commission.

In September 1988 the UK case was thrown out by the court on grounds of admissibility – it agreed with the Commission that no formal decision had been taken and only 'an intention' had been announced. To bring a soundly-based case the UK would have to find a contract where it had been frozen out of contention. Until then it was lumbered with the 'decision'. The UK is unlikely to take the case further and believes its point was clearly made and supported in earlier hearings. An opinion in June from the court's advocate general had suggested a UK win. The Commission had clearly escaped on a technicality.

A full-scale review of the way that consulting contracts are awarded is needed. The Commission's attempt to achieve the aim of quality contractors with restricted tendering fails on both counts: there are widespread doubts about the quality of the work even with its European origin; and despite cutting down on the number of firms bidding, the Commission's procedures still involve fifteen stages of vetting. And regardless of the checks the system still relies too heavily on the 'ethical' performance of the official. The review should focus on reducing the checks and putting them in places where they act effectively.

But EC aid to the Third World does not just come in the form of funding for capital projects and consulting. There is also food aid. Many ACP countries are very under-developed and unable to cope with short-term disasters such as floods, famines and earthquakes. They require quick assistance to cope. The European Parliament's close alliance with the aid movement and its championing of Bob Geldof's Live Aid pleas for Ethiopia put EC food aid centre-stage.

But the Commission has practical difficulties delivering up to £500 million of food aid a year. There have been complaints that shipments sent to Ethiopia, Somalia,

Mozambique, Kampuchea, Thailand, China and many other countries are arriving short, in poor quality and badly packed. It led to reforms in January 1987 with the details of ten years of mismanagement following in a Court of Auditors report in August 1987. This covered deliveries of food aid since 1976 in more than twenty countries and those handled by the Commission's food aid disputes panel, which had dealt with complaints since a 1980 review.

Two directorates in the Commission handle food aid: agriculture and development. Both have responsibilities in getting the surplus stocks out of the intervention warehouses and to the Third World state. Coordination could be better and at one time the two directorates published different figures for the food aid shipped. Both needed their own statistics and 'harmonisation' was undertaken. Common sense would suggest a joint task force, but civil service rivalries persist.

The 1987 regulations aimed to end disputes over who paid transport costs, and for example, that milk powder was delivered with vitamins where that was the instruction, and that the powder was not stale. It aimed to stop butter-oil suppliers from substituting vegetable oil for butter and saving themselves one third of the cost of part of the manufacturing. This type of fraud had been committed as far back as 1976, the auditors explained. Quality checks were not good and deliveries deteriorated in hot countries.

There was some dispute over the scale of the problem when the auditors reported. From the total 8,000 'lots' of food aid in the ten years, 90 'deliveries' had been uncovered as 'unsatisfactory' during 1981 to 1985. But a delivery did not exactly equate to a lot and the Court said the 90 cases could relate to one or more consignments or between 200 and 400 lots. This suggests 2.5 to 5 per cent were faulty. But this too proves to be an underestimate since the 200–400 lots were from a five-year period and should be compared to only half of the 8,000, because these come from a ten-year period. This makes between 5 and 10 per cent faulty.

Press reports at the time lambasted the Commission for its incompetence and prompted Lorenzo Natali, the Commissioner for development, to write a letter to *The Times* spelling out the levels he thought were faulty. He

***Table 10.3* Faulty deliveries scrutinised by auditors**
(Based on 90 unsatisfactory deliveries analysed by the Court of Auditors, including 10 with two classified problems)

Problems with amounts delivered:

– one-off consignments	4
– chronic shortfall	5
– late replacement of earlier delivery	4
– costs wrongly paid by recipient	3
	16

Problems with type and quality of product:

– not the type ordered	4
– poor quality	19
– quality deteriorated in shipping	9
	32

Problems with packaging:

– unsuitable packaging	1
– fragile or damaged packing	13
– defects in packaging or handling	6
– defects in markings on packing	11
	31

Problems with time and place of delivery:

– delivery after date requested	8
– delivery after period of shortage	8
– doubts about delivery date	3
– delay causing change to delivery point	2
	21
	100

compared the 90 to the 8,000 and repeated his error in a parliamentary answer to a Tory EuroMP. Natali calculated a one per cent failure rate and said this was less than the two per cent reported to the Commission.

The dispute mirrors those over farm fraud statistics (see Chapter 5). The Court of Auditors refused to put a clear figure on faulty food aid deliveries. It said: 'The problem is not so much one of assessing how representative these few hundred lots are in relation to the 8,000, as of using this sample to analyse the reasons for the shortcomings and to suggest remedies.' Once again the Court missed the point that the pressure for reform would depend on the level of abuse. If only one per cent were going astray, then ministers could shrug their shoulders. But if the figure was ten per cent, then it was much more serious.

There were many other reminders of international farm fraud issues. The auditors detailed a litany of doubtful shipments where one aspect or another had gone awry. To anyone with a knowledge of the means to rip-off the EC farm policy in Europe, the results should have been predictable. The added ingredient was Third World countries with poor management skills. The conclusions told the same message: 'The greater part of the problems stem from the over-complexity of the regulations and practices relating to standards, responsibilities and guarantees in the sphere of food aid.'

The auditors were not wholly impressed by the 1987 reforms. 'The Court has made various recommendations, bearing in mind the present scattered distribution of responsibilities. The Court nevertheless wonders whether an even more effective way of tackling this problem might not be to set up, as a matter of priority, procedures which were simple and unequivocal.' The message to the Commission was clear – further reforms were needed. Either that or more deliveries would turn up in a condition that made them worthless to the hungry of the world.

The development field suffers from the same problems as the rest of the EC and its institutions – but in double helpings. Spending on aid projects suffers from twice the level of bad management and waste as spending on developing the European regions. If there is an overseas jaunt then officials, MEPs or auditors have twice as far to

239

go. And if there are personnel problems, then they are twice as intractable. One such case involved the headquarters staff of the European Association for Cooperation. Only years of litigation forced the Commission to accept them as its employees.

Another Brussels-based EC development organisation has found itself outside the jurisdiction of the European Court and aggrieved employees have found themselves in a no man's land between Belgian and Eurolaw. The Centre for the Development of Industry receives £5.6 million a year from the EDF to help emerging industries in the Third World negotiate sales and industrial ventures with EC companies. It provides consultancy to take practical European technologies to ACP countries. It offers a partly private sector alternative to straightforward project aid.

CDI has fought messy cases with two of its forty-plus officials. In the first, it is believed it paid out FB3 million (£46,000) in back pay and interest despite the Belgian courts refusing jurisdiction. In 1988 an official was dismissed by Isaac Akinrele, CDI director, in a dispute over relocation expenses. The official had claimed these expenses for both himself and his common-law wife. Akinrele queried the larger claim, saying the two were not legally married. He refused to listen to the official's pleas that he and his wife had been together for ten years and were accepted as married in their home country.

During 1988, the Belgian courts told CDI to accept arbitration as a way of settling the dispute as the official tried to claim his job back. There has never been any question of his competence. Other CDI staff claim the dispute is syptomatic of the lack of an employment code and CDI's five-year employment contracts. These run concurrently with CDI's own funding from the EDF and grant no long-term job security to CDI's experts. Staff claim it hits morale and hope that in the next five-year review, CDI's status will be upgraded and staff given a detailed set of regulations along EC lines.

Staff describe Akinrele's overall attitude to staff issues as 'feudal' but he refused to explain his decision on the latest dismissal or in general. It is understood that in the court case, he believes his only sanction against the official was dismissal and that there were no lesser sanctions. In a letter to the author, Akinrele wrote: 'I would like to tell you categorically that it is not conventional nor in keeping with the ethical responsibility of an international organisation to disclose personnel matters taken in confidence and trust with third parties.'

A second letter seeking more detailed information on the two specific disputes and suggesting that taxpayers' money was at stake received no response. It is unfortunate that international civil servants are unable publicly to put forward proposals to improve their operations. CDI offers the enterprise-type incentives that are popular with EC governments and ought to be encouraged. Instead CDI is on the defensive. According to one insider, CDI is 'bitterly resented' by the Commission which wants everything under its own roof.

The shape of the EC's future Third World aid budget will be decided in 1989, for introduction when the existing convention runs out in February 1990. One aim is the creation of a more permanent organisation with the policy options of cash and target areas remaining under five-year review. This makes it even more necessary that this review concentrates on creating efficient organisations that provide value for money. The quality of spending ought to be a priority.

Much of the discussion on future policies will take place at the joint assembly of EuroMPs and delegates from ACP countries. These six-monthly events have become widely criticised as jollies for EuroMPs. (Each EuroMP expects a regular foreign trip as a member of twenty-odd parliamentary delegations to countries or regions outside the EC. In addition MEPs claim funds for political group trips. About 80 per cent of claims are turned down, though this has not stopped Jean-Marie Le Pen, French National Front leader, making controversial trips to Guadeloupe.)

The six-monthly ACP events alternate between a Third World country and a European city. The trip to Arusha in Tanzania in January 1987 prompted some measure of reform. The target for criticism is usually the same: the number of interpreters and the use of first-class air flights. MEPs like to speak their own language wherever they are and this led to a reputed 127 interpreters and translators accompanying the 66 MEPs to Arusha. It was said there were ten linguists for two Danish MEPs and four Greek interpreters for a single Greek MEP. All three MEPs were said to speak other languages fluently.

Arusha was probably the nadir of these trips, with one MEP paraded topless before the readers of a Sunday newspaper as she sunbathed at the poolside. A specially organised charter flight was badly used, as instead MEPs claimed their right to a first-class flight. After the cheaper trip to Lisbon in Summer 1987, Lord Plumb, the Parliament's president, instituted reforms. At Lomé, Togo in March 1988, the number of officials accompanying the MEPs was cut to 101 of which 52 were linguistic staff. MEPs could speak in eight languages but only listen in four. Documents were only translated into English and French.

The cut in costs was less dramatic – from £450,000 at Arusha to £385,000 at Lome, or about 14 per cent. The same charter flight was on offer and attracted the same small numbers. Many MEPs began their trips early by visiting ACP states to see projects. One such trip uncovered a hospital in Benin with over-sophisticated equipment. Such trips are regarded as worthwhile by MEPs but many ACP delegates, who speak English or French, can't understand why further cuts on linguistic services are not made. They point to the much larger UN organisation with only six official languages and documents mostly in either English or Spanish.

The EC could easily cut its languages to two for these Third World jaunts. The opposition comes from MEPs themselves who don't like having their perks taken away. It is doubtful if just English and French would prove a restriction to their effectiveness. The other way to cut costs would be to hold the assemblies in Brussels. Just holding the assemblies in Europe would cut the MEPs' costs – mainly in air flights – to two-thirds of the present bill. Since a sizeable number of the ACP delegates turn out to be their countries' ambassadors in Brussels, there could well be a saving on the ACP side too.

Development ministers from EC governments have their own joint meetings with ACP countries. In June 1988 they jetted off to Mauritius for their annual meeting. In alternate years, meetings are in Europe. Journalists were being charged FB22,000 (£340) for the round trip. Governments were cutting languages to four or five – those from the large EC countries. Minor language interpreters began complaining that they were losing their overseas trips.

The humdinger of development meetings will take place when the next five-year convention is signed, probably in Lomé, in 1990. This will attract government ministers, MEPs, officials, and journalists. Part of this bill will come out of EC coffers and the rest from governments' own resources. In either case, a modest use of languages and the filling of charter flights by MEPs and their entourage would set a good example. It would be a fitting statement on how the next phase of development aid will be handled. It would say to Third World countries that they could expect sound management of quality spending.

11

MAFIA:
THE GROWING GRIP
OF ORGANISED
CRIME

With fourteen deaths in one week in Autumn 1988 the Sicilian Mafia was back in business with a vengeance. First to die was a judge due to hear appeals from mafioso facing long prison sentences. Next was an anti-drugs campaigner after an outpoken television condemnation of Mafia heroin pushers. Others to be shot were mafioso themselves as rival factions fought for power. The deaths came as the Italian governments in Rome pledged new resources to fighting violent organised crime in its southernmost region. It looked as though they were needed straight away.

Before this carnage the Mafia had appeared to be on the decline. Criminal investigations had led to large-scale trials and more were planned. Laws to seize the Mafia's massive investments in legitimate business had taken effect. A growing political consensus in Sicily and in Palermo, its capital, was another positive sign. But in the agricultural sector, where European Community subsidies are at risk, millions of pounds in Mafia fraud is still being uncovered. In public works, where national and EC aid is being increased, the Mafia retains a hold.

And the squeeze on the Mafia has forced some to set up shop in other parts of Europe. UK and West German authorities have both had to deal with Mafia villains and in the latter country it is a growing threat, exhibiting the same pattern of drug dealing and EC farm fraud found in Italy.

Carabinieri, bullet-proof double glass doors, metal detectors, two more protective doors, one of metal, and closed-circuit television check visitors along the palace corridors to the office of investigating magistrate Giovanni

Falcone. He is the hammer of the Sicilian Mafia and led the successful maxi-trial attack which put 338 behind bars in December 1987. He says the Mafia is active in drugs, gun running, construction and agriculture. Drug trafficking is the best known of its activities, but public works the most important, says Falcone.

He stresses the strong links which the Mafia retains in agriculture. 'There is not an old Mafia and a new Mafia. It is always the same as in the past. The power is always in the agricultural fields. Some of us believed that in the past, the Mafia achieved large power when it went into the cities and were introduced in buildings, roads and construction, and that is true. But the Mafia is always linkable with agriculture and its power is in the hinterdom, not only in Palermo and in the big cities.'

Agriculture has had long connections with the Mafia, which is originally a rural culture. In Sicily the areas around Palermo, the capital in the north west, Trappani, further to the west of the 200 kilometre-long island, and Catania on the eastern coast have been hotbeds of Mafia activity. The proportion of mafioso in any community is low – some studies of Calabrian towns suggest one per cent – but the influence is extensive. Sometimes those involved are not true mafioso, men of honour, but friends or businesses where the Mafia has invested its illegal profits from drugs.

Anselmo Guarraci, Socialist EuroMP from Sicily, says: 'In Palermo there were two or three big farmers who were Mafia men. There were other farms friendly or connected to the Mafia. And there were big farmers with no Mafia connections. All three types went after European Community subsidies. The big Mafia farmers organised cooperatives, as did the friendly Mafia farmers and there were also non-Mafia cooperatives. These operations were regular. There was no monopoly of EC subventions. Everyone had the same possibility.

'What is criminal is the Mafia overseas with drugs in the US. The farms and cooperatives ran the new businesses to use this money. The political struggle has determined that this is not normal and there is a big battle for the elimination of the Mafia in the world of agriculture. We have good results in the courts blocking this. Falcone has condemned large farmers from Palermo, Catania and Trappani.'

Guarraci says that in 1988 the cooperatives of small farmers do not complain of Mafia harassment. The divisions between cooperatives are more on political lines: they are affiliated to Socialist, Communist or Catholic parties. Where there is fraud, it is no different to fraud in northern Europe. The reasons were prompted by the situation in the market, a failed crop or the late payment of subsidies. Where the earnings from agriculture are particularly poor – as they are in Sicily – then this increased the tendency to defraud the EC.

Even the Mafia drug barons retain their links to Sicily. Falcone, the leading Mafia investigator, quotes the case of one 'big boss' who lives in Canada and Venezuela but maintains a cottage in a small Sicilian village. 'They are still linked to their native town but they don't live there. They achieved a power because they are always linked. That is the power. It is not only organised crime it is more psychological.' He says their home fields are still farmed and though they may be in another country, the mafioso are interested in new techniques of agriculture. 'There is still that link with agriculture.'

Falcone believes this farming is within the law and that no EC subsidies for production aid, price support or farm restructuring are being defrauded. The wine sector, where the Mafia was active for years, has been cleaned up. It is better controlled and offers less scope for a range of ingenious scams, he says. Hundreds of trials over the last 20 to 30 years have tackled wine fraud. Partinico, a town 40 kilometres south west of Palermo, was the location of a classic example which Falcone believes was controlled by the Mafia. The town took the national record for sug... consumption per head as volumes of wine were boosted.

He says: 'The wine sector was a problem. There were some regions of Sicily which apparently made wine. It was wine made with water and sugar. They called it wine and imported it to France and this was an activity controlled by the Mafia. There are a lot of trials in relation to these activities but we have finished some of the processes (trials). In Partinico the Mafia did not control this business directly. A big part of the citizens were involved, they were not necessarily Mafia men. But we are sure that it was controlled in its entirety by the Mafia.'

Pancrazio De Pasquale, a Communist EuroMP from Sicily, put the wider EC spotlight on Mafia fraud on its farm funds. In 1985 he made his reputation as an anti-Mafia campaigner in the European Parliament with outspoken attacks. The Communist Party has been in the forefront of the fight against the Mafia in Sicily and in the national parliament in Rome. De Pasquale was instrumental in getting the European Commission to examine the issue as the fight against the Mafia faced a tough test – the Italian measures were beginning to bite and the repercussions had been savage.

The Commission's report is not comprehensive and covers a mere seven pages. It relies nearly completely on interviews with officials from the agricultural and judicial authorities. It was carried out by staff from the Commission's specialist agricultural anti-fraud unit. After a visit to the ministry of agriculture in Rome they spent a week in Sicily talking to officials in the regional administration, the regional institute for wine, fraud experts, the Guardia di Finanza, which is the financial police, and the chief prosecutor.

Table 11.1 **Agricultural spending in Sicily**
(£million)

	1982/83	1983/84	1984/85
Citrus fruit	55	184	173
Durum wheat	35	38	37
Wine	48	59	112
Olive oil	16	42	21
	154	323	343

(Table shows the levels of agriculture subsidies in the main sectors in Sicily during the period covered by the Commission's investigation)

The report spelt out the sums at stake. The EC had spent £820 million in Sicily in the three years from 1982 to 1985 across the four main agricultural sectors of citrus fruit, hard durum wheat, wine and olive oil. They were huge sums and the level of fraud reported looked small beer by comparison, with only £6 million wrongly paid in fourteen cases over the three years covered. Citrus fruit, where 50 per cent of the spending took place, had suffered twelve cases involving £5.7 million (but like most EC fraud statistics, they had their limitations, as Chapter 5 has noted).

The Commission itself thought the sums were an underestimate. It said: 'The ratio of the amount involved in irregularities notified to aid paid may seem low for Sicily, but the figure is not a final one and is, as it stands, seven times the EEC average. Nor is it certain that all fraud to the detriment of Community funds has been discovered by the authorities, this being true for all the member states.'

Putting a figure on Mafia farm fraud is not easy and of uncertain value. It is not clear which farming interests are controlled by the Mafia nor that they are breaking any law, including defrauding EC farm cash. It is probably the wrong question to ask. The two issues of farm fraud and the Mafia need to be tackled separately in the EC context. Fraud on EC agricultural subsidies is widespread and needs to be countered wherever it appears. Measures must be tough enough to block the most devious schemes from organised crime wherever they operate.

Specific measures against the Mafia should uncover the source of their investment, such as money from drug trafficking, and disbar them from access to EC funds. Criminals who increase their wealth by investing in farming should not be able to get an extra return on their investment from the European taxpayer. There also has to be a check on the violent intimidation of the ordinary farmer by the Mafia wherever it exists.

The EC ducks the source of investment and intimidation issues as it ducks many issues that cut across its policies. Crime is not part of the Treaty of Rome. On farm fraud, it has a clearer responsibility to act. In practice, the two will be handled by the same judicial authorities and the Italian criminal code includes sanctions against fraud on EC farm funding. For the record, the Commission quotes Sicilian judicial authorities as attributing 'only ten to fifteen per cent of the fraud discovered in connection with schemes financed by the CAP' to the Mafia.

Much of the belated Italian efforts to tackle the Mafia and farm fraud in Sicily follow this pattern, according to the Commission in 1986. Guardia di Finanza inspection teams had been boosted by officers from other regions; citrus fruit intervention was surveyed by officials from a board drawn from different authorities; at least five per cent of durum wheat applications were checked against on-the-spot inspections; the 'sensitive' wine distillation was supervised by several government ministries; controls over olive oil also satisfied the Commission.

The conclusion of the report to the Parliament was optimistic. On the Mafia, it praised Sicilian officials for their determination and courage which 'has already yielded results: only recently there have been a large number of arrests and convictions. A priority objective for the authorities concerned should remain that of improving the reliability of the controls, the efficiency of the departments and the resources at their disposal. Several officials visited stated, however, that they were prepared already to demonstrate the effectiveness of their work to interested MEPs.

'The information obtained also shows that the impact of the Mafia on (EC farm) expenditure is less than was thought and that its main influence is on non-CAP areas.'

The Parliament's budgetary control committee, which monitors EC fraud, rubbished the report as soon as it appeared in February 1986. The conclusion – 'less than was thought' – was strongly criticised. There is no real back-up for this statement in the report, which appears to be based on interviews with Italian officials responsible for cleaning up the sector. MEPs said the report was 'of little substance, bureaucratic and superficial'. The report appeared on the eve of the maxi-trial in Palermo and MEPs wanted to know if there were violations of Community regulations.

The Commission stood by its report in 1988. On

wine, its rosy view had been upturned in 1987 by a European Court of Auditors report which lambasted the Italian controls, particularly in Sicily (see Chapter 6). On olive oil, where a 1984 Court report said fraud was running at 30 per cent, the Commission claimed controls were 'strict' or in the safe hands of producers' organisations. The setting up of a private sector-style audit agency proved this to be hopelessly off-beam (see Chapter 5). But the Court did not name the Mafia in this wider-than-expected fraud.

(The Court of Auditors or the Italian Agecontrol olive oil agency, claim they rarely, if ever, come face-to-face with the Mafia. One Agecontrol auditor says: 'We read in the newspaper that there is some involvement of the Mafia and Camorra (Naples version of organised crime), but we have never had any direct contact.' It is unlikely that auditors reviewing the books and paperwork would easily uncover it. Their tests are not geared to do so. The auditors are better at pointing out the environment in which it thrives, which is what they have done.)

The motives of De Pasquale, the Sicilian MEP, in pushing the issue are also questioned. Commission officials say they were political. Many believe his main aim was to discredit Christian Democratic opponents in Sicily. The older generation of Christian politicians has been linked to the Mafia. De Pasquale is no longer playing on the farm fraud issue. The Mafia has also been dropped from the agenda of the Parliament's budget control committee. Italian Communists have rarely played an active role in this committee, leading colleagues to question their interest in the quality of EC spending.

De Pasquale has since taken on the chairmanship of the Parliament's committee for regional policy, and in March 1988 welcomed Leoluca Orlando, the Christian Democrat Mayor of Palermo, to Brussels. The committee was considering two reports on renovating the historic centres of Palermo and Lisbon, the Portuguese capital, with EC grants and loans. De Pasquale later took Orlando and the mayor of Lisbon off to meet Jacques Delors, the Commission president. The aim was to put more resources into the centre of Palermo where the population has declined.

Table 11.2   EC spending in Sicily in the 1980s
(£millions)

	1981	1982	1983	1984	1985	1986	1987
Agriculture	9	5	3	5	7	4	2
Employment training	6	9	12	9	14	17	24
Regional aid	108	39	50	119	28	35	105
Small business	6	17	4	–	–	–	–
	129	70	69	133	49	56	131

(Table does not include the subsidies paid on crops; this agricultural spending covers improvements to farms or irrigation schemes; in most cases this EC money tops up national spending and only represents between 10 and 20 per cent of total public funds)

Palermo is one target for the greater share of EC regional funds that will be spent in Sicily and Southern Italy. The city population in the centre has declined from 130,000 to 35,000, though overall it has risen from 400,000 to 730,000 in the last 30 years. The aim is to shift the spending balance towards the centre again and L50 billion (£22 million) in loans was lined up by mid-1988. Buildings from Byzantine, Arab and Norman architectural styles have fallen apart with neglect, and one aim is new homes. Inner-city renewal is just small-scale funding.

Since 1983, anti-Mafia laws have forced bidders for public contracts, like recipients of national or EC grant aid, to be vetted. Each applicant must submit a statement that neither he nor any member of his family has ever been involved in Mafia activities. A similar control is made of companies and each are checked by the Sicilian prefecture against central computer records in Rome. If an applicant is on the Mafia blacklist then funds are frozen and investigations begun. Applicants may then face criminal proceedings.

Orlando has also introduced open competitive bidding for public contracts in Palermo. Those over L1.4 billion (£600,000) are published in the EC's Official Journal. Price uplifts during the contracts are outlawed and payments made on contracts completed ahead of schedule. The gains by tightening up on L320 billion of contracts between August 1985 and the end of 1987 were estimated at L77 billion by the brave Mayor of Palermo. But the reforms are not a complete guarantee that Mafia business has been eradicated from the public works sector.

The 41-year-old mayor admits himself there is still some way to go. Orlando said during his visit to Brussels in 1988: 'I am not saying there is not corruption. It does exist.' He hoped that market forces and money from Brussels would set Palermo on a new course. And the open tendering has also attracted criticism from genuine Sicilian contractors, who claimed that the influx of northern Italian companies was relegating their role to subcontract work. The large Mafia businesses were squeezed but smaller Sicilian firms were not being given the chance to grow. Forming consortia was one way around this.

De Pasquale, from across the political divide, joined Orlando in approving the strategy of open contracts. The Communist EuroMP said: 'The Mafia is not only in the public works sector. It affects all parts of the economy. In Palermo the public administration is fighting it with determination. The Mafia prospers in the dark where collusion is possible. If the public administration is open and vigilant as it is in Palermo, it is not able to prosper.'

The policy of injecting public funds to improve the economy of Sicily makes sense. A better standard of living and improved communications between the country areas and the city will go a long way to rendering the Mafia an irrelevant alternative to genuine economic prosperity. The additional closer integration of Sicily into the Italian and European economy will add to this effect. But as new money follows earlier tranches, the danger remains that the Mafia will take its slice on the way. Anti-Mafia measures will have to be strengthened at the same time.

The geographical position of Sicily cannot be changed but its links with the rest of Italy can be improved. The grandiose schemes to build a fixed link across the Straits of Messina have symbolic attractions and would replace the ferrying of train services across the ten-kilometre channel. Completing the motorway along the north coast from Messina to Palermo would do more to speed road freight and improve the capital city's connections. It is just one of a number of major public construction projects being planned, for which the vetting of contractors will have to be in place.

Brussels authorities are relying on national controls as they double spending on EC regional and employment training in southern Europe. They say that only a small proportion – between 10 and 20 per cent – of any project will be EC money. But the sums still amount to billions of pounds and this approach is foolhardy. Italy's central government has often welcomed EC pressure to tighten its controls in the face of domestic opposition. Given its sometimes shaky attack on the Mafia, a rousing call from Commission president Delors would, in this case, have more than symbolic value.

But poor communication links and infrastructure in Sicily have not stopped the Mafia becoming an international operation. The different 'families' or groupings have used Sicily as a staging post and processing centre for drug-running from the near or far east to the United States. The illegal fruits of this crime have returned to the Italian island disguised as payments for agricultural exports and picking up EC farm subsidies as an added bonus.

In 1988 Michelangelo Aiello, a former Christian Democrat mayor of Bagheria, twenty kilometres from Palermo, was on trial for his alleged part in defrauding the EC of export refund subsidies. He protested his innocence. It was just one aspect of a massive drug-smuggling operation which netted hundreds of millions of dollars in the US and led to trials on both sides of the Atlantic. The export refund scam was the last lucrative stage in the recycling and laundering of drug money which led to eighteen convictions in New York in April 1987 and further ones in the Palermo maxi-trial in December 1987.

The US case was dubbed the 'Pizza Connection' because cash from drug sales was invested in pizza franchises. Some of this drug-money returned to Sicily via tax havens in the Caribbean and Switzerland, to appear as payments for exports of fruit juice to Romania, Bulgaria and Lebanon. The exports themselves never took place. Falcone says: 'We found it when we searched for evidence of drug trafficking. This evidence was not useful to us at the beginning. The exports were covered by payments from Switzerland and from accounts with dirty money.

'That is the charge and we have sequestered a lot of money. And on the side, they were refunded with taxes (subsidies). This is part of a large Mafia association. This is one of the aspects that links with drug trafficking.'

On the surface, the exports made some sense – payments do not always come from the country where the produce is delivered. But international inquiries, including contacts in the UK, proved the consignments to be non-existent. The choice of countries in the Eastern Bloc or at the centre of civil war had its purpose in disguising this. Lebanon has been used in other EC farm frauds to provide forged certificates of delivery (see Chapter 5). Falcone says: 'The problem was to ascertain the origin of the money. It did not come from the buyers of the produce but from the US.'

The added ingredient in this scam was the claim for EC export refund subsidies. It was the icing on the cake of a sophisticated and ingenious illegal operation. To Falcone it comes low on his priorities in tackling the Mafia despite 'millions of dollars' at stake. In one year alone, the fraud is believed to have cost £4.5 million. He says: 'It is very difficult and takes a very long time to ascertain these frauds. And the more deeply you search the evidence, the more sophisticated they become. They (the Italian authority which pays farm subsidies) did not understand anything.'

Falcone says this 'Pizza Connection' EC export refund fraud case is only one of many, though it is probably the largest. 'There are other cases being investigated. There are a lot of documents that we are watching and there are a lot of men who are suspected. We believe we will have evidence in there of similar cases. It is impossible to quantify (the size).'

These frauds on EC funds show once again that national authorities are not putting in sufficient controls or not applying the existing checks vigorously enough. Specifically, the physical checks that the quality and quantity of the goods actually exported were in line with the subsequent paperwork were found wanting again. Total checking of this will never be possible but a reasonable level of, say, ten per cent can be implemented. Together with additional checks targeted on larger consignments or known troublespots, such as Sicily, a much improved deterrent would be in place.

The European Commission's visit to Sicily in October 1985 and its subsequent report indicated that some targeting by Italian agricultural authorities was under way. It also believed that the judicial authorities were tracking down Mafia activity in the farm sector. But Falcone says he is too hard-pressed with fighting drugs and public works corruption to give it much attention. There is a clear need for greater resources, from the Italian judicial service, to fight Mafia abuse of EC farm funds. The Commission must press for this before international export refund fraud takes off.

But the Mafia is not confined to Sicily, Calabria or even Italy. We know from newspaper reports, from books such as *The Godfather* and the Pizza Connection case, that this form of organised crime has spread to the US. Less well-known is its spread through Europe. Falcone confirms that in the UK, several Mafia men were successfully convicted in 1985 as part of an international drug trafficking operation. He adds: 'Germany is now very concerned about this problem and I think they are right, because there are several Mafia men in West Germany. Now they are concerned. In the past they did not care.'

German local and federal police tend to dismiss the claims of Mafia in their midst. They say they cannot tell if Italian criminals are Mafia or not. 'The Mafia does not issue membership cards', one spokesman said. Crime is dealt with wherever it appears and whether it is carried out by Italians, Turks, Chinese or Germans. But robberies and extortion by Italians have been recorded in southern Germany and these are Mafia-style operations. One federal police spokesman admitted: 'I think that Mafia members are trying to extend their business across the Italian borders into Germany.'

But in September 1988 the German Interior Ministry went public about its fears, though without mentioning the Mafia by name. The police spokesman commented: 'What the Ministry published was concern about organised crime, not in the US sense of the word and not organised crime in the Mafia sense with payments for judges, lawyers, ministers and high officials. There is very serious concern that it does not get to that stage.' Federal ministry data suggests that its concern, based on wider evidence, is greater than among police on the ground.

As in Italy the main Mafia activity involves the supply of drugs, but with some interest in the agricultural field through international trade. Some of the mafioso in Germany already face charges and arrest if they return to Italy. They are based in the south of Bavaria and Baden-Wurttemberg around the cities of Munich and Stuttgart and have bought into legitimate businesses. In some companies the directors remain German and went without suspicion for some time. Elsewhere the violent activities of protection for shop or bar owners and the trade in heroin and other narcotics was more obviously criminal.

By 1988, German prosecutors had begun up to 40 separate proceedings involving a number of firms and up to 100 people altogether. And with the Mafia often operating in the shadows behind legitimate business, experts suspected there was much more still to be uncovered. One investigator said: 'Many professional crime people in Germany, including those in the Ministry of the Interior, said we will never have Italian style crime here. This has already proved to be wrong for the south of Germany. A couple of years ago this was a widespread opinion. Now it is difficult to make a prognosis.'

Seizures of drugs have varied from DM350 million (£110 million) to DM5 million. The frauds on EC funds so far uncovered are much smaller – in the range of DM20,000–100,000 (£6,000–£31,000). Of the 40 proceedings, it is reckoned about a quarter involve agricultural fraud spread between Stuttgart and Munich with maybe two in Bavaria. The total of EC funds at stake is estimated at DM2 million (£625,000).

Cattle fraud has been the major Mafia scam in the German agricultural sector. Exports have been faked or there have been mis-declarations of the number of cattle or their ages. In one case, cattle were bought by a Swiss firm, outside the EC, but stayed there only a day before carrying on into Italy. This gained the German exporter an EC export refund subsidy for the declared export to Switzerland. An export to Italy would only gain a much less valuable EC monetary compensation amount. The imports into Italy carried paperwork showing a purchase in Switzerland or other faked documentation.

It is also believed that more than one of the cases involved the corruption of a customs official. This would not be the first time that transiting goods through Switzerland to Italy to coin an EC export subsidy had been tried with some connivance from a Customs official. (Nor is the corruption of customs officials the preserve of southern European states. The UK may like to think it could never happen on its patch but Customs and Excise faced its own corruption scandal in 1988, though it did not involve the Mafia.)

And does the Mafia influence the EC's own machinery in Brussels? Some UK Tory EuroMPs have claimed it does but have no evidence to back it up. One claims that the management of the wine sector (see Chapter 6) suggests that Commission officials are in the pay of Mafia. But he admits he is 'talking generalities. I have not been into the specifics.' Commission officials are wide open to manipulation from anybody from the Italian government to the West Bromwich Widgetmakers Association, but there is no evidence of specific organised crime *payola*. Most experts, including Falcone, dismiss it.

More often the finger has pointed at Salvatore Lima, a popular Christian Democrat MEP from Sicily. He is a former head of the Office of Public Works in Palermo in the 1950s and later became City mayor and member of the Italian parliament. His name cropped up again in 1988 in allegations made by a mafioso turned informant. Falcone says: 'There has never been a judgement against him. He has been talked about for lots of time. It was not serious enough to invoke (his immunity).' (European Parliament immunity prevents criminal actions against its members unless the Parliament votes to waive this wide-ranging get-out.)

Uncovering the Mafia and keeping up with its latest tricks requires dedicated efforts. In April 1988 there were new swoops on Mafia drug activity in what some observers nick-named 'Pizza Connection 2'. The hunt was on for heroin refineries in Sicily and Calabria as a drug trafficking swap of US cocaine for Italian heroin cut the need to launder profits. In any case the latest wheeze for recycling dirty money was on the starting blocks: art treasures, such as pre-Christian sculptures, were being illegally dug up in Sicily and sold to US collectors.

Perhaps art relics will replace non-existent farm exports as a cover for money laundering. It would at least end the claim on EC subsidies. In Sicily itself, a major trial in 1988 was to tackle Mafia control of water supplies to farmers in the Palermo area. A number of Mafia bosses were in the frame for theft and misuse of water, which is state property. Water in sun-soaked Sicily is a precious commodity to farmers and the level was raised and lowered at Mafia whim. (The EC wasted £100 million in regional grants on water projects in Sicily but a Mafia role was never established.)

In August 1988 Falcone, the most dynamic and high-profile of six anti-Mafia magistrates in the fifteen-man pool of investing magistrates in Palermo, threatened to resign. Falcone had earlier been passed over for the job of chief investigating magistrate and clashed with Antonio Meli who got the job. Plans for three more sizeable trials in 1988 were side-tracked as prosecutors and judges fought over their own tactics. Ciriaco De Mita, the Italian Prime Minister, called on Falcone and other wavering colleagues to stay as the government's resolve to fight the Mafia wavered yet again.

In September Falcone's stand and the pleas for central government support in the anti-Mafia fight were heeded. Domenico Sica, Italy's top terrorist investigator was drafted in alongside secret service operatives. Even he was shortly to note that dealing with an estimated 20,000 mafioso and their sympathisers might prove more trouble-some than the tight knit Red Brigade terrorist cells he brought to book. It was clearly going to be a long job fighting the Mafia.

Before the upsurge in violence in Autumn 1988, many Sicilians believed the Mafia to be 'on the defensive' if not beaten. Others argued the fight was reaching its most crucial test as corruption among the politicians and the public works sector is rooted out. Many ordinary people believe it does not touch them and are uninterested by strident anti-Mafia propagandists. Violence on the streets of Palermo had subsided from its peak in the early 1980s. But the threat remains and a new modern prison is being prepared to replace the Aulo Bunker by the port. The fear, as some Mafia men get early release on health grounds, is that the cycle of violence will be repeated.

12 1992: WHY THE SINGLE MARKET WON'T WORK

The European Community is aiming to become a single trading bloc by 1992. It is the one policy which will dominate over the next four years. Governments, European commissioners and officials wax lyrical over the boost it will allegedly give industry and the economy. They say that by the end of that year the conditions will be in place to promote growth, trade and a new technological era. Instead of frontier barriers, red tape and nationalistic preference, consumers will be able to buy the latest high-tech products at similar prices from fit and hungry European companies in any of the twelve countries.

But is the EC really going to shake off the years of dead-hand bureaucracy, lawbreaking and political jockeying overnight – or even in the eight years it has given itself to put 300 detailed policy proposals in place? And will the measures work and produce the claimed £150 billion in savings for industry and up to five per cent extra growth? Will people as well as lorries speed through Customs posts? Or will it merely hand US and Japanese companies juicy markets on a plate? The negative aspects are being dismissed but job losses in the short term could be severe, as the prospect of EuroThatcherism is sold hard.

Even the UK with its pro-business government is reluctant to follow some aspects of the EC's free market rulebook. Its interpretation of VAT law has prompted a series of claims. Its defeat on zero-rating of industrial buildings for VAT will cost over £150 million a year and a large chunk of the 1989 Budget law to put right. Its unwillingness to go along with a plan to simplify the way

VAT is levied on exports will slow down commercial traffic with the rest of Europe.

Let's take one industry to see if this latest attempt to form a European market-place will take off. Telecommunications is a sector expected to be number one by size by the year 2000. The Commission and its 'cost of non-Europe' studies make great play of the opportunities here as new technology comes on stream and phone companies – PTTs – are deregulated. It has ambitious plans to take away their extensive control over terminal markets and to provide services such as telex and data transmission. With the opening of public sector buying, further integration into a single European market-place ought to take place.

The progress so far is disappointing. A 1984 recommendation to put ten per cent of PTT contracts out to Europe-wide tender was widely ignored. First there was a problem over the way governments would report the results to the Commission, then no one could agree what the results meant and finally the figures were buried altogether. Because of this failure, the Commission has resorted to a binding directive to open PTT buying in phases. The threat of court action was also necessary to permit suppliers of terminals, such as phones, fax machines and modems for personal computers, to break the PTT monopoly.

PTTs, particularly those in Germany, Italy and Belgium, proved a hard nut for the Commission and its competition commissioner, Peter Sutherland, to crack. Lengthy approval procedures remain a technical barrier to foreign suppliers of equipment after the monopolies were dismantled. Even the privatised British Telecom has been criticised on the time and cost of certifying equipment for connection to its network. Eventually the Commission applied a little used, but draconian, power to issue a directive off its own bat to free the market. Governments were furious and told the Commission not to do this again.

Europe-wide specifications, or standards, are at the heart of making the 1992 philosophy operate in the telecoms sector. It ought to stop each country's national telecom manufacturer spending billions on research and development on its own unique equipment. Instead companies will scale-down these costs, perhaps merge to save more costs, and sell longer production runs of telephone exchanges or handsets to a much larger market place. But so far progress is slow in agreeing these standards despite a 1986 recommendation to do so backed by the twelve governments. Putting this in place is already a year behind schedule.

In 1988 the Commission was pondering the best way of putting the next generation of telecoms back on track. New digital services, which will replace existing equipment and operate more like computer systems, face being bound by national barriers. It is expected that voice traffic will still flow between countries, but prospects for sending a high-speed fax or an electronic message from one European country to another are looking distinctly gloomy.

It is unlikely that the plug to connect the phone or terminal to the wall will be the same throughout Europe. In the face of Commission opposition, there are two European specifications for the material for the plug. The electrical connectors themselves are the same but there is a lightweight plastic type and a more rugged 'German-type'. One is all right for irregular use, the other is good for 10,000 times. So long as countries do not oppose terminals with the cheap plug, then there is no problem. But once countries insist on the 'German' plug, then there is a new barrier.

It sounds a bit like the electric plug saga all over again where the UK remains in a minority of one for good historical reasons – it decided on three-pin before joining the EC. One simple way round the telecom terminal issue is a simple 5p adaptor. If the Germans insist all equipment carries their tougher plug, then the Commission may take them to court. But in any case, the latest generation of equipment is only due to arrive in any quantity in 1989.

And the hidden strategy of the Commission, if not the PTTs, is to jump from this generation to the next as soon as possible. The so-called narrow-band digital system is so late and so badly planned that the EC is already pumping hundreds of millions of pounds into satellite and optical technologies. It is a high-risk gamble but has the possible advantages of catching up with the Japanese on high-definition television – the consumer revolution of the 1990s. Television manufacturers from across Europe are already cooperating on the R and D and common HDTV specifications look a realistic possibility.

Closely-allied EC rules on satellite transmissions, agreed in 1986, have also been breached – or at least in spirit. Commission officials had hoped that all future direct satellite television broadcasts would follow an advanced – MAC – specification as a forerunner to HDTV. But Rupert Murdoch, the press and television magnate, has decided his latest channel will only comply with the old-fashioned PAL-type of television emmission. His satellite is not covered by a government-agreed directive. The Commission can huff and puff but the EC is to blame – its directive has a gaping loophole.

The test of the telecom and television strategy, like the rest of the 1992 package, will come through taking on and beating the Japanese and US economic challenge. The era of excuses and anti-dumping duties – trade measures to counter alleged Far Eastern sales below cost – will be over. The protectionism and its cursory scrutiny from the Court of Justice will be found out. Europe will have to prove itself with cheap and efficient technology and the business nous to sell effectively. It will first have to do this in its own backyard.

The Treaty of Rome encourages the free movement of goods around the EC countries, subject to limited safe-guards, and ought to guarantee exporters easy access to European markets. International markets such as Japan may be regularly shut off by insuperable barriers, but the EC ought to be easy meat for its own club members. Not so. Each year the Commission investigates 1,000 cases where trade in the EC is being slowed or stopped altogether by national trade barriers. 300 of the complaints come from industry itself, some from EuroMPs and the rest uncovered by the Commission as part of its regular monitoring.

The bulk of complaints 'related to national rules which made the sale of goods, domestic and imported, subject to technical and quality requirements concerning such things as composition, dimensions, wrapping, name, labelling, performance and so on'. Various cases already

Table 12.1 Trade between EC countries
(expressed as a percentage of gross domestic product)

	Imports		Exports	
	1986	1987	1986	1987
	%	%	%	%
Belgium and				
Luxembourg	44	42	46	43
Denmark	16	14	13	13
Germany	12	11	14	14
Greece	16	17	8	9
Spain	n/a	(see note)	n/a	7
France	12	12	10	10
Ireland	33	33	35	40
Italy	12	9	11	9
Netherlands	29	28	40	34
Portugal	n/a	23	n/a	18
UK	10	12	7	9

(This table shows how much trade is being conducted between EC countries. The aim of the 1992 programme is to boost these percentages by reducing the barriers which prevent it growing further. No separate figures for Luxembourg are available, though overall it imports and exports about 90 per cent of its gross domestic product. Belgian-alone percentages are only marginally higher than above. A Spanish statistic for 1987 imports of 1 per cent appears to be an error and is inconsistent with other data which suggests a level above 7 per cent.)

taken to the Court of Justice back the Commission line that such legislation breaks the Treaty 'even if it has no discriminatory or protective effect, once its restrictive effects are out of proportion to its objective'.

Detailed statistics for 1986 and 1987 show the Commission acted against a range of trade barriers erected between EC countries. It acted where Greece had slowed down import clearance by restricting the number of customs posts for certain products. Maximum price regulations are also illegal under the Treaty and the Commission acted against national regulations on prices for drugs, cigarettes and biscuits. French makers of particle board had to have their products re-inspected before sale in Germany. The Spanish introduced an elaborate approval system for industrial goods.

The French had excluded franking machines made in another EC state from its market while Italy was refusing to register used buses from abroad if they were more than seven years old. Denmark was insisting on re-usable bottles for beer and soft drinks, Germany had put restrictions on imports of vermouth; the UK and Belgium had refused import licences for codeine, the painkiller. Sales of beer in swing-stopper bottles was barred in Italy. State aid granted by the British government was conditional on the Japanese recipient buying at least 60 per cent of its supplies in the UK.

The restrictions did not just cover goods but extended to businessmen providing services or employees sent to work abroad. The Greeks had nationality requirements for tourist guides, lawyers, architects, engineers, land surveyors, pharmacists, doctors and dentists. France did the same for land surveyors and valuers.

The list is a long one. In fact there are as many trade barriers within the EC as there are with the US. The US list, published each year by the Commission, includes items which have led to serious confrontation – multi-million pound trade wars. The list of barriers within the EC is more difficult to establish definitively but equally frustrating to exporters. The reasons range from protecting local jobs, preventing accidents and keeping grubby litter off the streets. In most cases a change will hit the public purse or put a national industry in the full heat of European competition.

Settling the disputes and removing the barriers involves lengthy correspondence between the Commission and the governments involved. These lead to European Court cases – more work for expensive lawyers. But a lengthening line of products, cassis from Dijon, France, beer from Germany and pasta from Italy backs the principle. If Germans want to drink Watneys Red, or

Italians want to eat pasta made from soft wheat, then that is their right. The products can be called 'beer' or 'pasta'. Health fears are dismissed. It is up to consumers to decide which products they prefer.

Many of these cases involve food where national or cultural traditions are at stake. Germans are rightly proud of the ingredients laid down by the centuries' old *Reinheitsgebot* law on beer. They are challenging another case where rival European sausage makers want to call a product a 'sausage' which includes soya meal. Defending Europe's heritage will prove a major challenge for 1992. The Germans will insist on very thorough labelling of food products either via a new European directive or further national rules.

And exporters to the UK have found a handy legal weapon to use when the UK authorities put up their trade barriers – usually in the agricultural sector. French turkey farmers in 1982 had successfully shown in the European Court that the Ministry of Agriculture and Fisheries imposed an illegal ban on their produce. MAFF claimed the French turkeys would bring a contagious poultry disease into the country. The restriction just happened to be imposed before Christmas and at the same time as UK poultry producers were complaining of imports.

The clever move by the French producers was to sue the MAFF for £19 million in damages in the UK courts. Their trade had risen from £650,000 in 1979 to £4 million in 1980 and was expected to go higher. The turkeys were clearly good value to the consumer and the French claimed loss of business between September 1981, when a ban was imposed, and November 1982, when the UK lifted it after the European ruling. Legal rulings have slowly established that ministers can be sued when they get things wrong, and the French won their case in the High Court in October 1984.

The government appealed and surprisingly won in the Court of Appeal in 1985. The case headed off to the House of Lords where an important precedent was expected to be set, one making it clear that the government was liable when it didn't respect European law. The MAFF chickened out. It settled the claim out of court for £3.5 million. The ministry suggests it got off lightly: 'It is considerably less than was claimed.' But most lawyers think otherwise and that the government was too scared of the consequences of losing.

EC law experts believe this area of law is ripe for further development and that the principle extends beyond agricultural trade though this is the 'high exposure area'. They suggest similar cases on financial services. If the UK government refuses a banking licence under planned EC directives and the bank successfully proves it is an unfair trade restriction, then it will cost the UK government dear. Lost profits from bankers tend to be a bit higher than turkey traders.

It may be one of the few examples where business can make up its loss from trade barriers. But it meant hiring the best legal brains, years of perseverance and expensive legal fees. Most companies expect doing business in Europe to be a good deal more straightforward. That is what many hope the EC will provide in its 1992 plan.

The Treaty of Rome in 1957 to set up the EEC should have led to just that – a European economic community. But in 1987, EC leaders happily celebrated thirty years of the Treaty without recognising their miserable failure. The grand names of post-war continental European history were invoked, but there was precious little analysis of what had gone wrong. One truth is that the EC had been side-tracked by just one industry – farming. As Richard Cottrell, Tory EuroMP for Bristol and Bath, said: 'The Community has spent the last four decades not on the building site of Europe, but in the farmyard.'

The appointment in 1985 of a strong European Commission team led by its president Jacques Delors, a centre-left former French finance minister, brought the economic community plan to the top of the agenda. (The Gaston Thorn-led Commission from 1981 to 1984 had lacked clear leadership, and the Luxembourger came close to not being re-appointed at the beginning of 1983 after his first two years. To be fair, it had a difficult start-up. The first appointment as head of his private office, a key role, had a nervous breakdown before formally taking on the job and his replacement was shot dead after just six months.)

The new impetus given to the single market policy was

set by Delors after he visited government heads during the back-end of 1984. It was one of four options he believed could be his four-year Commission's central task. Governments were less enthusiastic about expanding the EC into defence, strengthening the European Monetary System or major institutional reform. The first would have cut across the Western European Union and the North Atlantic Treaty Organisation, the other two would probably have meant taking power from capitals, and that is never popular.

When Delors shared out the portfolios among the then fourteen European commissioners (Spain and Portugal were to join a year later with their three commissioners), Lord Cockfield, the former UK Secretary of State for Trade and Industry, took the internal market and financial markets brief. Internal market is the inelegant title for removing trade barriers between the EC countries themselves. But whatever the title, Cockfield knew its importance and grabbed it by the scruff of the neck.

Cockfield is a man of wide experience. Courtroom lawyer before the Second World War, Inland Revenue commissioner after it, he was chief executive of Boots, the drug company, in the 1960s. He was also a cabinet minister as Trade and Industry Secretary. He set about laying his detailed plans with vigour. They would 'complete the internal market by 1992'. A timetable would focus attention. A white paper emerged in June 1985 containing 300 detailed measures that needed to be put in place. He had met his first deadline by having it ready in time for the six-monthly summit of government leaders in Milan the same month.

The paper was well-written and frank. It pointed out the EC's successes, such as the customs union, and the failures. It said progress peaked in 1977 with major VAT harmonisation. 'But thereafter, momentum was lost partly through the onset of the recession, partly through a lack of confidence and vision. The recession brought another problem. The Treaty specifically required not simply the abolition of customs duties between the member states, but also the elimination of quantitative restrictions and of all measures having equivalent effect.

'Originally it was assumed that such "non-tariff

barriers", as they are commonly called, were of limited importance compared with actual duties. But during the recession they multiplied as each member state endeavoured to protect what it thought was its short-term interests – not only against third countries but against fellow member states as well. Member states also increasingly sought to protect national markets and industries through the use of public funds to aid and maintain non-viable companies.

'The provision in the EEC treaty that restrictions on the freedom to provide services should "be progressively abolished during the transition period" not only failed to be implemented during the transitional period, but over important areas failed to be implemented at all. Disgracefully, that remains the case.'

It was all a bit of a mess. But the Cockfield paper said the mood was changing and governments were keen to try again. It then divided the task into three parts, covering the removal of physical, technical and fiscal barriers. In practice this meant ironing out the different health and safety standards for products from one country to another and tackling the distortions that different tax rates caused to trade. The paper admitted that the third – tax – part would be 'contentious'. Governments had given the Commission only a weak mandate in this field.

The Commission wants the frontier posts to disappear, and vehicles and people to speed through European borders unimpeded. Doing so means removing checks at borders for VAT, excise duties, the veterinary health of animals and plants, vehicle safety, quotas on lorry trips and collection of trade statistics. Many could be done elsewhere during the journey – via spot checks – or removed altogether. Laws on immigration, illegal drug trafficking and terrorism are mainly outside the EC treaty but the Commission hoped that governments would remove these from frontiers as well.

Commercial traffic may get an easier deal post-1992. Even lorries carrying livestock and crops will cross most borders without checks if officials continue to make progress on introducing inspections and health certificates at origin. For instance in 1988, the stamping of special transit documents by customs was cut to just on the

Table 12.2 Cockfield white paper – slow progress

	number of proposals in white paper	adopted or partially adopted	still to be agreed	still to be proposed
1. Removal of physical barriers				
– control of goods	84	30	14	47
– control of individuals	11	3	4	5
	95	33	18	52
2. Removal of technical barriers				
– free movement of goods	102	45	20	15
– public sector buying	7	1	2	2
– free movement for labour	18	7	4	2
– common market for services	35	12	18	9
– capital movements	3	3	–	–
– industrial cooperation	23	3	14	7
– application of EC law	4	–	–	–
	192	71	58	35
3. Removal of fiscal barriers				
– value added tax	17	2	8	2
– excise duties	13	1	10	2
	30	3	18	4
total number of measures	317	107	94	91

(Some measures have been withdrawn since July 1985 and others do not require governments' approval; those adopted are those up to September 1988; a number of measures have since been dropped and the number still to be proposed is 87, though it is unclear in which areas.)

entry-side of the border instead of on both sides. The main paperwork had been cut by customs simplification world-wide. And the EC's own much touted Single Adminis-trative Document (SAD) for standardised customs control had done away with 150-odd forms that were used in Europe before 1988.

But the SAD has its limitations. Some customs authorities don't use all eight parts of the SAD. This is not a problem for industry, which complained instead about the lack of SAD computerisation. Many large companies were already sending paperwork via computer lines and wanted to include Customs in their network. Only two or three EC customs are ready for this. Different thresholds also affected SAD use. Goods exported from the UK don't need an SAD if they are worth less than £605 and in Spain there is similar figure of about £200. But in Germany there is no threshold and all goods need an SAD.

In any case, the SAD is supposed to be only an interim solution. In theory it will no longer be needed in 1993 when customs at borders are removed. But international freight and transit will still need paperwork. Many importers, such as Japanese electronic goods suppliers are expected to put their goods into a single European bonded warehouse. This means that import duty and VAT is paid in the country of the delivery and not at the warehouse. It will require a customs transit document for all movements. The UK allows some companies to issue their own forms subject to financial guarantees. The Germans won't allow this.

Pure EC trade ought to move easier and without documents. But any international business will still face trade paperwork. DHL, the express parcels service, is one of the experts in dealing with customs. Mike Clifford, its European customs director and ex-UK Customs, queries the impact of SAD and future developments. He says: 'In

271

my industry we have made few advances which are directly due to the simplification of customs. We have had to manage the customs function internally to best advantage. No advantage was gained from the formal use of the SAD.

'My belief is that in 1992, we, as an express carrier, will have to be right on top of (our own computer) systems so that we can identify the status of goods from non-EC countries, countries with trade agreements, EFTA countries, goods on international transit documents and goods travelling on "nothing" because they are from full EC members.'

The prospects of car and foot passengers entering the UK via Dover or other ports unimpeded still don't look good. Drugs, the fight against Irish terrorists and the need for checks on the rabies disease make it unlikely that a UK government will dismantle these controls. This is disappointing given the ease of crossing Continental land borders. The argument over whether customs should do their inspections on trains going through the Channel Tunnel or set up a centre at Waterloo station in London is depressingly similar. If the Continentals can do it on trains, why not the UK?

The second part of the white paper tackled the removal of technical barriers, freeing financial services and professions such as lawyers and accountants. And 1992 would not mean more detailed harmonised specifications for products. To continue would be 'over-regulatory, take a long time to implement, be inflexible and could stifle innovation', said the Commission. A minimum level of EC-wide standards will be supplemented by mutual recognition of national rules. If a product is acceptable in one EC country, there is nothing to stop it selling in all eleven other states.

Harmonised European standards will only be set for strategic industrial products such as electrical, computers, telecommunications, construction and foodstuffs. And the details will be delegated to the specialised industry bodies which already handle some of this task, instead of forcing ministers to argue detailed points late into the night. They will only fix the outlines particularly on health and safety issues. The scheme also needs certification of products and officials are already drafting papers on how to fill this 'institutional vacuum'.

The aim of certification is worthy enough: to coordinate the work of national organisations so that European consumers can buy goods – from toys to telephone exchanges – bearing a label of good European standard. Buyers will ask if goods carried the label. It is a European version of the 'kite mark' of the British Standards Institution. The danger is industry being buried under a new avalanche of paperwork from Brussels. Certification has to avoid creating new quangos. It certainly needs watching.

Products meeting the European standards will be automatically considered for public sector contracts open to EC-wide tender. This sector accounts for up to 15 per cent of a country's gross national product. 'Public procurement' is a key element in the single market package and one which the UK enthusiastically backs. It means that public authorities from the state electric company to a government ministry will advertise their orders throughout Europe. Building power stations, roads, railways or supplying a computer to run a tax system will be open to bids from all EC companies.

The economic benefit from open public sector buying comes through more competitive and cheaper buying by authorities. With a European public sector buying market estimated at £300 billion, there ought to be lots of gains for everybody. But in the past achievement of this goal has been dogged by obstacles. Two directives agreed in the 1970s to open up a wide selection of works and supply contracts were ignored. One official drafted in to shake things up says: 'From the outset there was a feeling of cynicism in many quarters in the exercise. No-one believed in it and no-one took it very seriously.'

Cynicism led to just 25 per cent of contracts over £750,000 for works and £140,000 for supplies being advertised, instead of the stipulated 100 per cent. When the Commission queried the way adverts were drafted, a third of its queries were ignored. By the mid-1980s, only 2 per cent of public contracts were awarded to firms from other EC countries and 75 per cent were awarded to 'national champions' under tenders which the Commission describes as 'tailor made'. Other techniques to avoid the directives included splitting large contracts into smaller ones so that they fell below the directives' thresholds.

These fiddles stopped large parts of the public sector from becoming a single European market place well before 1992. The Commission believed that dragging governments before the European Court of Justice in Luxembourg acted too late and was counter-productive. More recently it has decided to make examples of Italy, Ireland and The Netherlands. The official says: 'The contracting parties tend to regard the Commission's intervention as arbitrary and unprovoked interference. Moreover, this ineffectiveness does not encourage contractors and suppliers to approach the Commission for assistance.'

The latest 1992 initiative has toughened up the two original directives, expands public sector buying to water, energy, transport and telecommunication services, and proposes stronger enforcement powers. Politically, some aspects are difficult because they may take business away from inefficient local firms – the national champions – and hit employment. And there are dispensations for depressed regions so they can still opt for a local firm under certain conditions. The threshold before works contracts are subject to full EC-wide publicity may also be set as high as £7 million after political pressure.

Enforcement of the latest measures will prove the key test for business selling to the public sector in Europe. Given the EC's dismal record with the two earlier directives on public buying, the omens are not good. There will be new but narrower loopholes to exploit. The Commission plans a directive giving it the power to intervene and suspend a contract procedure. If agreed, rules will also give aggrieved companies the power to go to local tribunals to seek remedies or claim damages for their lost bidding costs. The Commission is hiring lawyers in Brussels and national centres to police the plan.

Public sector bidding can be open to abuse. In the worst cases it takes the form of corruption within the public authorities. The Mafia has controlled the public works sector in Sicily for many years (see Chapter 11). It can equally be badly managed as the Commission's development directorate well knows (see Chapter 10). To work well, it will need tough policing and a commitment by EC governments at home, and in resources for the Commission's efforts. If it comes off, it will be a major factor in creating the single European market.

The Cockfield package also offered a new initiative for the professions. A single directive would permit a whole range of professionals the right to move to another EC country and put up their nameplate without starting their training all over again. Experience in agreeing individual directives for each profession had proved enormously time-consuming – up to seventeen years in the case of architects – and the Commission was not prepared to face that hurdle again. A global directive was agreed in two years and individual professions can still come up with their own plans – but only later on. Engineers are likely to do this.

But the agreement on the professions' directive showed how difficult moving between countries will still be. The first proposal would have meant an accountant or lawyer spending thirty-three years in qualifying for the other eleven market places. Only later did re-testing become an alternative to a mandatory three-year adaptation period. The UK played a delicate trade-off for its 150,000 accountants by insisting that those coming from abroad had to be 100 per cent re-tested. In exchange its 'exports' were part of a 'quasi-legal' profession and could opt for the tests instead of the lengthy adaptation period.

Other limitations emerged in the financial services sector, where the UK aims to do well and capture a large slice of the European market. Negotiations soon revealed the time it would take to free insurance, consumer credit, unit trusts, banking services and stocks and shares completely. The basic aim of the strategy is to permit operators that meet their home country controls to operate throughout the twelve states. An insurance directive agreed in 1988 set a long introductory period up to the year 2000 in the less developed countries. It also only covered policies for large industrial companies.

The flow of money itself is to be freed. Exchange controls and bans on opening bank accounts in another EC country will be phased out. Once again there is a transitional period up to December 1992 for Spain,

Portugal, Greece and Ireland. There is also a hiccup on the tax front, with France fearing the flight of capital to tax havens and seeking some form of automatic reporting to tax authorities by banks. It was a danger over which the UK, without exchange controls since 1979, was unconcerned.

Major monetary reforms are not part of the white paper package, yet their effects on creating a single European economy could be as great as the 300 measures put together. If a single, Europe-wide currency could be established, it would cut into the heavy burden on exchanging currencies and the risks of holding foreign exchange. Early 1980s studies estimated the pure conversion cost to business at over £1.5 billion a year, but added that there was a high cost of defending parities even within the European Monetary System. Those economies outside the full EMS, such as the UK, had the added burden of currency risks.

Consumer studies suggest that some of these estimates may be on the low side. Before the 1988 holiday season, the Bureau of European Consumers Unions estimated an alarming cost of repeatedly changing currencies. Starting in Brussels with FB40,000 (£615) and changing currency in each EC country, a typical traveller was left with only FB21,300 by the time he completed his journey. Clearly banks were making a good return on foreign currency. Business is not so badly hit as consumers and buys its money in bulk. The survey puts the issue in its starkest terms.

The third part of the paper covered the removal of fiscal barriers. Unike the first two sets of barriers, these were less clear to see. Physical controls were highly visible; and technical barriers were well-known to businessmen who couldn't get their exports onto EC markets because of petty regulations. But one fiscal distortion is reasonably clear. This is cross-border shopping to take advantage of lower value added tax rates. It takes place when the Irish buy cheaper Northern Ireland goods, and Danes do the same in the north of Germany. In the first case 23 per cent VAT played 15 per cent, in the second it was 22 per cent versus 14 per cent.

Table 12.3 European VAT rates

	reduced %	standard %	luxury %
Belgium	1 and 6	19	25 and 25.8
Denmark	–	22	–
France	2.1, 4, 5.5 and 7	18.6	33.33
Germany	7	14	–
Greece	6	18	36
Ireland	2.2 and 10	25	–
Italy	2 and 9	18	38
Luxembourg	3 and 6	12	–
Netherlands	6	20	–
Portugal	8	16	30
Spain	6	12	33
United Kingdom	–	15	–

(The table shows the widely different rates that countries apply under the existing EC VAT code. The French set as many as six different rates, while the UK only sets one. The levels also vary considerably from the 1 per cent rate operated in Belgium and the 33.33 per cent in France. The Commission wants rates to be set in two bands – a reduced rate between 4 and 9 per cent and a standard rate between 14 and 20 per cent.)

Many are unconvinced that fiscal barriers exist or believe that a free borderless market will do the job itself. The Commission has failed to produce convincing evidence beyond the cross-border shopping problem. The comparison is made with sales taxes in individual states of the US. Both Commission and governments have used this comparison to support their case. The Commission says that because tax differentials are not significant, American states don't suffer losses of revenue. Others argue that in some cases the differences are quite high but still distortion does not take place. It is difficult to know who to believe.

Similar plans to bring excise duties on wine, beer, tobacco and petrol into line have attracted even more ridicule. They would be costly to some exchequers and have major impacts on consumer demand. The EC has been struggling unsuccessfully for years on proposed directives to harmonise excises. The duties are used to encourage wine drinking in France and Italy and beer in the UK and Germany. Sacred pursuits, you may say, and the excise plans run counter to some national social and cultural policies.

The VAT and excise changes are part of an eight-directive package but one directive stands a good chance of making progress. It will have a major impact on border controls. This would end the system whereby goods that are exported are zero-rated for value added tax. Instead, all goods 'exported' to other EC countries would carry their normal national rate of VAT. This would be paid by the importer in his purchase price. If he is a registered business he will claim VAT back from his VAT authority. The UK exporter will pay over the VAT to Customs and Excise as if the sale was a domestic one.

This plan will prove a major and tangible benefit to European business. VAT is the major reason for having customs at frontiers, contributing an estimated 90 per cent of their financial take. At present someone who can't prove that he has paid VAT, by way of an invoice, is hit hard on importing to another EC country. Typically on a £1,000 product he would pay 15 per cent coming into the UK, plus duties of up to the same level depending on the product. Non-declaration – smuggling – would prompt a further penalty perhaps tripling the bill. The individual traveller suffers little of this because of his allowances.

Prospects for the plan are good though the UK prefers a return to an EC scheme which the UK introduced and then dismantled five years ago. This leaves exports zero-rated and makes VAT on imports only payable on account, a number of weeks after physical importation. The UK disputes the extent and cost of the present 'fiscal barrier' to trade and says it amounts to only a quarter of Commission estimates or about 0.1 per cent of gross domestic product. Once again the UK seemed out of line with its partners and it meant lorries would still require customs inspection on entry.

Earlier, UK officials had suggested the government was behind the full VAT-rating plan. One had said: 'The UK believes it is essential. But there are major difficulties in it.' Because of the arguments over the more radical proposals to VAT rates, this sensible plan received little detailed discussion until autumn 1988. Linking computer systems is a complex task and the Commission may try to set up a grandiose central machine in its premises to grab some of the glory. It has plans for techniques to trap tax evaders and to capture trade statistics.

Table 12.4   Car prices excluding tax for three models

	Austin Metro 1.0 Special £	VW Golf 1.3 C £	Ford Sierra 2.0 GL £
Denmark	2,560	3,751	n/a
Greece	n/a	4,167	n/a
Luxembourg	2,988	4,282	6,360
Netherlands	3,061	n/a	6,427
Belgium	3,067	4,329	6,360
France	3,296	4,439	6,516
Germany	n/a	4,473	7,077
Italy	3,420	4,925	n/a
UK	3,717	5,404	7,551
Ireland	3,894	n/a	5,861
Spain	n/a	n/a	7,614

(Ranked according to lowest Metro then Golf price.)

(These figures from the European Bureau of Consumer Unions (BEUC) compare manufacturers' list prices of cars in July 1987 and are the most recent available. By choosing only models which are directly comparable, the survey has gaps in a number of countries and no figures for Portugal. To buy a car adds further VAT of 14 to 144 per cent plus additional car tax in some countries. Many countries charge over 20 per cent in VAT and in Greece, where the system is 'very unclear' it pushes the tax inclusive price of a car up to two and a half times the price in the lower taxed countries. Cars bought for a quick export are usually tax-free until final importation.)

Nor are different VAT rates the sole reason for the price distortions between countries. There are many other factors to blame such as different government subsidies, company and property taxes or anti-competitive pricing by multinational companies. Many of these are against the Treaty of Rome. Again consumer surveys show that distortions on goods are much larger than can be explained by VAT alone. Buying cars in the low countries instead of the UK still remains attractive for certain models but tax is not the reason. Price differences are also narrowing.

An 1988 consumer survey of high and low European prices showed that pop music compact discs cost 71 per cent more in Denmark than Ireland, blank audio tape cost 94 per cent more in Denmark than Germany and that Greek compact cameras were 129 per cent more costly than in Germany. It is impossible to blame VAT for anything but a small proportion of these price differences.

Table 12.5 Proceedings started by Commission against governments

	1983	1984	1985	1986	1987
By legal instrument:					
Directives					
– no national laws notified	140	222	257	268	260
– not properly incorporated	19	46	30	51	42
– not properly applied	27	17	14	54	125
Treaty or regulation breaches	103	169	202	143	145
total	289	454	503	516	572
By policy area: (ranked by 1987 cases)					
Internal market and industrial	111	172	152	119	177
Environment and consumers	35	65	69	134	159
Agriculture	76	91	149	116	83
Employment and social affairs	9	15	22	23	59
Customs and VAT	31	64	48	60	31

Transport	5	7	10	11	31
Other	22	40	53	53	32
total	289	454	503	516	572

By country:
(ranked by 1987 cases)

Greece	26	60	69	106	77
Italy	69	67	70	61	73
France	55	92	93	69	66
Germany	16	36	29	40	65
Belgium	34	55	68	56	55
Ireland	16	33	33	44	46
UK	20	34	29	37	44
Netherlands	16	28	48	30	41
Denmark	13	21	27	26	36
Spain				22	32
Luxembourg	24	28	37	43	26
Portugal				2	11
total	289	454	503	516	572

(source: fifth law report)

Agreeing the package of 1992 measures at EC level in Brussels is just half the task. Putting the directives into national law and making them work will prove a more demanding one if past experience is anything to go by. EC governments have a lousy record at putting directives on their statute books within the timescale and then taking any notice of them when they have done so. Environment policy is one of the worst (see Chapter 9). But in 1987 industrial and trade issues took over the lead in the number of breaches tackled by the Commission as businesses consider expanding their operations throughout Europe.

The lax way directives are incorporated into national law has most to do with the political and administrative set-up in the countries involved. Governments are given time to take remedial action before the Commission takes it to the European Court of Justice. Some governments respond smartly to the first complaint, others take longer. In a substantial number, an agreement is reached and the government avoids the shame of going to court. But a large number of infringement actions end up at the European Court in Luxembourg.

The cases that are heard in the court reveal the most unconvincing arguments to explain these governments' lapses. It is not surprising that the Commission wins the vast majority.

Table 12.6 European Court judgements won by Commission against governments

(cases won by governments are indicated in brackets; ranked on 1987 judgements)	1985	1986	1987	1988 (first 6 months)
Italy	8 (–)	7 (5)	18 (1)	14 (–)
Belgium	2 (–)	3 (–)	6 (2)	8 (2)
Germany	4 (–)	5 (–)	4 (–)	2 (–)
Netherlands	– (1)	1 (–)	3 (–)	1 (–)
Greece	1 (–)	2 (–)	2 (–)	7 (–)
Denmark	1 (1)	2 (–)	1 (–)	– (–)
France	4 (1)	4 (1)	– (1)	4 (–)
Luxembourg	– (–)	– (–)	– (1)	– (–)
UK	2 (–)	2 (–)	– (–)	4 (–)
Ireland	1 (1)	1 (–)	– (–)	1 (–)
	23 (3)	27 (6)	34 (5)	41 (2)

The Italians, the worst culprits, blame a series of failings for their poor record. In many cases, scarce parliamentary time pushed directives of 'little importance' to the back of the legislative queue. In other cases the government fell and everything had to be started all over again. Sometimes delays were due to consulting up to five or six ministries on the best way of implementing the new laws. If one had a problem, it often took six months to deal with. In a number of cases, a ministry had not been consulted before the directive was agreed in Brussels and later 'started a quarrel'.

In 1986 the Italians began to shake up the way they deal with European law. A Ministry of European Affairs now coordinates consultations ahead of directives being discussed in Brussels. In a drastic move to catch up, the government asked for powers to implement about 100 directives by government decree. A similar system is being put in place to do this process annually. The legislation for this was being discussed in 1988. The plan was for the European ministry to propose the directives in January each year and Parliament to approve the process in March.

Italy expects that this way of doing things will make sure all EC legislation is put on the national statute book within two years of agreement in Brussels. As the directives in the 1992 plan mount up and the EC total approaches 1,000 in all, the Italians still had about 200 to put in place. It was certainly an improvement.

The UK has a better – but by no means perfect – record. Complying with EC value-added tax directives is becoming a serious problem for the UK and it lost two cases in 1988. The first came in February, when the UK claim to exempt the dispensing fee charged by opticians from VAT was ruled illegal. The Commission and the judges disagreed. The second case involved the UK's claim to zero-rate a range of services including food, feeding stuffs, water services, fuel and power and construction works.

The Commission said that such widespread zero-rating was barred under a VAT directive. The Court confirmed that 'clearly defined social reasons' allowed the UK to zero-rate goods and services that are bought by the ordinary consumer. But it added that this did not cover industrial buildings and industry's use of sewerage services, gas and electricity. The judgement will lead to an overhaul of the UK VAT system in the 1989 Budget. In practice many businesses will reclaim the VAT but banks, finance houses and more crucially charities cannot – their bill will run to an estimated £160 million.

In the summer of 1988 the property and construction business began counting the cost. The extra VAT on industry was expected to disrupt the price of land, buildings and rents. The domestic sector could not be entirely insulated from this and one positive effect may be a lowering in land prices. City of London experts began wrestling with the small print of a government consultative document. This tackled building-by-building VAT options for large office blocks or factories and phasing in the measures over two to five years. Getting the law right is proving a complicated exercise.

Many more VAT disputes are in the pipeline to the European Court but this time brought by private industry against Customs. There were a number involving Tupperware-style party selling and Boots the Chemist, Cockfield's old employer, was mounting a separate challenge. Clearly Customs was having trouble interpreting Eurolaw but was that the real problem? Was it necessary for the EC to set such detailed rules? It was becoming an entertaining spectator sport as UK accountants and lawyers took to catching out the VATman. But was there a fiscal frontier to remove? Did 'Europe' really need to be involved to quite such an extent?

Going to court is an expensive business and one magnified by the extra step of a reference to the European Court in Luxembourg. Lawyers say the bill can rise to £100,000. Citizens and commercial firms should be able to rely on governments and the authorities in their own countries applying EC law. In many cases they can't. Only when the issues involve the wider European marketplace or larger sums are at stake, should it be necessary to incur the extra expense of trips to Luxembourg.

Different national implementations of directives will be another problem. Lawyers are predicting a strange pattern of product liability laws come 1992 when a directive to protect consumers from thalidomide-type tragedies is in place. (The Commission has queried the way the UK is handling it.) In principle the liability of the manufacturer has been harmonised. In practice, lawyers predict those affected will choose where to fight a case depending on where they can get the largest amount of damages and prove negligence in the easiest way.

It opens up a spectre within Europe similar to the 'forum-shopping' which so often takes accident victims running to the US courts where damages are highest. One top Brussels lawyer says: 'Take the case of a chocolate bar made in Germany, sold in France, eaten in Belgium and where the victim falls ill in The Netherlands. Depending on the issue the plaintiff might choose one of these jurisdictions. Leave aside where you can get more damages, it may depend whether you can recover your own costs.'

When companies have overcome the obstacles of frontier controls or more technical barriers, they will want to operate in a marketplace free from industry cartels and other restrictive practices. The Commission already has wide powers to act in this sphere. It can, and does, make swoops on companies rigging their industry's prices and can go on to fine them up to ten per cent of turnover, though its record fine is only £10 million. It also forces takeovers to divest where a monopoly is created.

During the last four years Peter Sutherland, the Commissioner from Ireland, has gained a reputation for enforcing the competition and state subsidy rules, which help national industries. He persuaded BA to meet tougher conditions after the UK's Monopolies and Mergers Commission waved through its takeover of British Caledonian. Rival operators will compete more easily on European air routes and keep the prices down for consumers. His scrutiny of state subsidies cut the UK Government's cash injection by millions when British Aerospace took over the Rover Group. Car-makers will compete on more even European terms.

Sutherland has proved that strong leadership and sound skills can work wonders. He is backed by a Commission directorate containing more than its share of top-notch officials. But it proves that with duff Commissioners at the head, the Commission's ability to regulate is mediocre. As one seasoned Sutherland aide says: 'When someone does a good job, it is seen as a miracle.' In 1987, Sutherland began forcing governments to recover state subsidies they had paid out illegally. This too added teeth to the Commission's watchdog role.

Table 12.7 State subsidies ordered to be repaid

	number of cases	£ million
Belgium	10	210
France	5	395
Germany	4	10
Netherlands	2	83
United Kingdom	1	1
	22	699

(The figures are for 1987, the first year in which the policy was enforced. In 1985, only £3.5 million was repaid and in 1986 £8 million.)

It is difficult to see why state subsidy policy was not tightened up years before. In many cases, governments had not asked for prior approval from the Commission, as was required under the Treaty. Now, governments face an immediate investigation if they fail to notify grants within the laid-down timescale. Governments were regularly rapped for paying out illegal grants but only asked to recover them – not ordered. In most cases they didn't bother to get the money back. The Commission is preparing a full inventory of grants, legal or illegal, and more tough action is expected.

Effective policing of competition and state subsidy rules may prove as important to business as any of the white paper measures in the European economy of the 1990s. Good businessmen can overcome the delays at border posts or the excessive petty regulations and paperwork in getting their goods into national markets. Many multinationals have already achieved it. But overcoming the financial muscle of a monopoly or the state subsidies supplied to home-grown industries is more difficult and expensive a task. It usually involves the uncertain element of politics.

The pace of takeovers will quicken as 1992 approaches. In the summer of 1988 famous names to change hands included the HP and Daddies Sauce of Lea and Perrins: it became owned by the French BSN Group. In the autumn, the UK's Grand Metropolitan and France's Pernod Ricard scrapped for Irish Distillers with its famous whiskey labels. In the insurance sector Belgian company Groupe AG was chasing the British Sun Life. And Ladbrokes, the bookmakers, made a bid for the Belgian tote. It was open season as corporate raiders such as Robert Maxwell from the UK and Carlo de Benedetti from Italy stalked the bourse of Europe.

But hostile predators may find obstacles erected in front of a takeover target. UK companies can be bought if the price is right and London has an established stock exchange with well-tested takeover rules. The French quoted company market is becoming more open, though government rules on inward foreign investment can be imprecise. Italy is fairly unregulated for takeover (or anti-monopoly) activity and most large deals are friendly arrangements. In The Netherlands, many companies are tightly controlled or have used share issues or restrictions on their ownership to thwart hostile takeovers.

German companies remain the most protected from takeover. Quoted companies are few in number and investment banks play an important role as minority shareholders. Other factors are management's scope not to enfranchise new shareholders. Limited financial disclosure also makes it more difficult for the predator to put a realistic value on a company's worth or to find out the true ownership. Opening German companies to hostile bids is more likely to come through the outcry after a few failed attempts than any EC moves to increase disclosure.

Privatisation may offer one route for foreign buyers to pitch into another country's shares. But French and British governments, the most notable proponents, have restricted overseas holdings to 20 per cent of capital. In the case of Rolls Royce, the UK pleaded national defence interests to keep the level to 15 per cent. It forces foreign shareholders to make a hasty sale or risk losing their money. The

Commission has intervened in both countries but 100 per cent looks to be only a long-term goal. With more privatisations in the offing the scrutiny is unlikely to ease up.

The economic theory of 1992 is compelling. As the customs and technical barriers are removed, companies are encouraged to 'export' or deliver to a larger domestic market. These are the immediate gains. Further gains come as sectors which were previously protected face increased competition. This is where successful companies, those with the lower costs, take over rivals to rationalise the means of production or obtain increased market share. If this is added to Europe-wide economic policies of expansion, then the impact is magnified.

Rationalisation is likely to take place in sectors making electrical goods, vehicles, trains, computers, civil aviation and telecommunications. These are mainly industries where state subsidies or state ownership have kept companies nationally based. Privately Commission officials admit: 'More than half of the industries and service sectors are going to be affected in a big way. Analysis show that it would start with bad news and then you would get the good news. You would start with slight job losses and then pick up in years two, three, four and five.'

After the initial rush of the free market 1992 package, trade unions and socialist politicians are beginning to make their moves. Their main demands are more state spending on employment training and the regions as well as legal directives to protect workers' rights. But the shape of the EC's budget up to 1992 is already mapped out and governments will be reluctant to open the debate again. Commission proposals on workers' rights are limited. Another prospect on the labour side of the economic equation is pan-European unions. Strikes by such unions would give multinationals a real fright.

On the trade front, the perspectives are less discouraging. Studies show that where countries import from outside the EC, the 1992 plan encourages them to 'import' from neighbouring EC countries, improving the EC balance of payments. Similarly lower costs make exports to world markets more attractive. The Commission estimates 10 per cent growth in exports and an extra trade surplus of

1 per cent of EC GNP. Much relies on the assumption that US and Japanese companies don't take more of an advantage from removed technical barriers and Europe-wide standards than home-grown companies.

The Commission says it is against a protectionist 'Fortress Europe' and in favour of open trading with the rest of the world. It is not clear that all EC governments, such as those in France or Germany, share this view. 1992 is a bargaining chip in the current Uruguay round of world trade talks, and the Commission already believes it is opening new markets in goods to European exporters. On services, it says it will seek reciprocal access before granting US or Japanese finance houses the advantages of Europe-wide backing licences and other juicy benefits in the financial service sector.

But the Commission is not the same as national governments. The French have been tough on Japanese products in the past. First they routed all Japanese video recorders illegally through just one tiny customs post, slowing them down to a trickle. At other times they have imposed higher import duties on electronic consumer goods than the rest of Europe. In autumn 1988 they queried the European content of motor cars made in the UK by the Japanese company Nissan. The Germans take a different protectionist line. Their numerous standards across a range of manufactured goods will keep out both European and overseas competitors.

One key test of the 1992 package will be the emergence of companies operating on a European scale and in strategic sectors such as silicon chips, computers and other high technologies. Airbus Industrie, a joint venture of aerospace companies, is a pan-European success story in technological terms and its aircraft sales are performing well. But it relies heavily on state aids and there are question marks over its management structure and efficiency. Many smaller, but similar, joint ventures are emerging from EC and industry research programmes and their performance will be crucial.

European governments and the Commission are whipping up a tide of euphoria over the 1992 plan to which business has responded by piling enthusiastically into conferences and seminars. Along the way consultants are coining a mint from studies and advice. But take a hard look at the risks. At the international level, a world recession could scupper the economic predictions of the plan overnight. In Europe itself the gains could disappear into the Golden Triangle between London, Paris and the Ruhr, leaving the peripheral regions of Europe even worse off. At the country level, governments could forget to police whole tracts of the regulations.

As always, economic success and prosperity will depend on business performance. The 1992 package offers only the framework for an efficient single marketplace. But without the package, manufacturing industry will be overrun by the Japanese and other Far Eastern suppliers in the 1990s. Sector after industrial sector will fall. By 1992, the package will probably be heavily watered down and the commitment to regulate it weak. A single currency alone would save tens of £billions in trade between EC countries. Like many of the likely measures, it strikes deep into nationalistic attitudes and these are the major obstacles to 1992 and well beyond.

CONCLUSION

Putting the European Community on the right track requires tough solutions and a commitment to back them at all levels. The evidence of mismanagement, fraud and lawbreaking is clear throughout the EC set-up: it operates in Brussels where policy is formulated and managed; and in individual countries where it is put in place. One remedy ought to be an emphasis on quality rather than quantity. The EC should hold fire on its grandiose schemes until it can handle the activities it is supposed to be handling today.

A US-style federated Europe should be taken off the agenda until the present mess is cleared up. The EC is wholly unprepared to take on a European Central Bank or security or defence initiatives. And more thought needs to be given to the policy areas it does handle. Some issues, such as those affecting the global environment, should be tackled at world – United Nations – level and only policed by the EC. Other issues are too petty and don't affect cross-border trade, the main *raison d'être* of the EC, and these should be left to national authorities.

This basic test – should this policy area be the EC's beef? – is often not made. Instead the European Commission wants to do the lot. From culture to defence it wants to make television programmes and say how the bombs will be built. The first it continues to do, the second it was stopped from doing in 1984, but may be trying to do again. It would do better by linking its plans more closely with other organisations such as the Council of Europe on human rights issues, NATO and the Western European Union on defence. A closer link with the International

Atomic Energy Authority could prevent duplicated nuclear inspections.

The EC and its executive Commission should concentrate on improving its performance. It should analyse much more closely the policy areas where it has no impact and consider dropping them. Cultural events and Euroflags on mountains would be a good starting place. It could easily disband some of its economic services and get the Organisation for Economic Cooperation and Development to do its forecasting for it. (It is already more highly regarded.) Its scientific Joint Research Centres, which sit uncomfortably beside policy-making, should be sold to the private sector.

Inside the EC organisations, many of the reforms to accommodation and personnel policy have been highlighted earlier. Staff regulations need an overhaul to give management greater flexibility. In return, management should end its scandalous rigging of recruitment. The right of appeal to the European Court should be curtailed and a high-powered European Civil Service Commission must replace the present staff directorate. Budget and internal audit also need centralising. Salaries and perks should undergo a review and compared with the private sector.

In the longer term, the Commission should be reorganised into a set of policy divisions, paying agencies and policing operations. Policy would become more strategic and focused on areas with a European dimension. Payment of subsidies for farming, the regions and employment training should be hived off and privatised. Agencies would be given a budget to hand out and be set efficiency targets. Under strong independent management, finance experts would move in and set up closer coordination with national agencies and clamp down on fraud.

The 'policing' operations would have similar wide powers but no cash to hand out. Instead a trade or commerce commission would police trade barriers within Europe, ensure that competition took place and that trade with the rest of the world was fair and that where it was not, anti-dumping investigations took place. Another inspectorate would tackle the environment, again working more closely with national efforts. The lack of coordination and distrust between EC and national civil servants is a major brake on EC efficiency.

Some aspects of policing, such as in the environmental field, should be contracted to suitable private organisations such as the Royal Society for the Protection of Birds or environment groups. Such contract work has so far only covered canteens and security guards in EC organisations. It needs to be considered much more widely.

Supranational inspectors and liaison officers would raise compliance levels but be politically difficult to put in place. Only Commission competition inspectors currently have full EC-wide search powers. Despite UK and Danish opposition, from sovereignty-type qualms, these Commission powers have to be extended to other policy areas. They are vital unless national governments suddenly start taking notice of EC laws and applying them. The current breakdown in law-keeping is no more than government-inspired anarchy.

Those who monitor EC spending, the European Parliament and the Court of Auditors, have to put their own houses in order. The Parliament spends £250 million of taxpayers' money and lets its own officials waste a huge proportion. Its members' attitude is usually of embarrassment or complicity. MEPs would do well to adopt US Congress-style monthly Golden Fleece Awards for wasted taxpayers' money. The Parliament should start by coming clean each month on its own waste before turning to the rest of the £25 billion a year which the EC spends.

Dealing with the Court of Auditors requires tougher medicine – its disbandment. This ten-year-old organisation, the youngest of the EC set-up, is a disgrace to the public service. The EC audit could safely be handled by one, or perhaps jointly by two, international firms of auditors.

Political scrutiny must also be extended, though here the solutions are less obvious. Politics are less of an exact science than management. Apart from treaties which require parliamentary ratification, all EC legislation lacks approval by an elected parliament. The European Parliament, though gaining the power to block laws and external trade agreements, cannot definitively amend them. In practice the amendments it proposes are often lost in a round of trade-offs between government officials and ministers before a new law is agreed.

As much as 80 per cent of Europe-wide industrial legislation may be set in Brussels by the mid 1990s, but commentators are wrong when they complain that the Commission will set these rules. It only makes proposals and has the right to withdraw them if their purpose is lost in negotiations. Governments, meeting in secret, have the final say. Only in one or two countries do national parliaments have a veto, though even this breaks down when EC voting is by a majority of governments. In future either the European or national parliaments must be given their say.

Many believe the practicalities of putting European legislation through each national parliament make this a bad means of reform. They say that the European Parliament ought to carry out the scrutiny function. So far governments have yet to propose more power to either parliamentary system, preferring to keep a system which gives their own private club the last word. As with many other aspects of the EC set-up, the people of Europe deserve better. Given past performance, the prospects for this type of reform or any other radical overhaul of the EC machinery are pretty slim.

INDEX

Meyers, Jules 178
Middelhoek, Andre 73, 89, 93, 95
milk 119–20, 125, 163–4, 172–94
    Luxlait scandal 88, 172–7, 179,
    181–92
Millan, Bruce 47
Mitterand, Francois 136
Moat, Andrew 34
Moeller, Claus 45
monetary compensation amounts
    (MCAs) 105, 112, 121
monitoring 293
    Agecontrol 127–31
    auditing 76
    coastal pollution 199–203
    development aid 223
    farming 101, 105, 110, 123–5
    tobacco 164
    wine 138–9, 152–3
Morel, Jean-Claude 40
Moynihan, Colin 213
Murdoch, Rupert 263
Murphy, Michael 72, 81

Natali, Lorenzo 239
National Audit Office 70, 77, 80,
    116
Netherlands 107, 110, 120, 122,
    125, 197, 204, 218, 235, 261–90
    trade barriers 263–8
        fiscal 276–84
        physical 269–72
        technical 272–6

O'Halpin, Eunan 71, 75–6
O'Hannrachain, Eoghan 60–3
O'Kennedy, Michael 36–7
olive oil
    Agecontrol 127–30
    Mafia 248–9
    report 117–18, 122, 145, 159,
    169
organisation
    antifraud unit 126–7
    Commission 119, 131
    Court of Auditors 69, 71–3, 77,
    85
    Luxembourg milk sector 175
    polycentricity of EC 2–19

Orlando, Leoluca 250, 252
overexpenditure in Parliament
    50–68
    de Compte affair 52–9
    election funding 65–8
    rents 60–5

Pandolfo, Filippo 131, 150
Parliament, European 293–4
    Court of Auditors and 71
    location of 2–7, 13
    overspending
        de compte affair 52–9
        election funding 65–8
        rental 60–5
        staffing 21, 28, 37
Pauvert, Maurice 95–6
Pearce, Andrew 64–5
Petersen, Ole Bjorn 17
Pflimlin, Pierre 7–8, 60
Pitt, Terry 58
Planchard, Jacques 88
Plumb, Lord 58–63, 65, 242
Poeton, Bill 47
policy 292
    farm fraud 108, 114–15, 123–5
    rental 16
    single market 261–2, 272, 275
    staffing 22, 46–8, 76–9, 90–2
    trade 268–72
pollution in UK water 196–220
    cleaning up 215–16
    coastal 196–203
    drinking 205–11, 217, 219
polycentricity of Commission
    2–19
Poos, Jacques 192
Prag, Derek 7
Price, Sir Norman 70–5, 80, 86–7,
    97
Price, Peter 3, 5, 51, 222–3, 230–1
production
    tobacco 159–60
    wine 134–6, 138, 141, 144–6,
    152, 155, 157
Prout, Christopher 67
Provan, Jimmy 62–4

Quin, Joyce 216